Secret Animal Business

SECRET ANIMAL BUSINESS

A Celebration of the Secrets of Animals, Their Forgotten Language and How They Can Help You and the Planet Heal

Copyright © 2009 Billie Dean. All rights reserved. Printed in Australia. Apart from any fair dealing for the purposes of private study, research, criticism or review, as permitted under the Copyright Act, no part may be reproduced by any process without written permission.

Inquiries should be addressed to the publisher.

First Edition. ISBN 978-0-9806272-0-6

Published by:
Wild Pure Heart Productions
PO Box 61
Braidwood NSW 2622 Australia
www.billiedean.com
info@billiedean.com

In Association With:
Conscious Living Co-Creations Pty Ltd
www.consciousliving.net.au

Cover design by Wendy Slee
Book design by Liz Campbell
Back cover portrait by Andrew Einspruch
Photos by Billie Dean and Andrew Einspruch

Note to the reader: This book is an informational guide. The information in this book is not designed to replace treatment or advice from trained animal health professionals.

The stories in this book are true, but the names and circumstances have been changed to protect to the privacy of those involved.

Praise for Secret Animal Business

This is a book to touch the soul. So many books in today's world are fodder for the brain, but luckily, this book is not. Secret Animal Business is a book for the heart. Whether we like it or not, know it or not, every author carries a signature energy. When I read a book, I am also reading the author; so as I read this book I read Billie Dean. And this is what most impressed me. I could feel a strong soul with a clarity and determination to shine a light into an arena that for a long time has remained a shadowed place. I have shone my light, and continue to do so, but each writer's light is unique and different . . . and needed.

Read this book with your heart as open as your eyes. If the mind begins any protest, tell it to be quiet, and keep on reading. Allow Billie Dean to inner-touch your life, offering you a new and exciting direction into Nature. Telepathy with all living things is simple . . . and as easy as our busy, complex minds will allow. Nature is waiting for you, offering a new life . . . be in it!

– Michael J. Roads, author of the bestselling *Talking with Nature* and *Journey into Nature*, and more recently, *Conscious Gardening and Through the Eyes of Love*

Social visionary Billie Dean takes us on an incredible journey into the minds, hearts and spirits of the animals who share our lives. Her use of story paints a picture so illuminating that it leaves us wondering why we didn't see this truth long ago. Secret Animal Business is wonderful, and provides us with insight into becoming a better person, not only for our animal friends but for humanity.

– Rebecca Booth, founder of *Elementals Equine Therapies*

I wish this book had been around when my first dog entered my life. Our time together would have been even richer than it was. I have long believed that animals and people needed more harmony, but Secret Animal Business takes this to a whole new level. Billie Dean spells out how enriching it can be to connect to nature, whether it is the cat on your sofa, the wombat outside, or the stones in your garden.

– Patricia Hamilton, publisher, Conscious Living Magazine.

Secret Animal Business takes you on a journey that will surely open you more fully to the animal kingdom. Billie Dean writes not only from her generous heart, but from her soul's wisdom. Secret Animal Business is a book whose time has come. Open your heart to Billie's insightful wisdom, and you'll come into a deep relationship of compassion, joy and understanding with all beings.

– Pamela Talbot Adams, animal communicator and author of *Angels Who Come With Fur and Four Paws*

Billie's book is an absolute joy. It moved my soul. Her understanding of animals is pure magic and she shows us how the animals can teach us unconditional love. We are at a time of unprecedented change on our planet now and only unconditional love will work. Let us learn from our animal friends. Everyone should read this book.

– Anne Hassett, international psychic and author of *Reading Your Child's Hand* and *The Secret Power of the F-Word*

Secret Animal Business

A Celebration of the Secrets of Animals, Their Forgotten Language and How They Can Help You and the Planet Heal

Billie Dean

Wild Pure Heart Productions

SSSSSSSHHHHHHHHHHHHHH...

The Animals Have A Secret . . .

And that secret is as old as time . . .

They want you to listen...

To their voice in the silence . . .

And understand their mission...

Which is to help you

Become a HUMAN ANGEL.

Hello, I'm Billie Dean

Like you, I was born telepathic. Except that for me it didn't fade away. My sensitivity was attuned to an empathetic communion with nature and animals. I always felt their joy and pain. I intuitively understood them. And even though I grew up in an ordinary household and learned to keep my thoughts to myself, sometimes it all got too much and I would have to speak up and try and defend the lives I knew were precious, sentient and animate.

Just like now.

Nobody believed a ten year old.

But after decades of being this way, and with animal communication clients around Australia and around the world, I think people are ready to hear the amazing truth about animals.

The cat in the living room, the dog in the kitchen, the horse in the paddock, the budgie in the cage, the dolphin in the sea, the kangaroo in the bush...

It doesn't matter what fur, feathers or skin an animal wears...

They are all souls, like us.

And they are already angels.

Why Do Animals Need People to Become Human Angels?

This is the core of my work as an animal advocate, and I feel a real urgency to help people understand the truth about animals and of life as we know it – or don't know it.

We are in a time of tremendous global change.

We are in the time of the Earth Changes, as foretold by indigenous prophecy from around the world. This is what I call the 2012 Phenomenon. The first introduction I had to 2012 was through the Hopi Prophecy in 1978. This talked about needing 144,000 rainbow warriors to help create a shift in human consciousness which would herald a Golden Age of peace.

I wanted to be one of those warriors.

Because of my work with indigenous peoples, I was sought out in the early 1990's by a man of the Hopi Nation to write about the Earth Changes. He talked about finding safe places. And when I asked about how to find safe places, another Native American Elder said:

"Billie, there are no safe places, only safe people."

So what is a safe person?

And how does that person create a safe place?

A safe person is one who has awakened and is aware of their connection to spirit and to all life. A safe person walks with respect and honour, mindfulness, reverence and integrity. A safe person has raised their vibration to a certain level. A safe person does their personal work, has dumped their stories and works in world service. They are Earthkeepers. A safe person understands and lives by the Universal Laws, takes personal responsibility for their world, and lives in right relations.

As time went on, I noticed, in my work as an animal communicator, the animals were giving guidance to their people which encouraged them to change. I began to see a pattern. It fell into place when I began studying the shamanic healing methods of the Inka of Peru through the Four Winds Society. Here it was again. Rainbow Warriors and a prophecy of a Golden Age – a time when the world was once again populated by people who were earth honouring. But now I heard more – that people could take a quantum leap in evolution, and become homo luminous, children of light, or human angels.

Of course, when enough people become human angels, we will have a Golden Age of peace, because these people will be peace, and when you are peace, you project peace and peace becomes a self-fulfilling prophecy.

We are now in a time in history where it is possible to become a fully realised human being. Imagine a planet full of avatars or enlightened beings. People who Walk in Beauty. And all we have to do is our personal healing. And walk in the world in an impeccable manner.

I launched my new transformational school Rainbow Fianna: Wisdom School for Earthkeepers in 2007 to help awaken human angels for animals. This book is based on my teachings because it is no longer enough to teach people to listen to the silent language of animals. You have to help humans shift their perspective, accept personal responsibility and co-create their lives. This is what the animals are wanting right now – for humans to step up.

We'll talk about all this as the book unfolds. But I'm writing this part of my book as the devastating Victorian wildfires rage and it drives me to stress the point that if we want to stop the suffering of the animals we love, we have to now become what we are destined to become –

Human Angels.

And the sooner we do it, the sooner the Earth Mother will take a sigh of relief and settle into her own beauty, because –

We Are All Connected.

So, if you have never come across the idea that everything in life is connected and everything in life is animate, then please enjoy this hero's journey into the secrets of the animals, because they are the first tribes of this world – our spiritual elders – and they hold a key to unlocking the part of you that is asleep and disconnected from your Mother Earth, and the entire galaxy.

And by opening your mind and changing your perception of life, the animals will help you break free of the chains of cultural numbness and invite you to live a life of authenticity, of love, and of great beauty and joy.

Secrets of the Animals

They are Spiritual and Psychic.

They are the first tribes and the holders of great wisdom.

They have a Voice and a Language you Can understand.

They are teachers and healers.

They reincarnate across species.

They have free will.

They have intelligence and connection to the Divine.

They are angels without wings.

They are helping you become Enlightened.

They are helping you become Human Angels.

Secret Animal Business

For my husband Andrew and daughter Tamsin – my hearts, who do so much incredible work and give so much. I would be lost without you.

For Sollie who holds a special place in my heart and who always wanted me to write his story.

And for Pip, Chockmah, Binah, Pucawan and Reka – my first animal teachers. And to Suki and all the others, a huge thank you for all that you did and still do. Love and gratitude to you all.

XXX

Contents

Introduction 1
The Beginning 6
Part 1: The Journey of An Animal Shaman 8
Chapter 1: The Training of An Animal Shaman 9
Chapter 2: The Beginning 33
Chapter 3: Wosco 38
Chapter 4: Sinjin 40
Chapter 5: Omar and Rosie 44
Chapter 6: The Filly Who Saw Her Own Death 50
Chapter 7: Mala 53
Chapter 8: Lucy and Maryanne 57
Chapter 9: Jo Jo and Sandy 63
Chapter 10: Sollie's Story 66
Part 2: Animals in the Age of Enlightenment 80
Rainbow Fianna: Wisdom School for Earthkeepers 81
Rainbow Fianna's Guidelines for Apprentice Human Angels 83
Chapter 11: The Path of the Human Angel for Animals 84
Chapter 12: Secret Animal Business: Soul's Journey 86
Chapter 13: Animals are Angels 91

Chapter 14: Enter the Stillness 93

Chapter 15: Aho Mitakuye Oyasin 96

Chapter 16: Animals Were the First Tribes 100

Chapter 17: How Can One Own a Soul? 104

Chapter 18: Change Your Words and Change Minds! 106

Chapter 19: The Animal Point of View 110

Chapter 20: Opening Your Mind to the Psychic World of Animals 113

Part 3: Communicating with Animals 122

Chapter 21: About Telepathy 123

Chapter 22: The Wider Ramifications of Learning the Silent Language 128

Chapter 23: The Right Mental Space for Communication 132

Chapter 24: The Art of Telepathic Listening 133

Chapter 25: Learning the Silent Language 138

Chapter 26: Being Polite with the Animals You Speak With 145

Chapter 27: The Practice of Telepathy 150

Chapter Distance Communication with Photographs 163

Chapter 30: Communicating with "Pests" and Wild Animals 165

Part 4: The Secret to Harmonious Animal Relations and Secrets the Animals Want You to Know 170

My Vision 171

Chapter 30: Animal Care as a Spiritual Art Form 173

Chapter 31: Understanding Animal Behaviour 175

Chapter 34: Love, Acknowledgement and Seeing the Good in All 210

Part 5: Animal Health And Healing 214

Chapter 35: A Holistic Approach 215

Chapter 36: Diet for Dogs and Cats 218

Chapter 38: Diet for Horses 235

Chapter 40: More on Health and Healing 243

Part 6: Death, Dying and Euthanasia 252

Chapter 41: On Death and Dying 253

Chapter 42: When Your Animal Friend Is Dying 262

Part 7: Creating a Better World for Animals 272

Chapter 43: 2012 and the Fifth Dimension – The New Earth 273

Chapter 44: Dreaming in the New World of Peace 277

Chapter 45: Help an Animal – Change Your Diet 280

Chapter 46: Animals and Spiritual Practice 283

Chapter 47: The Power of Right Thinking 284

Chapter 48: Ritual and Ceremony 290

Chapter 49: Making a Commitment to Happiness 291

Chapter 50: Animals as Shamanic Teachers 303

Chapter 51: Animal Medicine and Messengers 307

Chapter 52: The End of Animal Suffering: Brave New World of Animal Stewardship 329

Chapter 53: Animal Communication as a Business 332

Chapter 54: What I've Learned from Animals and their Secret Business 336

Acknowledgements 338

Bibliography 339

About the Author 342

Index 346

Introduction

Thomas the cat was missing. He was an old cat who you could set your clocks to, according to Abby. He never went anywhere. And now he was gone. Abby was in a panic. It had been more than 24 hours.

I was in a bookshop when she called, and took a minute to tune in to Thomas while I waited in a queue.

Thomas was disgruntled. "I'll be home at 8 PM," he said testily, obviously annoyed at being disturbed.

"Are you okay? Is everything alright?" I asked, echoing Abby's fears that he might be doing the great cat final walkabout.

"I'm on secret cat business." He'd say no more about it.

To Abby's great surprise, Thomas indeed came home at 8 PM, none the worse for wear, and took up his place in the kitchen like he had never left.

– Excerpt from Billie's client journals

There's an old quote from Pawnee Chief Lekota-Lesa, which is on a poster in my bedroom and on a horse calendar on my desk.

> *In the beginning of all things, wisdom and knowledge were with the animals, for Tirawa, the One Above, did not speak to man. He sent certain animals to tell men that he showed himself through the beasts, and that from them, and from the stars and the moon, man should learn.*

And from Job 12:7-8, we also get:

> *But ask the animals, and they will teach you*
> *or the birds of the air, and they will tell you*
> *or speak to the earth, and it will teach you*
> *or let the fish of the sea inform you.*

This has been my truth for as long as I have been in this body this time around. There's not a time I can remember where I wasn't able to commune with nature and the animals. It's a part of me, like breathing. And always, the animals, the trees, and the spirits have been my teachers.

We've all heard the Australian terms "secret women's business" and "secret men's business", which I first heard referring to sacred Australian Aboriginal mysteries. They were things I wasn't allowed to know because I wore a white skin. A white skin over a native soul.

There was something about the Aboriginal culture which called me, and when I was about 10, at a time in Australian history when it just wasn't done, I wished I had the easy rapport with horses they seemed to have. I knew there was something "other" about our indigenous people, and that "other" sang to my soul.

As I grew older, those "secret business" terms were bandied about in Western culture. We'd laugh and say of a shopping expedition, "We're on secret women's business." But to me, the sacredness of the phrase always hung in the air like a promise. Like a door I needed to find a key for.

Along the way the animals in my life tended the soul wounds of my youth when I lost my parents, and became my guides and shamanic teachers. Tough lessons of loss and heartache. When I look back, I can see how the animals shaped me, chiselled away at my armour, and built my self-esteem. They taught me to listen and trust, dance lightly with energy, walk in complete integrity, be mindful, and to understand the truth of the life we are living. So many lessons to be grateful for.

So when I came to write a book about the sentience and spirituality of animals, I realised that all my life I had held a key to one of the ancient mysteries of the cosmos. Secret Animal Business is just that. It's about the forgotten language of the animals and nature. It's about a secret, sacred world which needs to be known about today, not just for animal welfare, but for our own, the planet's and even the galaxy's.

As I write, the Earth and the future of humanity stand on a precipice. We are engulfed by our own midden heap of anger, hate and violence. We live in cities which shout at us to drown in a mire of materialism, cluttering our minds, souls and cupboards with stuff we don't need. We are programmed by television, advertising and the media to stay distracted from reality, to stay numb and drugged. Western culture has created nations of zombie-like people suffering from depression, living mundane lives devoid of real meaning, joy, happiness or peace.

It's time to change this.

It wasn't too long ago that we lived closer to nature. We understood the vital connection between our humanity, animals, and the living Earth. Studies have shown how being in nature affects our moods and our children's mental, physical, emotional and spiritual development.

But let's take it one step further. Today, nature is represented not just by meadows and trees, but also by the animal companions who share our homes. Our furry and feathered friends have souls that are misunderstood; the language we once shared, forgotten. Embracing this mystery, exploring the potential of our connection, opens a door to a world of exciting possibilities.

And let's take it another step. Even nature has a language which we can all understand. Being with our animal companions and with nature, and understanding the true meaning of their many messages to us, can help put us on the right track in life, and make life rich with meaning.

It's time to remember that all of earth is alive, and that the rivers, stones and trees all have a voice, as does the horse and cow grazing in the field, the cat curled by the fire, the owl hooting in the trees and the ants on the sink. We can have understanding and mutual cooperation. We can have communication. It's time human beings remembered they are part of the web of life, and to stop being a predator trying to remove everything they don't understand or is inconvenient. We see this attitude in our overflowing pounds where thousands of animals are killed as if their lives had no value, and we see it in the way we carelessly mow down old growth forests, wipe other species to extinction, and view Mother Earth as something to develop, exploit and harvest.

At other times in history I would have been burnt at the stake for talking about the secret, silent language of animals and nature. And indeed, my soul shudders with ancient memory. But today it is impossible to stay silent when so much of humanity is crying, and our animal companions and Mother Earth are being treated in intolerable ways. Because of our disconnection. Because of our cultural numbness. Because of the way we are being encouraged to think.

And today, there is talk of the Great Shift in human consciousness – and a change which is already occurring. If we want to avoid falling completely in the midden heap and obliterating the planet, we need to make changes in ourselves fast. Saving Mother Earth is not just about going green, it's making a commitment to grow up as a species and embrace the mantel of love, peace, and unity.

It's about understanding the basic metaphysical tenant that thoughts become things and what you focus on expands.

And it's about listening to the voice of nature and the animals, following their guidance, and ending their suffering at the brutality of human hands, by recognising that **all** life is precious.

Thank you from the bottom of my heart for taking the time to read this book and going on a journey to learn Secret Animal Business. Thank you for your open mind. In the following pages I will share with you my experience of over half a century of communion with the silent world, what the animals are saying right now, how we can be of service to them, and how this helps our own soul's journey and the planet.

Aho Mitakuye Oyasin
(In Honour of All Our Relations)

Billie Dean
Ballyoncree
February 2009

Secret Animal Business

The Beginning

The mist is thick as you travel the narrow dirt road down into the valley. You pass the sacred grove of ancient pines and wind your way through gates and curious wild horses who look up from their grazing. Suddenly you see a blue farmhouse with welcoming light, and a feeling of calm and safety overcomes you. Beautiful it is, and beautiful too are the shadows of more curious horses and the excited barking of happy dogs.

This is Owl Cottage where I live with my family and all the animals we have given sanctuary to. Inside we sit by the warm fire, drinking hot cocoa from earthenware mugs. The room is small and cosy, bright with Navajo-style rugs and blankets, feathers, stones and crystals adorn the mantel, and incense burns. Books dominate the walls and shelves. Cats and dogs drape themselves all over the furniture and you, and because you are an animal person, you enjoy the exchange. And then I tell you my story, and the animals tell you theirs.

Owl Cottage

Secret Animal Business

Part 1:
The Journey of An Animal Shaman

Chapter 1:
The Training of An Animal Shaman

In my journey back through space and time, I wound up in the loving embrace of my celestial parents. "The road won't be easy for you," they said. "But you must remember."

I came back to this time and place with tears running down my cheeks. Their love had made me feel whole. I knew my Destiny and I knew my true parents were always with me. I saw myself choose my Earth parents Susie and John. I knew their love wouldn't last. I knew the road would be rocky. But that wasn't the point of my existence. The point was to be one who remembers. And I hadn't failed.

– Excerpt from Billie's journal, 2008

Pip

Pip the fox terrier nudged me in the leg. My beautiful, brown-haired mother was about to make a big mistake and we both knew it. A house in the country. This was the answer to prayers I didn't even know I had asked for. I just knew it was right. Space, freedom, and something "other" called to my soul. There were spirits here. And possibilities. I'd never wanted anything so much as to move here, as I stood with my Mum, Dad and Pip, drinking in the peaceful atmosphere, staring at the old world house with the yellow door.

We stood in an enchanted garden of beautiful, big oaks, and vibrant autumn-coloured trees of red and gold. My feet crunched on the fallen leaves. The crisp, autumn air sang to my spirit. Pip and I wanted this place. We wanted to live here. I willed my mother to say "yes".

My Dad too, stood there looking hopeful. He cut a vibrant figure with his black hair, blue eyes and love of life. A house out of the city was his idea. And it wasn't surprising that I loved it too. We were alike in many ways. I loved that house with every part of my four-year-old body. And I've never forgotten it. Perhaps because it was the last time I remember my family as a happy one.

"No, John. I don't think so."

Mum's reply left me crestfallen. I could see a darkness hanging over my family, even though I didn't know what it was. Pip hung close to me, sending me love. We got back in the car, and in silence, drove back to the city and the dark flat we called home.

Mum and Dad divorced a couple of years later and I knew Mum was dying from a brain tumour. Perhaps I couldn't put it into those words, maybe Pip "told" me, in the easy communion we had together. But I knew she was going to die. I knew the watch she gave me for my sixth birthday was a farewell gift.

To help me through the rough patches, Pip encouraged me outside on my scooter and together we'd run wild and free to the parks and by the waterfronts. There was sunshine on my skin, wind in my hair and Pip at my side. That's when I was truly happy. No adults, no restrictions. Just Pip and nature. Like Pip, I lived in the moment. We were inseparable. Every night he'd curl up with me on the bed, providing warmth, comfort and love, keeping me from the arms of the loneliness and fear that threatened to crush my spirit.

I missed my blue-eyed, laughing dad. And my mother had become an absent shell, wrapped in her own misery and illness. I missed her too.

I came home from school one afternoon to find with a shock that Pip had disappeared. Mum's nurse told me that Mum couldn't handle his barking and he'd gone to live with my godparents in the country. They had talked about it, and I had protested, but I never believed the day would come. It was like

Pip and I

he'd died, the ghost of his lively presence filling the flat with a physical emptiness that made his absence even more unbearable. It hurt. My body hurt. I couldn't get my bearings. I hated the dark, silent oppressive flat. I hated the world. I couldn't wrap my arms around my dog for comfort. I couldn't bury my face in his fur. I was alone. Completely alone. I flung myself on my bed and cried hot tears into my pillow. I was seven and didn't think life could get any worse. I was lost without Pip.

I could feel Pip's presence trying to comfort me in the way he always had. And in the way he had of communing with me, he told me we would be together again.

I just didn't know how. I didn't believe him.

He was constantly in my mind during the following months – but I didn't realise until decades later that he was trying to reach out to me, to communicate. I didn't try to communicate back.

Pip showed me how a relationship with an animal could be. We were in perfect harmony. We understood each other in a language without words. I knew he understood everything I said. He parented me better than my parents, and I was empty without him. Adrift. Alone.

As mum's illness progressed, I was sent to live with some neighbours with four children and a cocker spaniel called Brandy, who I adored. The last time I saw my mother was on my eighth birthday. I didn't know it was going to be the last time. I was polite and thanked her for the ugly, frilly, pink underwear I knew I would never wear. She was like a stranger to me, sitting in the bed with a black eye patch and a death sentence.

She died a week later and I found out from my best friend at school. It wasn't until I reached my home at the neighbours that afternoon, that it hit me that I was parentless - and homeless. Deep inside, I was terrified.

New Life in the Country

That night I was surprised to find my mum's sister standing in the living room. "Do you want to come and live with me?" she asked. I ran into her outstretched arms. Like an abandoned puppy I was so incredibly grateful for a new home with my aunt and uncle. They lived in the country in the same town as Pip, and they had cats, two children and a huge pine tree, which I used to climb whenever life got too much for me. They introduced me to horses and riding and a love of the Australian landscape that imbedded deep in my heart. Pip and I never lived together again, but I saw him often and we would spend hours together in the easy harmony we once had.

I didn't think much about my affinity with Pip. To me that was normal. But I did wonder how other children could carelessly hit trees and bushes with sticks. Couldn't they feel it, like I could? How could people thoughtlessly stamp on ants and how could people be cruel to animals? I was completely traumatised when my uncle chopped the head off a duck with an axe, and I was chased around the back yard by this headless duck with blood spurting from her neck. I was then asked to eat her for Sunday lunch! I sat staring at the plate, my stomach heaving and my eyes swimming.

It hurt and bewildered me to see adults riding horses with such heavy hands that the horse's mouths bled, and witnessing farming activities like cattle branding, tail docking or sheep shearing always left me feeling sick.

In my family I was considered "too sensitive". And decades later my husband bought me a book called *Are You Really Too Sensitive?* by Mary Calhoun, which really helped me understand my "ultra sensitivity", and why I had so much information coming at me all the time. Growing up in a household where the word "psychic" was just never mentioned, it helped me gain a perspective of myself as an adult that was hard to get my head around. The concept of Billie and "psychic" just didn't compute. I wasn't one of those people who could see the future of another. But being an ultra-sensitive was a gift, and something to hone and develop. Sometimes my ultra-sensitivity left me feeling scared, overwhelmed and sad as a child. I also began to feel that no one really understood me. This was something that became a bit of a mantra as I grew up.

At ten, I was small and intense. That was when I was invited to go out with a shearer's family to experience "the back of Bourke". This was red country – dry, very thirsty and to my eyes, bleak. Red soil to the horizon and not many trees. Desert country.

Lisa and Cherry wanted to make a cubby house. That sounded like fun until I saw them run over to a grandmother tree and strip branches from her. Pain and distress hit me in waves.

"Can't we make a cubby out of sheets and towels?" I begged them.

"No, this is more fun."

Please don't do this.

Why didn't they understand the tree was struggling for every drop of moisture? That she needed her branches to create food to survive? Couldn't they feel how thirsty the ground was? Each branch ripped from her skin was like hairs ripped from my own – only worse.

"You're killing the tree! You're stealing her kitchen!!!" I was crying, distressed.

Lisa and Cherry, in their dresses and socks, laughed at me. "Billie's silly!" Now part of the game was to upset me, and giggling, they ripped off more branches. The tree was in shock. It was like rape.

Like a berserker on the battlefield, I lost all reasoning and control and flew at them with my fists, and when that didn't work because there were two of them, I bit and scratched. Lisa screamed for her mum. "Billie's gone mad," she sobbed.

"You're killing the tree's kitchen," I yelled. "Without that she'll die."

Cherry and I rolled in the red dust, and fury fuelled us both. I was hauled to my feet and when I looked up, came face to face with Lisa's mum. My heart sank. I knew I had no chance of making a grown-up understand. "How dare you?" The mother shook me, slapped me hard, and told Lisa and Cherry to continue their game. Cherry stuck her tongue out at me as they ran toward the tree, giggling.

Like a wild creature, I ran into the bush alone to lick my wounds and hide. I didn't go back until nightfall. *"I'm sorry. I'm sorry,"* I sent to the tree. Tears streamed down my cheeks. I'd failed. It was a hollow, helpless feeling.

Chinta

I didn't see my Dad much as I was growing up. He'd remarried and had a new family. His new wife didn't need a moody pre-teen who probably reminded her of Dad's former love. As a devout Roman Catholic, I'm not sure she was keen on the public reminder that Dad was a divorcee in a time when divorce was still a dirty word. She tried hard to mother me and I was sensitive to tensions that weren't talked about. I was also jealous of another woman in Dad's life – as young girls can be.

So I spent a lot of time with Chinta the golden Labrador who filled up the empty spaces with her maternal love. I spent hours cuddled up to her in the laundry where she lived, when I was sad or lonely – or in trouble. She told me I was loveable in a world which didn't seem to embrace me. And she gave me two gifts which were much needed – companionship and strength. I felt more at home with Chinta than I did with humans. As with Pip, we shared a common view of the world, and a deep understanding of each other.

"Why is *she* here?" I asked Chinta one miserable afternoon when I'd been yelled at for something. "She's so different to Mum."

"All beings need love," Chinta sent me.

"I can't love her, and I won't."

"All beings need love, and humans are the thirstiest of all."

I didn't want to hear what Chinta was saying. But her teaching stayed with me, and years later I understood the wisdom of her words.

Ants

A few months after the drought-stricken tree incident, I had another chance to stand up for the life of another species. I was sitting in the car waiting for Dad on a hot summer's day in the country. One of my Dad's junior employees had been sent to keep an eye on me. He was about 18, bored, smoking and idly stomping on ants with his black-shoed foot for amusement.

I was deep in a book when I realised a wrongness in my body. A subtle cry for help. The boy was dragging on his cigarette, his thoughts far away when I yelled at him, seeing him through a haze. "Stop that!" I said. "Ants have a right to life too."

He purposefully killed a few more, grinning at me. Furious, I leapt out of the car and launched myself at him, my tiny body hitting him in the stomach. I don't know what would have happened if Dad hadn't re-emerged right then. The boy saw I was crying, and instead of anger, I saw puzzlement. He had no idea why the life of a few ants meant so much to me.

Stone People

When I was eight, I would walk home from school, apologising to the stones I tripped over. *"Sorry. Sorry. Oops."* When I caught myself saying it aloud, I'd quickly be quiet. I knew nobody would believe me about the stones who whispered to my soul, some asking me to pick them up in the same way a tarot card begs to be chosen, or a crystal.

I had a collection of stones in my bedroom, and sometimes I would take one and hold him in my palm. Intuitively, I'd understand that these were beings who were alive and had a voice. I sensed their desire to help me heal, or just be there like a friend, even if I could not have put it in those words.

I was in trouble enough for my over-sensitivity, so I kept quiet about it all. But my interest in stone collecting was encouraged, and I was introduced to fossils and geology. I loved it all, but not for the reasons adults thought. When I held a stone, I felt the ancient strength. They spoke of grounding, of Mother Earth, of long-forgotten times. If I closed my eyes and concentrated, I felt my energy settle. The stones called me, stirring up a longing for something "other".

I also sensed that "other" in the indigenous people of our land. The stockmen who worked the cattle stations had not only a rapport with their horses, but seemed to have something else, which later I would understand to be a pure connection to the land. My interest in them was not exactly welcomed in those days.

Years later, when I was free to study with the indigenous peoples of many lands, I learned that the stone people were indeed alive, and were revered and employed in healing and ceremony.

Today my home is decorated with piles of stones and rocks who have requested to come inside and hold the energy for me. I now have a mesa, or medicine bag, made up of 13 stones, or *kuya*, which I use to heal others and myself in the tradition of the Inka Q'ero.

Horses and Tree People

Despite never feeling as if I really fit into the family I was raised with, I loved them all and often wished I did fit in. I loved my cousins and living in the country. I loved horse-riding every Saturday with Dod Sleeman, the old stockman who took a handful of kids all over the surrounding countryside on horseback every week. This was heaven. The horse I always rode was a grey pony called Skeeta. Skeeta was worried about a lot of things and he would shy and spook, but I wasn't afraid and learnt to soothe him. What I also learned about horses in those days was that a lot of men treated them like things, and that really disturbed me.

We were galloping on the Common, men and young people alike, on a crazy ride rounding up horses. It was wild and exhilarating. But then I noticed more than one of horses the men rode, had bloody spittle in their mouth.

"Your horse's mouth is bleeding," I called out to one man.

"She'll be right," he said with a grin, but when he wheeled away I felt the horse's wince of pain in my own mouth. It made me aware of the metal in a horse's mouth and how it could hurt. And I always rode with light hands and a loose rein.

There were a lot of times when I was unhappy, feeling the odd one out, and the sharp pain of other species. Sometimes I felt like I was going to shatter or break. And then I would find solace high in the old pine tree out the front of our house. She would wrap her spirit arms around me, and I would warm in her embrace. I knew I would never fall, and I would stay there until I was ready to face the world again.

Years later, I learned that it was typical of the Celtic shaman to spend a lot of time high in trees. Pine trees still hold a special magic for me. Today I have a row of ancient pines and have created a special ceremonial place among them, where on the full and new moon I speak with them and ask for guidance and wisdom.

Boarding School, Surfing and Dogs

I was ten when I "knew" I was going to be a writer or a vet. But until the following year, when I walked into the large, imposing, wood-panelled office of Miss Roberts, the headmistress of the boarding school I attended, I had no idea that being a vet could be bad.

"You want to be a vet?" she boomed, peering at me through her glasses across her massive desk. I thought she looked like a tall, skinny chicken past her prime. She terrified me.

"Girls aren't vets. They're not big enough or strong enough to wrestle cows and horses. It's a horrible, messy job and it needs very high marks in science. No my dear, choose something else. What else would you like to be?"

My tongue stuck in my mouth. I loved animals and until that moment, it had been a secret passion to work with them. To help them. What if she damned my other secret passion – to be a writer? I closed my eyes tight. I couldn't say the words. I couldn't have two dreams killed in one blow. I shuffled my feet, staring at my toes.

"I – I don't know."

Miss Roberts smiled at me. "Perhaps a nurse, like your mother?" she suggested, putting one skinny hand on my shoulder. "A good choice. Welcome to high school."

Boarding school was like a cage. I hated it. It was very difficult being an ultra-sensitive in that environment. It was very regimented, with regular checks of your underwear to make sure you wore regulation bloomers, and being subjected to pat downs to make sure you didn't bring back contraband like sweets after a day's outing with the family.

There was much disparity in wealth, and also between boarders and daygirls. Instead of the school encouraging self-esteem in their students, I spent six years with mine being bruised, and feeling very much the second-class citizen.

I channelled my energies into starting the school's first paper recycling run when I was 12. Even back in the '60s, I was worried about the future of trees. I cared deeply about the environment, animals, and the struggle of the oppressed people – the Africans, the Native Americans, and the Australian Aboriginals. It bothered me that they were being oppressed. At 15, my hero was Martin Luther King.

I had enough self-awareness to know I was different, but I also "knew" that side of me would blossom when I was released from school. Even so, I would spontaneously have flash backs of past lives and would channel writings at various times.

I was 14 when I discovered the joys of surfing during our annual holidays at the coast. And always, the stray dogs would come and be with me whenever I walked the shores alone or sat on the beach watching the waves. My favourite time was early in the morning, before the rest of humanity arose, and I could be alone in nature with a handful of surfers and dogs. I'd rush out of bed, head down to the beach, and always somehow collect some dogs to throw sticks for. They would just appear out of nowhere, their faces alight with the joy of dog, and either sit beside me or draw me into a game. I didn't think anything of it, but was always grateful for the company.

It didn't occur to me then that the dogs were looking for anything more than a game. But today I understand that the dogs "saw" who I was, and were looking to talk, to protect and to do service. They saw my sadness, and sought to cheer me up with games of throwing sticks. They saw how I was attracted to solitude and nature, and reminded me to write everything I noticed, felt and remembered. They wanted to sit beside me in the sand, strong and protective – true friends.

I owe those angel dogs so much, and yet they never asked for anything more than a game in return, lighting my heart and spirit with their merry grins and laughing eyes.

Much later I learnt that Pip had sent them to me.

The surfing culture, with its cottage by the sea, home grown veggies, whole foods and love of nature and animals, shaped my outlook on life. It introduced me to health food stores, healthy eating and the surfer's lifestyle which I longed for. I saw my future in a weatherboard cottage, with trees, veggie garden, dogs and miles of deserted beach where I could surf to my heart's content.

The dreamy surfer teenager worried my family though. I wasn't fitting in again, preferring to "hang out the back" on a borrowed board of my cousin's with all the other surfers, than sitting in the sun on the beach looking pretty and meeting boys. Worse, I wasn't much fun at parties, preferring early nights and my lone early mornings.

"Where's your lipstick?" my grandmother would say disapprovingly, as she took in my dishevelled, sandy appearance and the white zinc on my nose. I knew she would never understand the spirit of Mother Sea, and the power and freedom of catching the perfect wave. I wasn't ever much good at board surfing, but I honed body surfing to a fine art, enjoying the relationship between the sea and myself. It touched the wild inside me, nurtured my spirit and numbed the rawness of my inner wounds. When I was in the sea or wandering around the coastline on my own, it felt like the only time I could be myself. Nature and the elements were my friends. I could shed the restrictions of my culture as easily as I shed my T-shirt. And as I surfed, I understood the true meaning of life and touched the Divine in all. But I couldn't verbalise all that. So "social misfit" was the next worried phrase that was attached to me.

By 16, I was constantly threatened with expulsion for being rude and wild, even at the same time as I was shy and had, what other students told me later, " a terrified look in my eyes." I was desperate to conform and be like everyone else, but I was an empath and felt too much of the world. And at school, there were no animals to keep me company and safe.

I was angry, hurting, and confused by a life which didn't make sense to me. It seemed repressive and cruel. My dad, who I adored, had disappeared from my life with his new family in a flurry of misunderstanding which we didn't unravel until years later, and my body responded to the loss of him with a nasty outbreak of plantar warts. Of course, no one understood that this was the root cause at the time.

The medical profession failed me completely and utterly. I was subjected to acid being poured onto my raw feet, and then, after months of this treatment proved futile, I was told I would never walk again.

I was 15. If I was a dog or a horse they would have shot me then and there.

I'll never forget sitting in the school hospital with my aunt and the doctors as they discussed wheelchairs for me. The doctor's voices were heavy with regret, and they looked at me with no hope in their eyes and a great deal of pity. My heart fluttered and everything inside me screamed out that the doctors were wrong. But I just sat there, curled up in a miserable ball of silence, too scared to speak. Inside, I was determined to walk and be free of pain.

I hobbled around on my crutches, studied folk medicine remedies, and came up with one to remove warts. I begged Percy the cook to let me "steal" a steak, which I was then to rub on my wounded feet and bury in the school grounds.

"It'll never work," sneered Sandra, one of my dormitory mates, as she watched me rubbing the meat onto my foot. I was barely holding it together, and her words were like cold water to my hope, making me flinch with their harshness. For the first time I broke down, sobbing with grief and despair.

"Don't you see I need to believe it will," I screamed at her through tears.

She stood there glowering at me.

"It's all nonsense," she said coolly. "You'll never get better, and certainly not like that."

"Leave me alone," I screamed again. "Just leave me alone. I've got nothing left to try."

"Shut up, Sandy," said a voice.

"Leave her alone," said another. I looked up and all the girls in the dorm had come over to intervene. They pushed Sandy and her big mouth away from me, and formed a protective cluster in my room. I was so relieved and grateful that they had come to my aid because the shred of belief I had was the only thing I was clinging onto. I felt if I let go, I'd unravel completely.

I didn't want to end up in a wheel chair.

"It'll work honey," said another girl.

"You've got to try."

I nodded and kept going, rubbing the meat into my wounded feet, willing it to absorb the warts, seeing my feet as whole again. Nothing more was said about it. But even today I'm grateful for those girls who stood up and believed in the possible when a situation looked impossible. And I'm grateful to Sandy, because I needed to cry.

This proved a turning point for me, because, even though it wasn't instant, I did heal, and by 16 was running around free of ugly, white, orthopaedic shoes and crutches. There never was any need for a wheelchair.

Today, as an advocate of holistic healing for both people and animals, I understand the power of emotional causation of disease, and also the power of belief. Belief was at the root of the folk medicine I tried, a tool to self-empower the patient and create conditions of hope so that healing could happen. This allows the body to heal itself.

The mind and emotions are powerful tools when used correctly for healing.

A couple of years later I was visiting a friend's parents when her Dad suddenly pulled me into a hug.

"You're a brave little girl," he said. "You showed courage and perseverance. You showed 'em you've got guts and inner strength. It'll stand you in good stead for the rest of your life"

I was really surprised by his kind outburst, and it gave me something good to hang onto. He shone a light onto some wounds with his words and gave me different view of myself.

It also taught me about the importance of words and acknowledgement, and how we all need to shine a light on people and animals, instead of destroying them with criticism, negative programming, and limiting beliefs.

The plus side of boarding school was having country friends. I was often invited home with them in the holidays. There I could be with nature. I could ride. I could be with animals and in the landscape I loved.

Because I was always off by myself, writing in my journal in the local parks, my aunt suggested I become a journalist. It was a brilliant suggestion, because I saw it as training for the writer I knew I would become. But my schoolteachers who knew me as incredibly shy were very concerned.

"A journalist?" asked my English teacher, who was my personal favourite. "Well, look, may I suggest that when you go out into the real world, you draw a bubble of protection around you." She looked at me with grave concern, shaking her head. I could see she doubted my ability to be a journalist.

"You're so very sensitive," she explained.

My history teacher had the same reaction. "I want you to look in the mirror every day and say "every day I am getting better and better." This was my introduction to the personal growth movement – in the early 70s.

Years later I bumped into my history teacher at the theatre. I reminded her of the affirmation she'd given me. "You were the shyest person I had ever met," she said. "And the only girl in all my years of teaching I have ever had to give that affirmation to."

Despite the odds, I landed a job on a suburban paper.

First Work – And the Beginning...

At 18, I was the entertainment editor of a large suburban paper, writing movie and music reviews. It was a fabulous life. I made up my mind to be a comedy film director.

My soul had other plans.

I became anaemic. And it wasn't a fun experience. The iron tablets the doctor game me made me feel sick, and I stopped taking them. One of my friends dropped around with one of Australia's first alternative magazines and told me to read it. There was a story about nutrition and how you are like a car, which needs to be fed good oil and petrol in order to run. I got it. I healed myself with fresh parsley and spinach in salads and discovered the delights of whole foods and vegetarianism. I didn't like meat and only ate it rarely because I thought I had to.

Discovering vegetarianism was liberating on many levels and I never looked back, despite it being considered "weird" back in the 70's in most circles.

I baked my own bread, made flower salads, spaghetti with lentils, and meat free quiches and stews, and friends would eat at KFC before they came to dinner in case I fed them the "lettuce leaves", they thought a vegetarian diet was. I remember being more amused than insulted when one friend said that her boss, a chemist, had become a vegetarian to lose weight, and he was "intelligent".

Some months later I became a sub editor of the same magazine, Nature and Health, and it's partner Simply Living. This was a whole new world in thinking and being. Writing about the magic of herbs made me want to study them deeper, and when I heard herbalist Denis Stewart use the word "esoteric", I just had to be in his herb class.

I also studied filmmaking and loved it, but the vegetarian, peppermint tea drinking me was an outsider with the other students. I was always made fun of by other journalists and filmmakers because I didn't drink or smoke, and my only vice seemed to be chocolate.

"How do you have fun?" they would ask. I couldn't explain to them that fun for me was journeying to the unseen worlds and learning what it took to be a healer, even though I knew I would never make it my career. To me, healing was connected to the Great Mystery, and I was fascinated by that. Little did I know where it would lead me.

Traditionally, the shaman of the tribe was a healer who called on the spirits out of time to assist in healing, and who spoke the language of the animals. This is the path my soul kept putting me on, despite all my efforts to the contrary.

Sollie, Binah, Chockmah, Pucawan and Reka

Most shamans have a mentor to teach them. I didn't even know the word "shaman", let alone understand that was the path I was on. But as usual, Spirit presented me with teachers and guides to steer me in the direction I was supposed to go.

Not only did I first hear about the ancient prophecy of 2012 and the promise of a Golden Age of peace through that dynamic 1978 herb class, but a fellow student suggested I read *Kinship with all Life* by J. Allen Boone because of my love of animals. When he told me it was about talking with animals, my heart leapt! I really wanted to do that!

By this time, I was in love and about to live a self-sufficient lifestyle in the bush with a lovely man and our three cats, Binah, Chockmah and Pucawan.

Binah was a scrap of a Blue Burmese, Chockmah was a chocolate Burmese who was a retiree from a cattery, and Pucawan was their son. We had a wonderful rapport, but I would never have called it communication. But that's only because I didn't consciously know what communication was. Again, the affinity I had with animals and nature was just natural to me, and I didn't think it was anything particularly special. However, I admit to being suspicious that something was up because those cats understood every word I said, and our relationship was exceptional.

And then I met Sollie, my horse friend. Sol would send me images as we rode, and we had a partnership and understanding that was beyond close. I "knew" when he wanted to go to the dam and when he wanted to gallop or canter. I "knew" his heart and soul with my own body.

Binah, Pucawan and Chockmah

While I call the animals my first true teachers, J. Allen Boone was certainly my guide and mentor. Here was a man whose words and writing truly spoke to me. He was the first person I had "met" who I resonated with on a spiritual level. He saw the world as I did.

Boone was a Hollywood writer who was given the movie star dog Strongheart to babysit, and *Kinship with All Life* is the story of how this highly educated dog taught Boone to communicate with mental images and humility.

Sollie

Images. That was communication? It was like a door opened. A huge "a-ha". That's what Sollie and the cats were doing all the time. And there was more. I empathetically felt what they felt too. Images, feelings, intuitive knowing – and whispered words. That was the silent language of the animals and nature.

I was already doing it. Had been all my life.

Oh.

It was incredible the way the animals had tried to get me to understand. Chockmah disappeared an entire Easter break once, before we built our house in the bush, and despite calling him and searching for him, I never heard a peep. He was on secret cat business. But on the last night, I stood in the bush where I had lost him, and said in a loud voice, "I'm going to the next door neighbour's for dinner and when I get back, I expect you to be home because tomorrow we're leaving early and this is your last chance."

Sure enough, Chocky was waiting for us when we got home, and when I checked with my senses, I felt intuitively that he hadn't been far away at all. As he wolfed down the food I prepared for him, Chocky told me that he didn't like "*being cooped up in the shed*" we used for a kitchen and that we were "*to trust the cats not to run away or 'go feral'*".

I agreed and felt thoroughly chastened by my cat. From then, on the cats ran free on the property and by unspoken agreement, slept with us

Secret Animal Business

every night in our tent where we knew they were safe and warm.

This was secret animal business. This was cat as teacher.

There were many experiences like that, which helped me understand that animals did understand our language, that there was a psychic bond between us all, and that animals indeed were far more enlightened than we humans and acted as our guides and teachers.

Inspired by Boone's book, I had to get a German Shepherd dog called Reka to teach me more about communion with animals, like Strongheart did. But Reka didn't teach me anything about communication. Her lessons were profound and had everything to do with love, healing, journeying, and understanding the psychic and spiritual nature of animals.

In the meantime my relationship broke up and I headed back to the city to study acting and write, temporarily leaving the animals in my partner's care while we sorted things out. I'd come home on weekends. It was a difficult time, and Reka showed me how deeply affected she was by getting distemper.

I was in the middle of my first professional play, and would rush home between shows on the overnight train. As soon as the season was over, I packed up my Sydney base and went back to the bush to nurse her full-time.

Two vets told me she wouldn't make it. But I was determined, and turned again to another mentor - the writer and animal herbalist Juliette de Bairacli-Levy. She recommended fasting until the temperature went back to normal, and had a routine of daily care which I followed judiciously. I wasn't going to let Reka die. She was only two and I loved her deeply.

Reka

Reka not only lived, she thrived.

Again I was being taught not to listen to the conventional medicine people when they said it was the end of the road. While there were other avenues to explore I wouldn't give up – for myself or my animal companions.

Andrew, Shaman Stuff and Animal Advocacy

I was deep in my shamanic phase, having been taught shamanic drumming and journeying by noted Australia author on shamanism Neville Drury. Neville was my boss at Nature and Health, one of several magazines I wrote for. I also ran a seminar called Healing with Humour, and I performed stand-up comedy.

Stand-up was tough and scary, but I was determined to master the art form of being at ease in front of an audience without the mask of a character. I loved comedy and felt you could help people through making them laugh and seeing their problems and issues in a new light. I wanted to make comedy films with meaning. And besides, that was how Woody Allen got his break. Maybe it would help me too.

I'd meditate every morning during my runs through the bush with Reka, and a gracious, strong Native American woman would come to me in spirit. If I held onto the memory or essence of her, I'd perform on stage with ease. If I forgot, my anxiety would get in the way. She was far more dignified than I was, possessing a quiet inner strength I admired. So at the same time as I was cutting my comedy teeth in Sydney's tough comedy clubs, I was deeply involved in the spiritual community, and growing my wings as an animal shaman – even though I would never have called it that. I just kept telling myself I was happily exploring spiritual things which interested me.

Reka allowed me to project my etheric self into hers and see the world through her eyes. It was something I did with many animals, learning to understand how it felt to be a soul in an animal's body. This is a form of shape-shifting, but I always longed to do a physical change – to become the animals I loved. That was what real shamans could do.

I was single and living in the city with Reka, three cats and two budgies. Sollie was still in the country with his friend, the pony Sebastian, and our goats. I visited every second weekend and for extended writing breaks. But it wasn't enough. There was a piece of my soul missing and it was a very difficult time. I felt split.

The animals were my refuge and my rock. Together we found homes in the city which suited our need for peace, space and wilderness. Reka would make sure I had my daily bush fix, and helped me explore the neighbourhood in the afternoons. On Sunday, I would drive her to the beach, and for a short time we even did dog training. I don't have fond memories of that.

Secret Animal Business

Reka was my best mate, and was even known to come into theatre rehearsals with me. She was often on the set of commercials and TV shows when I was an extra. Once she even got paid because they asked her to be on camera. She was loved by all my friends and family. She was my life.

By the time Reka was eight, I was married to the love of my life, fellow comic Andrew Einspruch, who I had met at a personal growth conference in Hawaii. An American, Andrew was a spiritual, vegetarian, animal-loving, non-drinking, non-smoking, non-drug taking comic like me. He was also very brave. I married him immediately and people were a bit stunned. How did I find another comic with the same values as me? Comedy was a tough scene and most of them were heavily into alcohol, drugs or both.

Some people thought I was just plain lucky. But it was more than luck – it was destiny. And that's a story for another time.

Andrew and I were often busy performing comedy, and I didn't want Reka to be lonely. So I asked her about it. "Would you like a friend, Reka, a pack mate?"

"I don't know. I've never had one."

"Well, if you were to have one, what would you like or look for?"

"Someone with a sense of humour."

We found Kai, a pup in danger of death simply because it was Christmas and the shelter would be closed. We asked some friends to pick him up and bring him over to us, and after an excited day of a bath and being introduced to Reka, I was awakened by a serious looking black kelpie/Shepherd cross pup sitting by our futon.

Kai and Reka, me and Andrew

"Kai, what is it?" I said, struggling awake and sitting up.

"Are you going to look after me?"

"Of course I am," I said, my heart breaking open a little, and I pulled him into a cuddle in my arms.

He and Reka got on incredibly well, and as Kai grew up we included them both in our comedy act, which we toured just a little. Reka and Kai, I'm proud to say, have howled "Happy Birthday" on stage and on radio, and one man's response was something which struck a chord. "I don't like dogs," he said. "But seeing you up on the stage with them was something else. They're fantastic. Thanks so much. I'm going to look at dogs with new eyes."

I began to realise something "other" was happening, more than Andrew and I understood.

I also had to get back to living on the land so I could be with my then three horses, two goats, three cats and three dogs all the time. We moved everyone to the Blue Mountains and I immediately fell over with adrenal burnout. I call this time my "shamanic initiation into stillness," and I spent it journeying and hanging out with spirit guides, who I came to know as The Tribe.

Kai, on the day he came to us.

I didn't know it at the time, but huge changes were afoot, and I was about to be placed firmly and squarely on a path that was my soul's choice, not mine. But when I look back, I see how the animals conspired with my soul to prepare me for this next big phase. And it didn't matter how unconscious I chose to be about it, they were determined to wake me up.

Andrew and I were writing children's books then, but my beloved Reka was failing. I had had some deep connections to the spirit world, and I called on my people in that world of infinity to beg for more time with Reka. They granted me that.

She was due to go to the vet that afternoon for some acupuncture, and was sitting outside on the veranda in the cold winter sun on a mat. Something made me not want to leave her side. I tried to sit in the sun for a little bit, but she called me back to give her the healing power of Reiki.

Kai came over and bowed to her, in a silent communion that I wasn't privy to and still I didn't figure out what was going on. I was giving her Reiki and chatting on the phone when she died suddenly, doing the death dance that I was to become so familiar with. I dropped the phone in horror and screamed.

"Noooooooooooooo". I had begged the spirits for more time and they had promised me. Two days? Only two days? I was numb with shock. Reka had been my constant companion for 11 short years, teaching me so much about healing and partnership. To lose her was like losing a child and I begged her spirit to come back to me.

"Reka, please come back, please."

Reka's spirit form looked at me, her golden coat luminous and glowing. She didn't look at me with pity, or even compassion. She looked at me with the strength she always had. And then in front of me, she turned into a beautiful young woman with long, tawny hair. This woman, like Reka, possessed an inner strength and beauty. I could tell she was someone special. She was tall, graceful and wild. She was Reka's soul in human form, and this would be her next incarnation. The vision faded. I was shattered, my heart in pieces, but I was complete. Reka's soul had moved on.

We buried her that night, after the sun went down. Kai watched stoically until the first clod of dirt went on her lifeless, golden body. Then he let out a howl of despair and jumped in the grave, digging her up. Andrew and I both broke down then, crying and cuddling Kai and telling him everything was all right, that Reka was gone.

Reka left me with a mission. She sent Andrew and I off to the worst pound in Sydney with an instruction to find a dog that carried an essence of her. We had to go on a particular day, and it was tough. I was shocked by the conditions in this pound, and it was even more desperate because I knew that many of these dogs would go to science experiments or death. The atmosphere was heavy with collective misery. I cast out my senses and counted eleven dogs I could take immediately. The only way I knew to choose was to honour the soul's choice and ask which ones wanted us to help them. But suddenly it was closing time and we were being asked to leave. I sent a silent: *"I'll be back,"* and did a double take when I saw a golden German Shepherd cross who reminded me of Reka – or someone. There was a moment of recognition between us. She and I locked eyes. *"I promise I'll get you out,"* I whispered. She looked terrified. Meanwhile the man on duty at the pound was a kindly soul and he picked up another Shepherd cross pup, who was reddish in colour and had a sad face. He thrust her into my arms and I knew I had found Reka's essence.

A whimper caught my attention. A little black pup who was now alone in the cage looked at me with an appeal in her eyes. My heart squeezed. "What about that one?" I asked. The guy pushed us along. He needed to close up. "She'll be right. She'll find a home. The pups always do."

That little black face has haunted me ever since.

Andrew and I named our new dog Tala, and she was the saddest dog I had ever met. It took her days to heal, but we were suddenly rewarded when we took her for a walk and she began splashing in puddles like any young dog. It was so spontaneous I had to laugh. She looked up at me, and grinned. I grinned back and a bond formed between Tala and I that remained the 14 years she was with us. She never left my side, walking with me from room to room when I went through the house, and hated it when I had to go away.

We went back for the other Shepherd, because I always keep my promises. She was so terrified in the pound that she hadn't eaten for a week. Her hair was falling out, and she had an eye discharge. She looked a mess and had that wild desperation that said she knew her time was up. The attendant, this time a man who was frightened of dogs, let her out of the cage. She bolted. He cursed, too timid to fetch her back. The dog ran down the isle of cages.

I squatted down and called her in the low, calm voice I use with animals. "Here girl, it's okay, you're coming home with us. Come on." Amazingly she stopped, and allowed me to touch her and pick her up. She was about seven months old. Animal experiment material. I sent her pictures of home and dogs, but she was too frightened to listen. The atmosphere was too oppressive. I hoped the other dogs in the car would be able to communicate with her, but when we stopped for groceries, she bolted again – in the car park. Again she responded to my voice and by the time we got her home, she stood on the veranda for a moment and looked around with awe. She looked at the house, the other dogs, the trees, the horses, the bush. And then she smiled, wagged her tail, and trotted up to me.

"*Thank-you,*" she sent. And then, tail high in the air, she trotted over to Andrew. "*Thank you.*"

We called her Twylah, for our Seneca teacher Grandmother Twylah Nitsch of the Seneca Wolf Clan Teaching Lodge, and she became a teacher herself. She and Tala became great friends, and she died 14 years later, a week after Tala's passing, exactly the timing they had come to us.

The black pup had indeed gone from the pound, but we kept going back. We re-homed dogs, and sometimes were even able to reunite them

The Sad Puppy – Tala

with their people when the pound staff failed to find phone numbers on collars. It was gruesome work, because you wanted to help all of them. It tore our hearts to experience the misery of their souls, and it left a stain on ours. It made me ashamed to be part of the human race. Death row and scientific experiments on animals is wrong for so many reasons, and while I still provide a service to animals in trouble to this day, I swore then and there I would do my best to stop this violence towards other species.

Twylah and Tala

At the same time as Tala and Twylah came into our lives, we were involved with the natural horsemanship community, and being made painfully aware of the plight of other horses outside that community.

Our own horse herd swelled in number. When an animal whose language you understand begs you to help them, you can't say "no".

I used to worry about how we were going to afford the now 10 horses, five dogs and assorted cats we had vowed to take care of forever. But Spirit kept sending me rainbows, and something deep inside me relaxed. I knew it was going to be fine. I didn't know where this path with animals would lead me, but I knew it was important for my soul, and Andrew's, too. I knew it was something we'd signed up for together in that place outside of time.

Today my life is a tapestry of stories from the many, many animals who have graced my life with their Light and their profound teachings. Our horse herd grew to 30, and our dog pack to eight. I know it is a drop in the ocean of need, but the animals needed someone who understood them at a deeper level to tell their story.

And this is that story.

Chapter 2:
The Beginning

Sue, the petite, brown-haired woman in front of me needed help for her dog, and my body was frozen in panic. "*It's time,*" whispered Sollie, who I was unsaddling after our ride with Sue. The autumn sun was still hot, and I felt sticky but exhilarated. Sollie had behaved himself. I had stayed in the saddle. All was well in the world.

So why were my legs turning to jelly?

I took the rope halter off my horse, who tried to stand on my foot. "*Okay,*" I sent back furiously.

I cleared my throat. "Eczema, you reckon, Sue?" A frown marked her pretty face. I could tell she was deeply worried about Marker, who she had adopted when she found him wandering around near her place.

Sollie let out a sigh, blowing on my plaited hair. Up until this time, the only people who knew I spoke with animals was my husband Andrew and my indigenous teachers and friends. When you walked the shamanic path, it was expected of you. "Go and talk to the tree," Grandmother Kitty, a Lakota-Sioux Elder had once instructed us. "She has much information for you."

As I had always spoken to trees, bushes, stones, and animals, this request was nothing out of the ordinary to me. But it was when my teachers in non-ordinary reality, The Tribe, asked me to talk with other people's animals that the trouble started. Other people were fine, so long as I didn't have to mention the word "psychic" in association with myself. I wasn't psychic. I was just sensitive. Filmmakers and comics didn't talk to trees or birds or dogs. They just didn't.

I had just spent six intense months with The Tribe during my shamanic initiation into stillness. The outer world called it Chronic Fatigue Syndrome; my naturopath doctor called it adrenal burnout. I saw it differently. I had been about to go against the whisperings of my own soul and go into television as a comedy performer.

Lying on my back wondering why my athletic body suddenly couldn't move had been frightening, and so was the prospect of a lost opportunity. And as Andrew and I were a comic duo, this effectively killed both our careers. We'd moved to a log cabin in the mountains with our large animal family, and Andrew found work as an IT writer. This was a waste of his comic skills, but it paid the bills.

To renew myself, I meditated. Every day I shamanically journeyed to that other world outside of time, and sat with the Tribe council. I was instructed in horsemanship by a spirit named Grandmother, and was called "woman of twin tongues". I had no idea what they meant, and always wondered if I was supposed to learn Apache, which seemed to be the tribe's language. I was initiated and taught many things during this time, and the veil between my world and theirs was very, very thin.

Then came the day when it was time for me to return to my world, and my health and do my work. "*You are the woman of twin tongues,*" I was told. "*Go and speak with other people's animals.*"

Oh.

At this stage, I had no idea why they wanted me to do this and the very thought filled me with dread. What would people think? I remembered past lives of persecution for that gift, and shuddered. I'd been burnt, stoned and ostracised for my abilities back then. It hadn't been fun at all. This was a big ask.

But I respected my Tribe's wishes. And I wasn't going to let them down. I dutifully printed a small colourful card that said "Billie Dean – Animal Communicator" on it. And promptly had palpitations and shaky limbs.

Today was no different. My hands were slippery and my heart beat wildly. This was a big thing for me. I took a breath and gave Sollie a hug and silent thanks. He gave me courage.

"Let's get some tea and we'll talk about it, Sue. There's lots you can do for it." I flung the lead rope and halter over my shoulder and strode purposefully for the door of our house. "And I also do this psychic thing with animals we could try. I can hear them."

Sue was behind me, and part of me hoped she couldn't hear me. But no such luck.

"Ooh, Billie, that would be wonderful. I'd love you to talk to Marker." Sue's voice was light with joy. I glanced at her. Her longer strides had put her quickly beside me. "Really," she grinned.

Inside, Andrew already had the kettle singing, and brought out one of my popular cocoa-laden, almond meal, sugar-free cakes. Our various dogs were lying around the kitchen floor, panting happily. Sue's face broke into a smile when she saw the cake. "Just what I need for the drive home," she said. She didn't realise how much she was putting me at ease. She hadn't blinked or tripped over the words "psychic" or "hear".

It made me realise how different people are, and how families and friends can often put you in a box without realising it. Sue was a new friend and was delighted to hear about my abilities.

Sue took a seat at the table and patted Suki, the kelpie with shining brown eyes. "Gosh Billie, they're all so silky. How do you get their coats like that?"

"Natural diet," Andrew piped up. I took a swig of tea to calm my shaking body. It was going to be all right. No rejection or death by fire here.

"These dogs all eat a raw food diet and, it fixes them up every time." Andrew proudly drew Twylah into a hug.

"Would that help Marker as well?" Sue asked.

"You bet." Andrew's eyes twinkled as he cut the cake. It was lovely to have a husband who supported and understood my holistic care of animals.

"Sue, Marker probably needs some oils in his diet as well, but I'm thinking the cause of his problem is emotional. It usually is. That's why I'm suggesting we talk to him," I said in a rush.

Andrew threw me a look. I shrugged. Sollie was right. It's time. And Marker, I could already feel in my own body, was miserable. I had to help him.

"So how do we do that Billie? When are you down our way?" Sue was keen.

"I can do it here," I said. "I just tune in. It's just telepathy. All animals have it. So do we. We've just forgotten. But I'll do it later, if it's okay with you. And I'll ring you tomorrow."

"Thanks Billie, that would be incredible. Marker is so precious to us, I'd love to hear what he has to say."

Andrew slung his arm around me as we waved Sue off, watching her red Landcruiser chew up the dust in the long drive way.

"Come on," he said. "Let's feed the horses and get you calmed down."

I smiled. The horses always calmed me down. They saw it as their job – when they weren't pushing me to become a better horsewoman and more confident, assertive person. Just like Grandmother from the Tribe. Sollie had been considered a dangerous, problem horse at one point. But I knew the fault was with me, and refused to give up on him. It now scared me to ride him, but I loved him deeply.

The autumn evening was starry and cool by the time I sat at my desk overlooking the bushland around our mountain home. I took a deep breath. My first professional consultation.

Sollie intruded into my thoughts. I remembered when I first saw him tied to a tree outside another log cabin in another bush. It was love at first sight for me and this round, chestnut, stock horse with the expressive eyes. My then partner made an offer for him and suddenly the horse and I were together, riding in poetry. Sollie would send me images, telling me where he wanted to go – to the dam, to the end of the valley, up the hill – and I would respond the same way. We were in perfect harmony and understanding.

I sighed. Those days were long gone. Sollie was teaching me things the hard way now.

I called Marker's energetic body into the room and invited him to communicate with me. He was very keen. I could "see" the hot spot clearly on his back and asked him about it. He said he was very afraid his new people would throw him out like he had been before.

"They're always worried about it, and I'm afraid of being a nuisance," he sent.

He showed me an image of two men in the front cab of a big truck, throwing him out. And I could feel the distress and fear in the Blue Heeler's compact body.

"Surely you came off the back of the truck?" I said, incredulous that

anyone would toss a dog as heartlessly as they would an apple core.

He sent me the image again.

I typed up my notes, as he showed me the full picture of what was going on for his body. The more his loving people fussed over his hot spot, the worse it got, because Marker thought he would be again "thrown away" and this caused him great distress. The stress he felt aggravated his hot spot. I spent some time assuring him his new people were far different to his former ones and would never "throw him out", and felt him relax. I had to get Sue and her husband to help break the cycle. I wrote down some blood-purifying herbs to send her which would help as well.

Finally, I asked him what would make him feel comfortable.

"*Calamine,*" he said promptly.

As a natural therapist I hadn't used calamine lotion since I was a child. "*Do you mean calendula or chamomile?*" I asked, knowing both would be healing and soothing.

"*Calamine,*" he insisted.

The next day I rang Sue and told her the story.

"Oh that makes perfect sense to me, Billie. Now I understand why he is so terrified of getting into the car," she said. "I know exactly what to do. I'll fill my hand with love and make sure I touch his sore spot. And I'll chunk down the car rides. I'll put him in, and then take him out. I'll put him in and drive a minute and then we'll both get out. It'll work. Just patience. Thank you, Billie."

I smiled and knew that was one dog who was going to be all right.

"Oh, and he said something about calamine lotion helping him. I wasn't sure I heard that right. Chamomile or calendula would both be good in an ointment," I added.

"No, he was right Billie. Calamine is what we've been using."

Chapter 3:
Wosco

Word spread about my ability to help animals through telepathic communication and soon I was speaking with other people's animals regularly. The work was enjoyable as I met caring animal people and fabulous animal characters with a wide range of interesting problems. And while it could be challenging and heart-breaking, rewarding and heart-warming, it was never, ever dull. With every animal client, my respect for the animal kingdom grew. And it was heartening to be involved with people who wanted to try a more enlightened approach to their animal's problems. Stephen's Rottweiler Wosco, for example, refused to go out in his new backyard.

"We've just moved," Stephen told me over the phone. "Wosco's been out in the yard once, and now refuses to go out again. We're at our wit's end. Can you help?"

I promised to see what I could do, and settled down at my desk to communicate with Wosco, who was on the other side of the continent in Perth.

He sent me a picture of tall trees being blown in a high wind. From his perspective, they looked scary, as if they topple any minute.

"They are going to fall down," he insisted. *"I've already been hit by one. Please tell my people to look for borers in those trees. They aren't safe."*

Wosco didn't want to say much else. And so I mentioned the borers to Stephen and told him that until the trees were made safe, Wosco would remain frightened of being killed in the backyard by a falling tree.

There was a stunned silence.

"The trees do have borers," Stephen said finally. "And now you mention it, the first night in the new place, there was a storm and a branch did come down. Wosco got a terrible fright. But we never thought..." His voice trailed off. "Wow."

Stephen told me a few days later that he had sat down with Wosco and thanked him for his concern about the trees. A tree surgeon had been brought in and the dangerous trees were removed. Stephen could tell when the backyard was safe by taking his cue from his dog.

"I'll never call Wosco a dumb dog again," Stephen said. "He's the smartest dog I've ever met, and from now on he gets my complete respect."

I was smiling when I got off the phone and I bent down on my knees and hugged Kai, who always sat under my desk as close as he could get to me.

"All dogs are smart," I told him fondly, ruffling his coat. "And one day everyone will understand that."

Chapter 4:
Sinjin

"So can you help me?" I was pleased the woman with the proper English accent couldn't see me as I stood in the living room, blue jeans sopping and a wet towel in my hand, watching a soapy black kelpie/collie cross roll delightedly in the dirt outside. *"You might have escaped for now,"* I sent to Suki, *"But I'll be out in a minute to finish the job."*

Suki laughed and raced around with an equally wet and dirty Kai. It was wonderful to see them so happy.

Mrs Mary Rowe's dog Sinjin, however, was not happy. He was a stud Maltese Terrier and a much-loved animal. But he'd gone missing again. Apparently he did it often.

"Sinjin, where are you?" I sent.

I immediately received an image of the bush and a sense of a cheeky little dog running around excitedly. *"There are lots of smells,"* he said.

"Your person is very concerned for you, and it would be kind if you returned home."

"That spoilsport."

"She loves you."

"I'll go home when I'm ready."

Very cheeky, I thought, and left it at that for the moment. I went to finish washing my own cheeky dogs, and gave them a thorough dry. They loved being towel dried and reminded me that I really was their mere servant. I threw the ball a couple of times and headed back to my office, where I checked in with Sinjin again.

"I'm still chasing smells and trails," he said.

"I need you to find your way home now."

"When I'm ready."

"I've got a cheeky one today," I told Andrew, who was working at his computer.

Mrs Rowe rang me the next day. Thankfully, a neighbour had brought Sinjin home the night before. I was worried to learn that Sinjin wore neither collar nor tag. As most people couldn't talk animal language, and Sinjin was determined to find release in "chasing smells", there was a strong possibility that he might get very lost – or taken in by a well-meaning stranger. If he chose to.

"Mrs Rowe, really, a dog like Sinjin needs to wear a collar and tag. He's an escape artist who relies on other people to bring him home. But what happens when he goes further away and people don't know you have Maltese? Please save yourself the stress of so much worry and get him a collar and tag, so at least people know who he is and can bring him home."

There was a haughty silence at the other end of the phone. "I have another problem with Sinjin," she said finally. "It's a long standing one, but I think you can help me."

I waited. "He screams and barks for three long days after he mates. It's unbelievable and I can't stand it anymore."

Sinjin sounded subdued when I tuned in, almost bored. The change from a happy, cheeky, dog bursting with vitality, humour and curiosity to this dulled dog was profound. Gently, I asked him what the barking and screaming was all about.

"I'm so small, " he said. *"I need to be heard."*

"Come on Sinjin, you're beautiful. People notice you all the time."

"No they don't. I scream because I protest. No one hears me."

"I think you'll find you are heard, just not understood. Do you want to talk about it?"

Sinjin was more than ready. *"They bring me a girl. Then they take her away. It makes me crazy. I cry for her. Why do they take her away? I need a mate. To keep. A girl to love and cherish."*

I saw a picture of dogs by a fireplace. A family of dogs sleeping peacefully, curled up together on the stone hearth. Blissful parents to eight puppies contentedly sleeping, some attached to their mother's nipples. Beside them, the fire danced, warm and bright. This is what Sinjin wanted.

Sinjin sighed softly. *"I'm happy as a dog. People may laugh at me because I am little, but I enjoy my freedom. I just wish they could understand me better."*

My heart went out to the little bloke. He had a big personality and his moments of running free were the only times he seemed really happy. No wonder he was such an escape artist.

"How can I help you Sinjin? What would make your life better?

"A wife and children. What else is there? I want to love and be loved. I scream because I am crying – and frustrated. Tell Mary I think she's fantastic, but she needs to learn the silent language. It's frustrating to be misunderstood. I don't come when I'm called because what is there when I do?"

Sinjin was getting more upset by the minute. I gently soothed him and told him I would see what I could do for him.

"It would be good if you could stay within your boundary."

"Tell Mary to de-sex me then. Cut off my balls and give me a wife. I'll not stray from her. I'd be content."

He sounded so angry and bitter then, and my heart went out to him. We talked about his unhappiness for a while and I promised him I would see what I could do to convince Mrs Rowe to retire him, and find him a permanent mate.

But Sinjin had some suggestions of his own.

"Perhaps Mary could take me around the boundary and show me where it is. Perhaps she could talk to me more in the tongue language and explain things – like telling me the girl I mate with is just a friend – not mine to keep. Perhaps we could come to some arrangement about finding me my own girl? Perhaps we could start afresh, with no misunderstandings?"

He was calmer then and I left him mulling how life could be instead of how it was. He was an intelligent and sensitive dog, and my job was to explain that to Mrs Mary Rowe. I wasn't sure she'd be responsive.

Sinjin looked at me and I saw light shine from his soulful brown eyes. I had to admire him for his pluck and courage. But there was more – Sinjin was indeed a teacher and a philosopher.

"It's OK, Billie, I'll live the life I live."

And I thought, you're right. That's all any of us can do. Live life the best way we can.

I don't actually know what happened to Sinjin in the end. Mrs Rowe said she'd think about it, but never asked for follow-up. But when I tuned in to Sinjin, he seemed at peace and I knew he had the spark and the spirit to grab whatever life handed him with all of his paws and make the most of it.

Chapter 5:
Omar and Rosie

Omar the cat was missing. George was on the phone and I knew he didn't know what to expect from me.

"We've tried everything. Done a letterbox drop, put adds in the local paper..." His voice faltered.

"Okay, that's good. You're doing everything you can. Even with a psychic consultation, you still need to put in the legwork. Has anything happened at home to make your cat run off? Any emotional upsets?"

"Nothing I can think of." There was a pause. I got an immediate impression of a dog, a bouncy brown terrier mix with a happy open face. "We're babysitting a friend's dog. We often do," he added. "So that shouldn't be a problem."

I assured him that normally it wouldn't. But I'd ask Omar if the dog had offended him somehow.

Lost animals are my most difficult clients. There's usually a lot of emotional stress from the humans, and sometimes, but not always, from the animal. When caring people take in lost animals, it's often impossible to get them back, and sometimes the animals themselves choose this. That's particularly hard for the original carer to hear. My success with lost animals comes from understanding that in life there are no accidents. There is often an emotional or dietary cause for animals to run off. And sometimes there is a spiritual lesson for their carers to learn.

With some trepidation, I called in Omar and was relieved to find him in good spirits and still in his body. *"Why did you leave?"* I asked.

"I wanted to go because I don't like the dog they are looking after. He makes me nervous. And it's not the first time he's ruled the roost at our place. He's so ... bouncy."

"Omar, the dog's gone home and now your people are worried about where you are."

"I'll make it home," he said confidently. *"But when I do, I don't want any of that tinned food. Or the dried stuff. It's addictive and it makes me crazy.*

"What sort of food would you like?"

"Fresh," came the immediate response. *"Oh, and I like white cheese, a little, and eggs and chives."* I chuckled. It's always fun to talk with a cat who knows his own mind. But then, most animals do.

"What?" George laughed cynically when I gave him Omar's message. "Omar never eats omelette, let alone chives."

"Omar insists he loves omelette, so if he hasn't had one, perhaps he'd like one. Maybe he needs one." I said. "Trusting an animal's instincts is always a good idea."

George wasn't buying it, but was polite enough not to say so. "Anyway, where is he?"

Silently, I asked Omar.

He showed me a picture and gave me a feeling of "left". A couple of blocks away there was a park. "You might try the park near you," I said to George. "That's where he seems to be."

The man snorted, gave a strangled thanks, and hung up. I knew he hadn't believed a word I'd said. While I get that sometimes, it still made me sad. And it made me wonder if Omar hadn't created this whole scenario to help his carer open up to a new world of spirituality.

I heard from George again the next morning just as I came in from feeding the horses. Three dogs bounced around me and my cats Binah and Pucawan wrapped themselves around my legs, begging for food. Andrew walked into the kitchen, saw me on the phone and whistled the dogs.

"Let's go for a walk," he said quietly to them and went back outside. Three dogs bounded after him.

"I owe you an apology," George began. "I didn't believe you when you said that Omar liked omelettes. Frankly, I thought you were a fraud."

There was a pause. I realised I was supposed to say something. "Fair enough. That's easy to do with something as esoteric as psychic animal communication."

"But when my flatmate came home, I told him what you said. Apparently Jim shares his chive omelettes with Omar all the time. I had no idea. I'm so sorry."

George and Jim had then high-tailed it to the park near their home. But Omar had moved on. Could I please tune in again?

I rolled my eyes in frustration. I really wanted to catch up with Andrew and the dogs. I loved our morning walks together. But this was a lost cat and I could tell George was feeling desperate. So I grabbed an apple from the kitchen and sat at my desk in the office.

"Omar, may we speak?"

This time his voice was less confident. *"I'm in a woman's house. I'm not allowed out."* He couldn't give me names or numbers, but sent me a picture of a tiny front yard with a tall brick wall offering privacy from the street.

I rang George back and suggested the two men do a door knock. They covered a four-block area around their home and near the park. Nothing. It was disheartening and I couldn't get Omar out of my mind.

I went back to my other work, caring for the animals and writing my children's books. Andrew and I had organised a performance night at the local café in the mountain village where we lived. We both looked forward to exercising our performing muscles again. This time we would share the stage with our writing students and other local writers and performers. I loved the warm feeling of community and acceptance, no matter what you did to earn a living. People here cared more about the kind of person you were rather than what you did, how successful you were, or how much you earned. Andrew and I felt completely at home.

It was the dead of winter and the café was packed. A log fire burned in the centre of the room and the atmosphere was loud, cheery and expectant. Harry, the tall, lean, blonde-haired, young builder who owned the café and Leslie, his beautiful girlfriend, who ran it, greeted us enthusiastically.

"This is a great idea, Billie and Andrew. We should do more of it. What can we get you?"

"Hot chocolate for two," Andrew said promptly. Neither of us could eat until after we'd performed. I squeezed his hand and found a table for us near the stage. I pulled out the script I was going to perform, a comic monologue about a girl who met Death. Across the room, Andrew was deep in conversation about water tanks with Harry, who made beautiful, rustic homes from timber slabs.

Andrew looked relaxed and happy. He wore black jeans for performance, and a thick Tibetan jumper against the bitter cold outside. I watched him from across the room, slightly envious of his performance confidence.

My familiar nervousness was like a snake coiled in my gut. I could no longer see the script in front of me I was so scared, but I read it anyway. Over and over. I was sure I would forget my lines. This would never do. I had to get myself together. I closed my eyes and silently called Binah, Reka, Sollie and any other of my animal friends who might want to help. Their familiar faces soothed me and I was sure they sent me healing energy. The snake in my gut oozed away.

Andrew's warm hands were on my shoulders. "Ready? I'm about to start."

I nodded and settled back as Andrew MC'd the night like the professional he was. He had the audience laughing and eating out of his hand. The room was relaxed – a terrific and supportive audience. I knew I didn't have to worry.

After the performance, Andrew and I tucked into a meal of pumpkin soup and damper. Leslie pulled out a chair and slid in to join us. "Billie we were wondering if you could speak with our old dog Rosie. We want to know if she wants an operation on her tumour and if she could stand a younger dog as company. We could swap you a meal for a reading if you like."

I readily agreed. Rosie was a lovely girl of mixed parentage. She was a sweetheart and a village fixture.

"You need to change her diet to a natural one," I said. "Rosie needs finely chopped vegetables or veggie pulp from the juicer. She needs fresh meat with it and Vitamin C. And she needs green. A supplement like spirulina, wheatgrass or barley grass. Or all three. They rebuild the blood."

I was channelling as I was going. I was surprised the communication was so clear even amidst the noise of the café. Rosie wanted to talk.

"She wants you to give her some herbs to cleanse her blood. I can help you with that. And she definitely doesn't want any more processed dog food. Yuck." Rosie had sent me a clear picture of a congealed mess in a dog bowl.

"What about the operation Rosie?"

"Not yet. I need the diet first."

"What about the companion?"

"There is a black dog at the pound. He's waiting for us. Not young. Not old."

By this time, Harry had joined our table and the couple were listening intently to what Rosie said through me. Harry nodded. "We can do that, can't we Les?"

It was good to see that people were so open to doing what they could for their beloved animals. "If you need any help with the diet, or anything, let me know. I'll get you some herbs and you might see our friend Susan." Susan was another animal sensitive who I'd met when Andrew and I were at the movies one day. She'd spotted our car full of dogs and decided we needed her. Susan dowsed over animal hair and used homoeopathy and herbs. She was very accurate and had tremendous success. Harry and Leslie agreed.

Three days later, I was sat in the office talking to Omar again. He was still stuck inside. *"Do you think you and George will be together again?"* I asked, wondering how on earth he could get home now.

"Oh yes."

"Are you ready to go home?"

There was a cat sigh, but a definite *"Yes"*.

A thought occurred to me. Something George had said. *"Apparently you're microchipped. Maybe you could try to get to the vet."*

"I'll see what I can do," Omar said.

George kept up his door knocking for a while longer, and I felt useless because all I could tell him was he needed to trust. Then eight weeks after his disappearance, Omar did indeed go the vet with his new person. The microchip was discovered and Omar was returned to a delighted George.

George told me they never babysat their friend's dog again, fed Omar nothing but fresh food and the occasional chive omelette, and never had any "trouble" with him again. Further, he wanted to explore the spiritual side of animals.

And Omar?

If cats can wink, then that's what he did.

Chapter 6:
The Filly Who Saw Her Own Death

The filly knew she was going to die. I felt her fear as if it was my own, an anxiety which gripped my body, making me shake. She sent me images of horses racing wildly around a track, crowds of people in the stands cheering them on. Then, trouble. Several horses crowded near the rails, racing to win. In a split second it was all over – a filly had smashed into the rails. Horse and rider tumbling, falling…

The picture faded.

"That's me," the filly said telepathically. *"I'll die on the track that day."*

My stomach clenched. I had communicated with racehorses before but never with someone whose fear was so overwhelming.

A rough male voice dragged me back to the phone conversation in my office. "Bloody filly plays up as soon as we get anywhere near the racetrack for training," he complained. "I was told by a mate to call you. Can you do something?"

The guy didn't even know I was a psychic. I had a feeling this was a consultation destined to be doomed.

I made soothing noises and asked him to wait a second. The filly was psychically in my ear, clamouring for help. And I didn't know how to help her.

"I've seen my own death on the rails," she said. *"But if I don't race, I'll end up dog meat. And I don't want that either."*

In my minds eye I saw her – a princess of a young filly, all chestnut and legs. She was full of life and spirit. Something told me the rough voice on the other end of the phone wasn't going to be receptive to what we had to say.

"If you don' t want to race, what would you like to do."

"*I want to be an eventer,*" she said promptly. "*I can jump.*"

I mumbled something about that sport being equally dangerous for horses. "*Not for me,*" she insisted. "*Racing is where I'll die. On the rails.*"

I spoke to the trainer. He was shocked.

"That was bloody quick. You haven't even seen the bloody horse yet," he said.

"I don't have to," I explained. "I'm an animal psychic. I hear their voice. I communicate with them using telepathy."

"Bloody hell," he said. "I don't believe in all that mumbo jumbo. She's got to race–"

"Or she'll end up dog meat," I finished for him. "She told me."

There was silence on the other end of the line.

"The bloody filly's got to bloody race."

"Couldn't you sell her to an eventer. That's where she'll shine. She can run and jump – fabulously."

"She's not mine to sell. She's got to race, that's all."

He hung up. I sat at my desk, trembling as the filly was in her paddock, miles away.

"I'm sorry," I whispered. "I'm truly sorry."

If a horse could cry, this one did. I felt her sadness and despair as her spirit crumpled. I wasn't going to let it go. There were other ways. The filly and I communed some more. I had to give her back a sense of her own personal power.

Trainers around the world have used people like me for years. It wouldn't be long before this particular trainer would be complaining about me in the pub, and one of his mates would mention that he'd heard about that in the USA or England. Sometimes people had to be introduced to a new concept more than once to understand it.

And, if she continues to play up, they might give up on her, and he might remember our conversation, and he might sell her to an eventer. Might, might, might.

I wished he'd given me his phone number. He hadn't even given me his name. I looked down at my nails. As usual, I'd chewed them to the quick. I resisted the urge for chocolate.

I felt deeply for the filly. She had a bold spirit and a sense of her own destiny. In the right hands she'd be a wonderful companion. She was busting to compete and to give her heart. I shuddered. How awful to be owned. To not be able to make your own decisions. To be gifted with the Sight and see your own death, and not to be able to free yourself from it.

I sat there, staring at my computer screen, pondering the problem. I had to trust, that this little filly had the strength to take care of herself. That the seed I planted in the trainer's head would bear fruit and she would be freed. Surely she was too valuable for the dogger's truck. Surely they would sell her.

Over the next week, my busy life crowded in on me. The filly left my mind, which was filled with other animals needing help.

But on Saturday, right in the middle of a course I was taking, I was suddenly hit with an overwhelming feeling of panic and fear.

"They're making her race," I thought as the realisation hit me. In my mind's eye, I could see her struggling. I knew they weren't listening to her.

As the filly joined her mind with me for several hours, I learnt a powerful lesson and came to a powerful realisation.

"*This is what it feels like to be me,*" said the filly. "*Know that and make a difference.*"

I made a vow then and there that horses would be treated with more respect in the future, and that I would work towards that so that this little filly did not die in vain.

Chapter 7: Mala

It was Saturday morning, the sun shone, and the local markets bustled. But as soon as I stepped into the old community hall, I felt something was wrong. People were smiling and friendly and everything appeared normal, but I felt uneasy. As I queued for organic fruit and veggies, I glanced at the familiar faces. There it was. Jan, who was into horses, looked tense and miserable.

I wandered over to her through the tea tables and stalls. "What's up, Jan? You look as if...."

"It's my mare, Mala. The vet's coming this afternoon to put her down."

"For goodness sake, why?"

"She's gone mad. She kicked her foal and nearly killed her, and now she won't let anyone near her."

"This is really serious. Let me help you," I offered. "Please. She might have something she wants to say. There must be an explanation for her behaviour."

Jan nodded. Her look said everything she didn't want to say: *You didn't see the way she was behaving. She's gone crazy*. But also: *Yeah, I should have called you.*

I gently squeezed her arm. "Don't do anything until you've heard from me, OK?"

She nodded again. "Thanks." She looked a little bit lighter, but my heart was heavy.

I left Andrew shopping and rushed home and into the office where I could think. I took a deep, calming breath as I reached for my pen and gently called the mare to me.

"Mala."

"I'm here."

"May I speak with you?"

Mala agreed. She was furious. I frantically scribbled her distressed words.

The story tumbled out. Mala had belonged to a man who had abused and beaten her, often with chains. Jan found her and rescued her. So far, so good. But then Jan took her home and soon decided to have the 20-year-old mare served by a stallion.

"I was raped," Mala spat, her eyes flashing. *"I went from one abuse to another with no time to heal. I was hurt and then raped."* She paused. *"I didn't mean to kick my foal. It* hurts. *It's so sore, "* she said.

As I blended my energies with hers, I felt a red-hot pain in my breast. Of course. Illnesses always have an emotional reason at their core. Mala's anger at being "raped" by a stallion so soon after her trauma, and at her age, caused her to create a nasty and very painful case of mastitis. No wonder she had kicked her foal. Suckling had probably hurt her terribly – and given her a shock.

I shook my head. The people had seen what they perceived to be a mare gone mad. And for that she was going to die. In reality, she was a mare in great emotional and physical pain.

I tried to explain that her carers didn't understand that she hurt, and that a vet was coming to give her a needle to help her sleep and pass into the spirit world. *"But I'm happy to try and prevent that, if that's what you want. I could argue for your life."*

I expected her to say "yes", that I should intervene on her behalf. But Mala didn't fear death. She welcomed it.

"I want the vet's needle. I've had enough of this life. But when I come back, I want to come back to kind hands. And I want you to make sure I do."

Her words hung in the air. *"I'll do what I can,"* I promised. It was a huge thing she asked, but she was the second horse to demand it of me.

I thanked her for speaking with me and sent her blessings and love. Her anger subsided and she looked at me with eyes like serene pools. In that moment I understood both her beauty and her pain. And also her gratitude. She had needed to ear bash a human.

I've found a lot of animals calm down after they'd had a chance to blow off a little stream and get things off their chest. Mala was no different.

I hurriedly dialled Jan's number and told her what the mare had said.

"Oh, I had no idea," she said sadly. "I'll let everyone know." Mala, she explained was agisted on a nearby property, and the property owners were just as involved with Mala as she was.

My hand shook as I hung up. I buried my head in my hands and cried. What a lesson this mare had to give, both to her carers and to me. And what a shame she had to give her life for it.

The next day I got another call from Jan. She sounded very subdued. "The foal died. Would you be willing to talk to her spirit?" There was a pause. "Maybe you can tell her how sorry we all are – about her mum."

"Of course."

I opened my mind to the foal's spirit. She was tranquil and bathed in golden light. Her message was simple. *"I only came to be with the one they called Mala. I wasn't meant to be here for long."*

I relayed the foal's words to Jan, and then didn't hear from her for a while. Outwardly, my life was normal, but inwardly I too had been touched by Mala's death. I saw everywhere how horses were harmed and even killed every day through human ignorance. Sure, there was a natural horsemanship movement and attempts to better understand equine psychology. But more than ever, I was determined to do my bit to make sure Mala's spirit, when it came back into a horse body, returned to kind hands. My experience showed that even big-hearted people like Jan could make terrible, even fatal mistakes.

Months later I got a phone call from one of Jan's friends. "We were all so upset about Mala that somebody's offered me another mare," he said. "And we want to know what she'd like to do."

I sat up straighter in my chair. Was I hearing right? A human actually respecting the wishes of a horse? He wanted to find out the horse's preferences? It was the first time anyone had ever asked me that.

"What would you like to do with the mare? What kind of life can you offer her?" I asked.

"I'd just like to go trail riding. And maybe later on down the track, perhaps she could have a foal. If she felt like it. Of course, it's completely up to her." The voice on the other end of the phone was hesitant and respectful. I was thrilled. Mala had done her work well. Her death was not wasted after all.

I psychically called his young mare, Bliss. I explained that the people had been traumatised by the loss of a horse and were now trying to be more respectful.

"*Good,*" she said. "*But how am I supposed to know what trail riding is or if I will like living with him. I don't know him.*"

I sent her a picture of her exploring the trails I knew were around the area where we all lived – pictures of the bush, stands of trees and paddocks with lush grass.

"*That looks alright,*" Bliss said.

"*Do you know what you'd like to do?*" I asked the horse. She thought about it. She was very young and didn't know her options, so could not express a preference. But she did ask one last question. "*Will I be lonely?*"

"I'm pretty sure there are other horses there."

"Good."

I asked about the foal. "*Perhaps they can ask me when the time comes,*" she said. "*I'm not sure I want to be a mother. But then, I might. It's too early to say.*"

I smiled as I reached for the phone. I knew Bliss would be all right.

Chapter 8:
Lucy and Maryanne

"Trust."

The ringing phone shattered the last vestiges of sleep as I groggily left the warm nest of my bed to answer it. It was so dark I tripped over a dog bed, stumbled into my desk, and cracked my knee. I cursed loudly, causing the dog on the bed to cower. Peering into the gloom I felt the soft fur and floppy ears of a German Shorthaired Pointer. Louie, I decided. "It's OK, sweetie, you're OK."

I grabbed the phone.

"Hello," I managed, sounding as professional as 6:00 AM would allow. The woman's voice on the other end was stressed and garbled. My heart sank. An emergency. For me.

"My name's Maryanne. I found your card. Someone gave it to me months ago. We had a wake for Lucy last night but this morning she doesn't look as if she wants to die and the vet's coming in half an hour to put her down."

I was instantly awake. If there's one thing I dislike, it's animals dying before their time.

"Just a second. What kind of dog is Lucy?"

"She's an Australian Shepherd, 14 years old."

"Right."

I pushed away all grumpy thoughts and silently called the name Lucy, holding the image of an Australian Shepherd. As I suspected, she was waiting for me.

"I don't want to die. I'm not ready to go."

"OK."

"You're right. She doesn't want to die. Cancel the vet."

"Thanks Billie, should I book her for an enema with the vet instead?"

"An enema? What's wrong with her?"

"She's got a massive tumour obstructing her bowel. She'll die if we don't get rid of the faecal matter."

I sighed. "Book the enema, I'll do some healing on her for you."

Lucy was waiting for me. I shivered. My bed held a very warm husband, a large German Shepherd and two cats. Very tempting. Outside I could see a world covered in hard, white frost. I hunted around for my discarded clothes and found warm socks and work boots, blue jeans and a couple of wool jumpers. I padded into the living room where I threw some more logs on the fire and stood there for a minute, warming my chilled limbs. A strong sense of urgency pulled me back to the office and my desk, where I spoke with all of my animal clients.

"Lucy," I called softly in my mind, inviting her energetic field into the office.

"I don't want to die."

"It's OK, the vet's been called off."

"But I'm still going to the vet."

I understood her fear. Some allopathic vets see death as an option when they've run out of answers. Sometimes I think they've been desensitised, as one vet explained to me, by people themselves who want their animals put to death to save themselves possible emotional pain, because they can't afford treatment, or because the animal has just become too much trouble. Other allopathic vets embrace no other forms of healing and sincerely feel there is nothing more to offer. But understanding the world of animal spirituality as I did, I could no more condone death for an animal without his or her permission, than I could for a human. And my motto was always, "Where there is life, there is hope."

The question hung in the air. Lucy had a tumour, which for some reason was inoperable. Would Maryanne's vet suggest euthanasia? And would Maryanne be strong enough in her convictions to stand up for her currently dying dog?

"We'd better work quickly," I sent to Lucy.

I put myself in a deeper trance. I knew Lucy was already in the car, travelling toward the vet surgery. How much time did I have?

"Lucy, what's this all about?'

"I'm in intense pain, it hurts. But I don't want to die. There's no one waiting for me on the other side. I've looked."

How she looked and knew that, I'll never know. I've always accepted that animals have extraordinary spiritual and psychic lives. Right now, my main priority was Lucy and doing what was needed for her soul's purpose.

"I need to live. Maryanne needs me."

"What about surgery?"

"I'd die on the table and I'm not ready to die. The cancer has weakened my body. I need building up."

"OK, do you know what caused the tumour in the first place?

"I thought I was no longer needed."

"So you're now ready to heal?"

"Yes. Trust."

Trust. I'd heard the word just before I woke up. Suddenly I knew this client was no coincidence. There was something for me here, too. A lesson which would unfold. I felt a moment of panic. Could I help this dog in time? And how?

Outside, the sun was beginning to rise – a rosy glow through a thick mist. I took a moment to calm myself and admire its beauty. I loved the thick mists which often graced the early winter mornings of my home. It clothed everything in magic and mystery.

Suddenly I knew exactly what to do. I called on Grandfather, one of the healing spirit guides from The Tribe. I asked for assistance working in the shamanic tradition of native people around the world. I wasn't sure what he could do, but his presence was always comforting, and I was convinced he'd saved my own dog Suki from tick poisoning once.

In my mind, I saw his familiar ethereal, tall lean body clad in blue jeans and a red long sleeve shirt. His long, silver hair was plaited, and his face was weathered and kind.

"It is not Lucy's time today or tomorrow. It will come soon enough and it will be peaceful. I have offered her healing and she has accepted."

I watched as light radiated from his old, weathered brown hands into Lucy's body and felt her sigh of relief.

"Thank you Grandfather. What else can we do to help this beloved?"

"A short light fast for a day or two with nothing but carrot juice, wheatgrass juice and healing herbs like Burdock and other herbal blood cleansers. Then a natural diet, no cans or dried food. When one creates cancer, the body is out of balance. She needs to put her body back into balance in order to live."

"Will she survive?"

"Of course. The tumour has already reduced."

"Do you know how much longer she will live?"

"There is no telling for this being who wants and needs to live. Her will is strong and she is accepting healing."

I thanked him again and went back to Lucy, asking for a final message for Maryanne. *"This is soul/spiritual work she is doing and it's more important than anything. Her work can wait. I don't want to be separated from her at this time.*

"Tell her I have been so happy with her, and that my soul has been rescued and nourished for my next life. My time has been so good and I am so grateful. I want so badly to tell her that. I am her, she is me, we are One."

Lucy seemed calm now, as animals often are when their message has been delivered or something important has been spoken for them. I sat at my desk, holding her in my mind, sending her gentle, warm Reiki healing energy.

Then Andrew, my husband, woke me up. I'd fallen asleep, my head on the desk.

"Must have been powerful." Andrew grinned at me as he walked past followed by a pack of excited dogs.

I blinked. It must have been. I never fall asleep during healings. Our family joke is that Andrew can barely meditate without dozing off. But me, I'm supposed to be the alert one.

I joined Andrew and the dogs for our early morning run up and down the hills and mountains of our home. The world was still white. I wished I'd worn mittens, but with a beanie stuck firmly on my head I decided I looked frumpy enough.

I walked inside just as the phone was ringing. Maryanne, I decided. No further drama I hoped.

But she was really excited.

"You'll never guess what happened."

I braced myself.

"On the way to the vet, Lucy started letting go some wind. I knew you were working on her and I knew something was happening. She started looking really uncomfortable, like she really wanted to go. So I drove faster, because I didn't want her to go in the car and we got to the vet and she popped out of the car still looking uncomfortable and then she let it all go, splat on the surgery doorstep!"

I laughed at the image. I could sense Lucy feeling pretty pleased with herself.

"Billie, thank you. The vet can't work it out but we suspect the tumour has shrunk."

The story of Maryanne and Lucy didn't end there. The tumour didn't disappear, but they learned to manage it, and it never grew to such a dangerous size again. Maryanne and I became friends. Like me, she was a staunch advocate of animal rights. She was bright, energetic, intuitive and passionate. She adored her two dogs and did everything she could for them. I liked her enormously. In the months that followed, she moved and had a baby girl who she was completely smitten with. But there was something wrong. There was a tension to her, a tightness, which belied her bright emails.

Is this why Lucy knew Maryanne needed her? Is this why she fought death so bravely? To provide comfort to Maryanne in the underlying unhappiness of her apparently happy life?

I was completely unprepared for what happened just 18 months after Lucy first brought us together.

Maryanne was killed in a car accident.

As I suspected, Lucy's health declined after Maryanne's death. Maryanne's husband called me to help Lucy on the day she was dying. I sat in the office trembling. I didn't know if it was Lucy or me who was trembling and I really didn't care. It had been a shock to lose Maryanne and I knew that neither of her dogs would survive without her. But now Lucy was still frightened and miserable and that I did care about. A lot.

"I'm scared of the big sleep."

"I know honey. How about I call my friend Pam to help you cross over. We'll both support you. It'll be OK."

Just then the room filled with a golden glow and I could see Maryanne's spirit holding out her arms to Lucy.

"Maryanne's waiting for you."

"Yes, but I'm still scared."

I understood. Lucy might have lived a few more days, but Maryanne's husband insisted on euthanasia. It was just too hard for him, and while I didn't agree with him, I completely understood, given the circumstances. Besides, Maryanne's spirit being present was to me an important signal that it was Lucy's time. I called Pam, another animal telepath, and asked her to also tune in to Lucy and assist her passing. Together we sent her peace, light, love and healing as she crossed over, and watched as her golden spirit launched into Maryanne's outstretched spirit arms. I smiled, wiping away the tears. Lucy finally had a friend waiting for her on the other side.

Chapter 9:
Jo Jo and Sandy

I drove through Sydney's chaotic streets to see my friend Juliet and her dog Jo Jo, a Border Collie. Normally I don't do house calls like some animal communicators do, but Juliet was a friend, and Andrew and I had been invited to lunch. He was meeting me there.

I pulled into the drive of her home, thinking sadly it was probably going to be one of the last times I did so. Juliet was moving to New Zealand.

As I jumped lightly up the steps to her front door, Jo Jo came bouncing out of the house and leapt up to greet me, barking frantically. "Hello, Jo Jo. Good girl."

I cuddled the dog, noticing she looked thinner and more tense than normal. But I put these thoughts aside as Juliet appeared and drew me into a warm hug.

"Thanks for coming. I'm really worried about her."

"My pleasure. It's the lunch bribe. Works every time."

Juliet grinned and beckoned me into her colourful, busy kitchen, where she was chopping vegetables for a salad. She'd already told me that Jo Jo appeared out of sorts and that she'd gone off her food.

"What's up Jo Jo?"

Jo Jo looked at me with big brown eyes and said nothing.

I shrugged. Lunch was something which smelled wonderful in a wok, and I was starving. Juliet chatted about her move to New Zealand and Jo Jo sank to the floor looking depressed. I sat on the floor next to her and put my hands on her body, sending Reiki energy. Jo Jo looked at me with sorrowful eyes. And then she closed them, drifting into sleep.

"Gosh look at Jo Jo, I haven't seen her so relaxed for ages. Billie, you really have a knack."

"Not according to Miss Roberts."

Juliet paused in her chopping to give me a quizzical look.

"A headmistress who didn't believe in women vets."

"Stuff her. Lots of women are vets."

"Well, she was right about me. I had no aptitude for science. I thought dissecting frogs was barbaric. The idea of surgery still makes me shudder and the only thing I was good at in school was English."

"And yet here you are. Is Jo Jo saying anything?"

I shook my head. "Strangely quiet. Or maybe I need lunch." Putting my hands on the dog was relaxing me. It was stressful driving through the city,

Juliet tossed the vegetables together and rummaged in her cupboard for a loaf of bread. I felt a wave of sadness wash over me. Not mine. Jo Jo's.

"Where am I going to go?"

"Juliet's taking you to New Zealand."

"She's not taking me. She hasn't said."

"Honey, believe me, Juliet would never go without you."

"But she hasn't said."

"Juliet, tell your dog you're taking her with you when you leave."

Juliet whirled around and stared at Jo Jo in amazement. "I thought she knew. Of course she's coming with me."

"Always assume they understand you when you talk to them, but never assume they understand indirectly," I told my friend. "You need to talk to Jo Jo like she is another human in the house."

Juliet groaned. "And I thought I was a good communicator! I guess I hadn't actually told her she was coming, but of course she is."

"Jo Jo, did you hear that, Juliet is taking you with her when she goes to New Zealand."

Jo Jo's eyes brightened and she thumped her tail. Juliet immediately sank to the ground giving her dog a huge hug.

"You silly girl, thinking I'd leave you – never, never, never."

I stood up, smiling at them, knowing my work here was done today. I could enjoy lunch knowing that Jo Jo had been able to voice the anxiety that might otherwise have made her so unwell she might not have made it to New Zealand.

It reminded me of another, similar case of doggy misunderstanding. I'd had a call from my friend Stephanie, who's boyfriend Gus was visiting her from interstate. Gus's dog Sandy had been rushed to hospital with severe bowel problems by the people who were taking care of him while Gus was away. Could I help?

I couldn't promise anything, but I said of course I'd try.

I quickly tuned in to Sandy. *"That woman will take him away,"* he said.

"No sweetie, not this particular woman. He's just visiting her and he'd never abandon you. And besides, if they hook up, you'll just have another dog-loving person to hang out with. Steph's a great lady. She loves dogs and she's fun to be with. She's a friend of mine."

I felt all the anxiety slide out of Sandy's body, and again, knew that everything that needed to be said had been said. Animals, like people, sometimes need to hear you say what you might think is obvious or unimportant to them. It's the same as the old story of the man who assumed his wife knew he still loved her when he'd only uttered those words once, at their wedding 30 years previously.

I wasn't surprised to get a call from Stephanie later that evening saying they'd heard from the vet who was astounded that Sandy had made such a spectacular recovery.

I smiled to myself. Miss Roberts might have been right all those years ago. Perhaps I wasn't cut out to be a vet. But I had an aptitude for listening with all of my senses and in that way I could still fulfil my dream of helping animals.

Chapter 10:
Sollie's Story

May 2003, Ballyoncree

It's Samhain in the southern hemisphere – All Hallow's Eve – a time for remembering and honouring those beloveds who have left us for other realms. A time when the veil between the worlds is at its thinnest. While my daughter paints a cardboard pumpkin, I'm aware that Sollie has come to visit, and I silently acknowledge his presence.

He's standing there at the stable in which he died, his round chestnut form filling the doorway. His big, sad eyes follow me as I take hay to the ponies standing in the yards. He's grazing in the yard near where he is buried and looks up as I enter the gate, sending me a silent whinny. He already knows that tonight I will conduct a ceremony to honour the first anniversary of his death. That I will light a candle and shed a tear and try to put aside the awful grief I feel at the loss of him from my life.

He's looking forward to that.

He never wanted to give me grief.

Sollie arrived one day 23 years ago on a visit. For me it was love at first sight. He stood under the trees, a bonny, chestnut Australian stock horse with a thick, white, blaze down his nose and big, round soul-filled eyes, which made his first people call him Sorry. Our neighbours had ridden over on him and another horse. I walked out of the door to greet my guests, and Sol looked around at me. Our eyes met.

He was four years old and for sale. $200 later, he joined my family. My own horse friend! I couldn't wait to explore the landscape on horseback. I couldn't wait to develop what I instinctively knew was going to be a deep and lasting partnership with this horse. And there was something more. I recognised his soul with my own.

I didn't want him to be sorry all his life, so I changed his name to Sollie, after the brightness and strength of the sun. We quickly settled into life together on the farm, going for long rides with my German Shepherd pup Reka.

We'd be out on the road and I "knew" Sollie wanted to go faster, just as I "knew" he wanted to head for the dam. He spoke to me in a language of pictures and feelings. Sometimes he wanted to visit a special place by the creek or even someone's house. It was the first time I was conscious of an animal sending me pictures, even though I felt their communications in my body and wondered at their perfect understanding of mine.

All the animal companions in my family were doing their best to wake me up to what would become my life's work. But it was Sollie who got through with our easy poetry together. Words came quickly after.

We rode all the time. During the drought I'd take him to graze the roadsides and we'd both shudder at the sight of dead cattle in paddocks. I'd ride him to visit neighbours and he'd crop grass while I sat on their different verandas, drinking tea. We'd take the long ride up our valley's steep road to get the mail. We explored the countryside around our farm, taking delight in both the landscape and each other. He was a lively boy who needed exercise, but we rode as one being.

And then, three years later, trouble. My relationship broke up, and I headed back to the city to sort myself out. Even though I was home most weekends to be with Sollie, I didn't realise how badly my leaving affected him. Although he never admitted it, I'm sure he felt abandoned. And he didn't like it when other people rode him when I wasn't there.

Instead of poetry, riding him became a nightmare.

Sollie charged down the steep road which led into our valley, and flew across someone's paddock, taking a sharp right and pigrooting as he went. I clung on for dear life, begging him to stop, a scream of fear stuck in my throat.

"Please stop, Sol, I don't want to hurt you. I don't want to pull on your mouth. Please stop," I whispered frantically.

He only stopped when we got home.

Shaking, I climbed down and unsaddled him quickly, tears pricking my eyes. There was a wall between us and I didn't know what was wrong. I rubbed down his sweaty body and turned him free. He looked calm and as if he didn't have a care in the world. When I asked him what was wrong, he assured me he was fine.

But I knew better.

This wasn't the Sollie who I knew and loved. The one who danced with me in complete poetry. This was a Sollie who was hurting – in his heart and in his body.

It was up to me to get the poetry back.

Sollie was being ridden by other people when I wasn't there, and he missed me. If I asked him about it, he would be in denial and tell me, "Everything is fine."

I remember going to a psychic about Sollie who told me what I already knew – Sollie and I had a deep, deep connection and it would be better if we were together. I vowed we would be together again, but knew it was going to take some time. So I left him in the country, not realising just how deep his love was for me.

I'll never forget the day Pucawan the cat went missing on one of my weekends to the farm. No one was there at the time, and I had to rush back for a meeting. I left food and water for Pucawan and sent silent messages to him that I would be back. All I got from him was the impression of a full stomach and rabbit holes.

I drove home with all my senses open, telling Pucawan to meet me at the house. As I drove the car up, there was my cat, in exactly the right place, rushing to greet me. At the same time, I heard the gallop of hooves. Sollie too, had rushed up to meet me. He was overjoyed I was home. I cuddled my funny, wild horse, and we spent some time blowing in each other's nostrils. Dark was falling but I didn't care. I had my animals with me, and I was on my land. I was home. It broke my heart to tell Sollie I had to leave the next day.

In the meantime riding was a challenge and I was losing the confidence of my youth. He'd take the bit in his mouth and zigzag to try and dislodge me. He'd go underneath tree branches and wipe me against fences. He'd bolt, pigroot and dance all over the place, making it hard to mount. He'd bite. And when I asked him what was wrong, he was silent, looking at me innocently. He wanted to be with me, but riding had become dangerous.

He didn't tell me he was being ridden behind my back, how angry he was that I had left, and how much physical pain he was in until much, much later.

My former partner tried to sell Sollie. After all, we were both headed back to the city. Where would either of us keep a horse? But when a man came to test him out, Sollie looked at me with pain in his eyes. "No," I said, surprising my partner and angering the prospective buyer. "He's not for sale. Not now. Not ever."

Sollie and I both felt a sense of huge relief. I didn't know how I was going to keep him, or why I should, but I knew I couldn't part with him, or him with me.

A short time later I fell in love with Andrew. The farm was sold and Andrew and I bought another. Sollie and the animals came with us, and for the first time in years, I felt whole again. Everyone, including Sollie, blossomed.

Riding was still a challenge, and despite my great love for this horse, I was now terrified of getting on his back. I was determined to change this and I refused to hurt him or pull on his mouth when he bolted. There had to be another way. I started looking everywhere for help. "You see saw the bit to get them to stop," said one person. "Buy a bigger bit," said another. "Martingale," suggested someone else.

It all felt wrong to me. This was Sollie. The love of my life. I might have hurt him emotionally, but there was no way I was going to hurt him physically as well.

I knew I needed someone to teach me horsemanship. If Sol was in denial, there had to be other ways of reaching him. Spirit answered my prayers. I picked up a horse magazine I never normally bought, and inside was an advertisement for a natural pathway with animals. "Kick to go" and "Pull to stop" were lies, it said. And I was immediately enthralled. That's the way I had been taught to ride and instinctively I knew there was so much more.

The advertisement was for training courses with natural horseman Pat Parelli, a course which was to bring Sollie and I back together again and turn my life around. At the same time, we studied TTEAM with Robin Hood, and again felt at home with other people who were out there making a difference to the lives of animals. It was all valuable, and I loved it.

Sollie and I entered a new phase of our life together. He'd become a problem horse, and I knew why, but lacked the horsemanship skills to deal with it. Telepathy wasn't working because Sol was in denial. According to him, he loved me, he was happy. Nothing was wrong.

I knew I needed to learn horsemanship, instead of the bush riding I'd been doing since I was six. I was instinctively natural. Not for me was the solution of bigger bits, or anything designed to control a horse through fear and pain. I felt their pain. It was not an option. Natural Horsemanship was a path to freedom that was to last Sollie the rest of his life.

My first instructor sussed Sollie out. "This guy is a major problem horse. We deal with them in Level 4. You're just a beginner. I wouldn't take him on. Start with an easier horse."

He didn't realise that I was as stubborn as my horse. I didn't just want to learn horsemanship. I wanted to be with Sollie. It wasn't about how good I could get with horses. It was about my relationship with one horse and how I could make that the best it could be.

And so we began. And on top of the lessons that taught him and me a new language of mutual respect, there was a pathway of the horse that is one of self-discovery and leadership skills.

There was also a round of chiropractors and acupuncturists trying to deal with the pain he felt but wouldn't admit to. For all these treatments Sollie was a perfect gentleman.

Sollie loved it. He loved the clinics and study groups we held at our place, the riding, the games, and all the other horses. Best of all, he was home with me where he belonged and he was never alone.

I quickly learned so many new things about my horse. If my energy was too big when we were playing together on the ground, he would be fearful. I learned I needed to dance lightly with him, and be calm and strong on the inside.

This idea of strength inside meant a lot to me, and eventually became something I taught. To be strong inside doesn't mean aggressive or dominant in any way. It is a way you hold yourself.

The Parelli training taught me a lot about helping Sollie be right, and slowly people stopped telling me he was dangerous, dense, or hard to teach. But they recognised he wasn't going to take me where I needed to go in horsemanship. He'd been physically damaged by one of the people who had ridden him behind my back and therefore unfit for the higher levels of training.

I didn't care. I wasn't giving up on Sollie and for me the training wasn't about becoming the best horsewoman, it was about becoming the best horsewoman for the horse I loved. The best partner for the horse I loved. That was the song I sung and it wasn't going to change.

I lived my life around my horse. We rode bareback and bridleless in the lazy afternoons, I would sit on his bare back and read out loud to him while he grazed around the house, I organised picnics with the dogs that I could ride to on Sollie. I played bending games on him when I was eight months pregnant, and after my daughter was born I taught her to ride on Sollie's broad back. He adored her and I trusted him completely.

When Sollie became challenged with his sore back and hips, I found and rescued Montana, a half-starved Appaloosa mare. She was willing and eager to please. A very different ride to Sollie. But after my first session with her, I watched as Sollie warned her off. "*She's mine,*" he said.

And later, when he was recuperating in a stable, I saw him telling her to "*look after her.*" Montana understood and respected our relationship. She agreed.

We moved again to a larger property and our herd of rescued horses grew to 20. Our place was a sanctuary, a horse heaven where horses roamed freely in huge paddocks and all gentled to our handling. Sollie had a girl friend too, a tiny Shetland called Samantha who adored him and was always by his side.

Sollie was no longer a problem horse. He was a saint. Still stubborn and single minded, I'd often have to convince him it was a good idea to go somewhere. He revelled in it. "*You need to be more assertive in life,*" Sollie told me. "*I'm teaching you to be more assertive.*"

My life revolved around thinking about Sollie – because he was thinking about me. He was always in my consciousness. I'd think of interesting rides we could take and games we could play. We never got past Level I of Parelli training, but we journeyed far, had fun and we were together. That's all that counted.

I first noticed something was wrong with Sol when I was in the middle of making my first feature film. We were shooting on our place and the pace was intense. He whinnied at me as I rushed past the pony paddock one afternoon.

"It's only for three weeks Sol. And we've only another week. I'll be with you soon."

I kept my promise and before the camera crew left, I had him hanging out with me in the yard. His coat looked off.

That winter he looked like a shaggy sheep dog.

"What's wrong Sol? What's wrong?"

"Nothing. I am well and happy," he would say.

I got out the acupuncturist vet. "Cushing's Syndrome." she said. "He'll live two years, probably – there's no cure and the cost to keep him on allopathic drugs is just prohibitive."

I'd never heard of Cushing's Syndrome but I was sure there was something I could do with alternative therapies. I researched on the net and there were a lot of Cushing's horses living happy, productive lives.

He went on a strict regime of natural therapies and next time the vet came out she was very impressed. "He's maintaining very well," she said. Except for a coat that didn't shed quite as easily as it had done the year before, there was no sign at all that he was anything but healthy.

But I knew he wasn't. Sollie was constantly in my head. He wanted his special treats, his meals, and attention. He wanted me. Sam was dumped. The herd was dumped. Sollie had become a loner.

One day there was a massive thunderstorm and after it was over I could see all the horses – except Sollie. Heart in my mouth, I called to Andrew to help me find him. I ran for the top paddocks where I knew he liked to go. And the shock of not finding him sent waves of panic through my body.

"There he is," Andrew said calmly. And I burst into tears of relief. He was grazing quietly by a Hawthorn tree. Alone.

"What are you doing here big buddy?" I asked him.

"Having a snack," he said.

I slipped on his bare back and headed him home.

Some friends came over for a trail ride and it was suggested that for a ride this long, I should take Montana. But again I felt compelled to ride Sollie. I wanted to be with him and Sollie was telling me he wanted to go. When my daughter wanted to come too, the decision was made. Without anyone calling or fetching him, Sollie trotted over, his ears forward. I saddled him up, Tamsin was put behind me, and the three of us had a joy-filled ride on a sunny autumn afternoon. Soul food. Pure bliss. Sollie had a ball and he handled it easily. I was in heaven. Nourished.

It was our last ride.

Soon after, he developed a number of health problems. He got laminitis and an abscess on his face. It seemed easy to treat, but things kept going wrong. Vets couldn't make it out to our place when they said they would, and when one of my healer friends told me of her dog who had died from an abscess, I felt the chill of premonition.

Sollie was not going to die if I had anything to do with it. I rang every healer I knew and some I didn't. Every morning I drained his abscess and it was healing beautifully. I tended his feet. He was on a range of alternative therapies to protect and heal him. He was getting more and more demanding, and wandered in to the laundry every night, making his presence felt, sticking his head through the door. I loved his presence and didn't care if he psychically and physically woke me up with a whinny every morning because he wanted breakfast. I didn't care if caring for him dominated my world. This was Sollie. My special friend.

Later I realised he knew he was going, as I did on one level. And we both wanted to cling to each other in what little time we had left.

I had an animal communication client and when I sat down in a light trance to connect to the animal in question, Sollie barged in. *"What's up, Sol?"*

"I am not your friend," he said. "I am your soul mate."

Frantic, I emailed my animal communication friends. "It's just a health hiccup," they told me. "He said he's not going to die."

But Sollie and I both knew better. Neither of us was willing to admit it.

I had a long chat to him one night. He told me he wanted to be in a book, and to be a movie star. I laughed. Of course you will be, I assured him. I felt a lightened sense of heart. Sollie would live. Nothing would ever separate us.

The next morning he wasn't in the yard. I had students arriving from all over NSW for an advanced, two-day animal communication clinic. I found Sollie in a stable where he had gone on his own. He looked at me with his large, soul-filled eyes. We both knew the time of denial was over.

"Sollie's dying", I screamed to the wind. "He's dying and I've got people coming in two hours and I can't cancel."

The people came and took one look at me with my horse at the back door of my house and lent me their healing gifts and energies. Perhaps they were supposed to be there. The vet came and told me he would be gone in 24 hours. She wanted me to agree to "put him down" now. Sollie threw me an anguished look. "*NO!*" he said, his eyes frightened.

"No," I said quickly. "That's not what he wants."

Sollie's communication was so clear, every student experienced it.

I'd read about all kinds of miracles happening to people and animals. If love could heal this horse, I would heal him. He didn't want to go. But he knew he was going. On one level I guess it was his time, but in the moment I couldn't see that. All I knew is that my best friend – my soul mate – was leaving me. And I was going to do everything in my power to make sure I had done everything I could.

I worked frantically all day. Andrew took over the class. We cancelled the rest. Sollie had homoeopathics every few minutes. He had Reiki and I appealed to my healing spirit guides, begging them for a miracle. But the miracle didn't happen. He responded to nothing.

Tears streamed as I begged him to respond, to stay with me, ignoring all the rules of healing and of spiritual truth, which is to honour the being's decision.

"*I am holding you back,*" he said, simply. Calmly.

"Nooo," I cried. "Look at how much I've learnt because of you. Look how far I've come."

Later that night, I prepared for a cold, long night vigil with Sollie. There was no way I was leaving him to do this alone. He'd been waiting for me, grazing in the back yard quietly. It was peaceful out there. If it wasn't for his telltale elevated breathing, you wouldn't know he was dying. When I came outside, he looked up with love in his eyes, and asked me to follow him. Wearing two horse rugs, he set off at a shambling pace out of the yard and for a long moonlit walk, saying goodbye to all his old haunts.

It was a full moon marked by a lunar eclipse. The moonshine illuminated the bare trees making the world look starkly beautiful. It was silent. It was magical. It was a night I will never forget.

He wanted to walk up the hill, to a favourite place by the Hawthorn trees. But he was tiring and I suggested he not over do it. He needed his strength. He agreed and took me back to the open stable where he sank down gratefully and dozed until dawn. I camped with him, curled up in a sleeping bag. At dawn, he lumbered to his feet, wandered out of the stable with me tagging behind, and walked by the ponies, giving a weakened whinny goodbye. Sam whinnied back.

My heart broke.

He wanted to go into the other pony paddock, where his long time mate, the old white pony Sebastian lived with his bay pony mare Saraid. A communication passed between Sollie and Bastie that I wasn't allowed to read and then Sollie barged into the stable, ordering Saraid out. He sank down on the fresh, clean straw. He didn't get up again.

I asked him if he wanted help to leave this world. He was obviously uncomfortable.

"*Then I'll be gone forever,*" he told me.

He was dying. He refused all homoeopathics, all help. The only remedy he took was Transition Essence – an Australian Bush Flower Essence to emotionally help with the process of passing over.

"Go Sollie, please go now," I cried. He didn't take his eyes off me. But I couldn't look at him. I sat in the stable holding him, trying to pass soothing energy to him.

Sollie's spirit slipped from his body at 8: 30 AM. His body lay quiet, still and peaceful, and I curled up to him, nursing his head on my lap. He was free.

I was alone.

Later, after he was buried in the backyard where he loved to graze, his spirit was everywhere, and so strong that sometimes I'd look up and do a double take. I thought he'd come back.

My heart froze with his leaving, like a glacier through my body. I felt I lived in a grey, cold world and no amount of hugs from my family could thaw me.

"*You've lost your friend,*" said Tala, my dog, understanding.

"Yes," I said. "And so much more."

Some people told me he was old. Some people told me to "get over it". Some people made disparaging remarks about my inability to work. But while a part of me was glad he was free from the pain in his body, the other part of me wanted to join him. I was in a ghost town of despair, an icy wind whistling around the derelict buildings of my mind. I was alone.

His death brought up feelings of grief, guilt, hurt, and abandonment. I had been touched by his deep, unwavering love for 22 years, longer than I had been married. But I was lucky I had Andrew. The horses were lucky too because I couldn't go in to the feed shed without feeling a shaft of pain that brought tears, swift and vicious.

"Why does it hurt so much?" I'd say to Andrew. "He was your life," he'd reply, giving me the space and permission to be as devastated as I needed to be. It was a year before I could start to feel gratitude for that life with Sollie, instead of pain.

So tonight almost marks the anniversary of his death. A year in which I have travelled on a journey of enormous adjustment. I haven't ridden. I have planned no picnics. I haven't read to another horse. But I can be among them again and the colours of life are vibrant. I love their beauty and it doesn't hurt so much to see the herd without his familiar shape among them.

Sollie told me more horses would come. And they have. And I feel an old stirring of joy as I watch them heal and fly around the huge open paddocks.

And although I might still cry at the loss of him, still mourn the lack of his physical presence in my life, I feel him beside me, urging me to horse play. To find joy with another horse again.

Montana checks every day to see if I am healed. Gypsy too, wanting me to touch her with soft hands.

Jaffah came, a red mare who barges in psychically to help others when they need help with their horses. And Erin, a lively grey pony, who makes me laugh.

It is only now that I can appreciate the truth that there is no loss. That Sollie and I are still together. He is there on the other side of the veil of illusion we have erected only with our mind. I miss his physical presence. I recognise the selfishness within that wants him with me on the physical plane. I recognise the journey the lesson of his death forced upon me.

We can still talk. I can visit him in the spirit world at any time. And I do. I know I can take as long as I want to heal.

It's Samhain and tonight I will light a candle. I will invite Sollie's spirit into the house and sit down with him and have a loooong chat. I will bury a crystal holding my sorrow in the soil in his gravesite in the back yard.

And tomorrow, I will call Montana. And we will ride.

Today, Ballyoncree

Sollie died in May 2002. I wrote his story in May 2003. My life changed dramatically with the death of my beloved horse.

I still see Sol and I still miss him. He took a big part of my heart with him, and I have a part of his. It's taken me a long time to recover, which is not what he wanted, but we'd been together 22 years, and it's hard to lose a love that's so profound. Over the years I've done work with many healers and psychics in different settings, and they've all seen Sollie in my field and in my heart.

He's never left me.

Sollie does a lot of work in the Otherworld, helping other horses make their crossing. Because he died naturally, he was able to make a choice

to get out of the cycle of reincarnation and live in infinity, that non-ordinary reality beyond time.

His wise, gentlemanly presence always soothes me when I think of him, and he still encourages me to play more with the other horses. I tell myself I don't have time. There's 30 horses here now and their spirits are each a balm to my soul. But there's not another Sollie.

Sollie tells me my journey with horses is far from done and I will get back to horses in a *"different"* way, joining my spirit with theirs, the way *"we used to"*.

He says I already know the horses who are my future.

And he's right. I've "seen" it and my heart beats in anticipation. There is something magical about pure partnerships with animals, when you become one being.

When you come from the perspective of a human angel.

The animals are beings of incredible beauty and wisdom, and I'm blessed to remember their silent language and be privy to the secrets of secret animal business.

Thank you Sollie. And all the others. Our journey, in truth, is just beginning.

Part 2:
Animals in the Age of Enlightenment

Rainbow Fianna: Wisdom School for Earthkeepers

My new students linger out the front of an old 1930's building, which was once a bank – our current school home. They know me from the photographs on my website and newsletter. I don't know them. It's a little disconcerting, but I shrug it off. Soon we will know each other. They are full of smiles and help bring stuff in from the car. I shoo them away from the room then, my desire to create a sacred space for teaching, something beautiful and alive, which talks to them in more than words about the world they are about to inhabit.

When my students re-enter the room, they notice the change in energy. From a cold and sterile place, the workshop space is now vibrantly colourful with indigenous blankets and prayer rugs from a wide array of cultures. Blues predominate. Splashes of yellow. Deep reds and vital green. These are colours found in nature.

The room has a warm and welcoming feeling now. There are drums, stones, feathers and pictures of native people, animals and countrysides. The room has been smudged with sage, an ancient technique to cleanse negative energies. The woody fragrance hangs in the air and mingles with the smell of incense. The candles are lit. Native music plays – soaring panpipes, didgeridoos, drums. When my students walk into the room, they walk into another world.

On another level, their teaching has already begun. The path of the shaman is experiential. It begins the moment they sign up for the course. And it doesn't end with the finish of the course either. It's about life, its Mysteries, and how you conduct yourself day to day. Do you walk in grace and Beauty, with ethics and integrity? Do you recognise all who come to you as a teacher and often as your mirror? Or are you still caught up in the web of angst, trying to unravel the threads of blame and complaints? My courses are not just about how to communicate with animals, although this is a big part of it. It is about walking in the world with intention and ceremony, bringing honouring to the land and to your life. It's about experiencing for yourself the whispers of Mother Earth and all her children, the sight of fairies dancing, and the call of Spirits.

We are blessed to have the entire building to ourselves. The students are in the living room, gathered around the fire, drinking tea, getting to know each other, and themselves. By the end of the week they will be ready to go home, but they won't want to leave. They will have found their true home, their spiritual family.

Out in the world, many of this tribe of people wear the face of the corporate West. They come from all walks of life. But their homes, like mine, are decorated with stones, feathers, books, crystals, colour – not unlike the world I have created for them. We are all the same. And once the newness, the shyness, wears off, they relax and are grateful to find their brothers and sisters. They completely understand when I tell them the importance of spiritual community, for out in the world they walk alone, surrounded by people who don't really understand.

Or do they? Our society does little to teach the indigenous ways of listening and respect. For centuries this has been considered primitive. But today, with the Earth's future dangling on a precipice, more and more people are voicing their discontent and finding themselves honouring an inner call to live differently. Perhaps people don't understand why they pick up a stone, or even know he has called them to do it. But they honour him anyway, and take the stone home.

This is the way the stone people travel.

I put on some music and ask my students to move and to shake off their journey, their strangeness. They are awkward and shy. I hear them groaning inwardly. Later they will dance with happy abandon. Now I let them off the hook with a laugh. "OK, good, that's over with. I'm not going to torture you anymore!"

The ice is broken.

We sit in a circle, as one would around a fire. And we begin with introductions. They have come from all over Australia, from Hong Kong, from America, from New Zealand. They are both sexes and all ages. There is something about this work which calls their soul. They desire to better understand their animal companions, and the world of deeper mysteries around them.

This is soul work. Soul talk. Soul remembering. It is a path to enlightenment, allowing animals and nature to lead the way. As it was always intended.

And so the journey begins...

Rainbow Fianna's Guidelines for Apprentice Human Angels

- See animals as teachers, healers, and connected to the Divine. They are our brothers and sisters on this walk through life.

- Always ask permission of the animals – to speak with, to heal, to breed, and especially to end their lives. Everything must be done with their permission.

- Work on yourself, so you are a clear channel, not projecting your own shadow onto their situations.

- Work on yourself, so you are a vehicle of peace and love, and can therefore be an Earthkeeper who consciously dreams in a world of peace.

- See challenges with animals as lessons, spiritual tests or initiations, and be grateful they have come to you as a teacher.

- There are no accidents or coincidences.

- Make animal care an art form and a vehicle for spiritual transcendence. Go about it with humility, understanding and impeccability.

- Understand that all life is precious.

- Do not kill any living being, unless that being is suffering and/or requests release.

- Envision a world where humans act like angels and their interaction with the Earth and the Animal Kingdom is nothing less than love, peace, sacred harmony, and right relations.

Chapter 11:
The Path of the Human Angel for Animals

In my school Rainbow Fianna: Wisdom School for Earthkeepers, I teach people the lessons I've learned from the animals. And there have been a great many. I also help people connect to nature, and understand how all life is animate.

In this book, I can't help you test and deepen your progress by taking you out to the wild horses of Ballyoncree, teach you a special fire ceremony, take you up our mountain, or have you experience nature, fairies, sacred wild messages or any of the many things we do in our retreats which help you become an Earthkeeper. And someday I hope you'll join me here so I can share these things with you. But for now, let me give you an outline of some of the things we cover in the school's foundation course.

And these are really important foundations for becoming a human angel for animals and the planet.

People come to my classes because they want to learn interspecies communication – some because they feel it would enhance their work with animals, and others because they love their own animals and want to understand them better.

To really come into a heart and soul communion with an animal and have the connection and partnership of your dreams, there are a few things I would like to bring into your awareness, like some shifts in the way we address and communicate with our animal kin, and some understanding of their psychic nature. I like to help people learn how to be still and really listen, and to understand another kind of life which is possible when we

Secret Animal Business

listen and really understand the animals who grace our homes.

So...

Let me introduce you to animals as I know them.

Chapter 12:
Secret Animal Business: Soul's Journey

Penny's dog Max was missing. He was a young dog who sounded bright and cheerful when I tuned in. "I'll be home on Thursday," he said.

I dutifully told Penny to expect him on Thursday and thought no more about it. A month later she rang me excitedly. "Max came home!" she said. "It was a Thursday – just not the Thursday we expected!"

What was he doing for a month – secret dog business? Max wouldn't say. It was, according to him, "his business". But he and Penny had a journey together and he'd chosen to come to her not once but twice now. What was that journey? How was this story going to unfold? And how was Penny going to grow in spiritual understanding from the teachings of an incredible dog like Max?

– Excerpt from Billie's client journals

Andrew and I were both working on a writing deadline. I was feeling stressy, and after working all weekend, longed for time in the spring sunshine. It was a beautiful, crisp, sunny day. Outside, green grass shimmered and horses beckoned. Working at my desk proved impossible. We have eight dogs, and it seemed like all they wanted to do all day long was go out and come back in, scratching at the door for help. They pawed at us hopefully, wanting food, wanting ball games. I couldn't concentrate for five minutes. When it wasn't the dogs, it was the cats asking for food, and when it wasn't them, it was the goat kids wanting their bottles.

It was annoying and our stress levels were rising. It also wasn't normal – or conducive to work.

Was it a lack of exercise or attention?

Were they mirroring our stress?

Finally I stood up from my desk and said to Andrew, "There's something wrong. The dogs don't want me to work today."

I took a breath and pushed away my tension, calling the dogs to me in that silent other realm.

"It's not the right time," came an answer. *"Follow your heart."*

I understood. To be a human angel, you have to live authentically. I was still jumping other people's hoops and not honouring my inner being.

And as it turned out, the deadline wasn't even a real one. I was denying myself nourishment time for nothing. The dogs knew this; I didn't. I was right to honour them – and my soul – and spend time in the spring sunshine.

Another time the dogs were going nuts, pawing us, jumping all over us and not letting us work. I could feel their tension in my own body and despite a really intense deadline I whistled them up for a walk. It would help them, and help me, even though I didn't think I had the time.

Down at the yards, the two baby goats decided to join us – just Polly and Peter, not the rest of the herd. This immediately alerted my other senses. What was the look that crossed Totem's face as he watched the baby goats go, and made the decision not to follow? There was something going on.

The little white goats pranced and danced across the creek with us and ran over to a water trough. There, another baby goat stood – alone, with a broken jaw, a swollen tongue, saliva dripping, and unable to drink.

He was from a herd of feral goats who wandered through our place, the same herd as the rest of our goats came from. We'd find them abandoned as babies and take them in, raising them in the house with the dogs until they were old enough to live outside at night. This goat was a bit bigger than ours, but their appearance soothed him, and made the humans less scary. I could tell he saw us as "other", but he wasn't really afraid. We were goat people.

Our dogs are very goat friendly, are working dogs, and know how to herd. They knew they had a job to do. But we, with our limited human thinking, thought that maybe the dogs should be in the house because they were young and liked to chase, and this little guy had a problem.

So Andrew, Tamsin and I wandered alone through the bush following and herding, sending out thoughts of help to this little goat, who knew we were help, and could see the babies were jumping all over us, but didn't quite know how to go about receiving the help we offered. Suddenly our three black kelpies appeared out of nowhere, and completely took over the situation. In no time the goat was quietly herded and held, by three determined but gentle young dogs. I was able to stroke the little, wild goat and soothe him. Andrew collected him in his arms and took him to an empty enclosure with our baby goats for company.

I apologised profusely to the dogs. They were right again; we had needed their help.

Tamsin called the new goat Valentine, and I gave him homoeopathic Arnica for his swelling and bruising, as well as Symphytum, Calendula and Hypericum for pain and healing. He had Emergency Essence for shock and trauma. Because I could smell infection, I gave Hepar Sulph for a possible abscess, silver colloid, and the Young Living Essential Oil Thieves. I gently syringed some slippery elm, honey and goat's milk into his mouth to see if he could swallow. I didn't want him to choke if he couldn't.

It was a Sunday and none of the vets I called could see him. I made him as comfortable as I could and also gave him a shamanic healing, clearing his stuck throat chakra, and illuminating him with Light.

I refused to think of his future, and Andrew and I didn't have the thousands of dollars surgery would cost. But we both knew we would go into debt if we had to. We would find a way.

The next morning Valentine told me in the language of silence that he felt so much better. The swelling in his mouth had gone down and he could now move his tongue. He looked at me with such love and gratitude that I had to blink tears. We both knew he wasn't coming back from the vet's. But it was something I wasn't willing, in that moment, to consider.

Andrew and Tamsin drove Valentine the two hours to our vet.

He examined the little goat in silence and shook his head. "The jaw's broken in two places," he said. "And there's infection."

He told Andrew even if we went to the specialist for reconstructive surgery, he wasn't sure how we would rehabilitate the little fellow, and keep him alive while he healed.

My grandmother always told me "where there's a will, there's a way." I live my life by that saying. So when Andrew asked me what we should do, I told him to phone the specialist. And then Valentine came through. "*No,*" he said. "*I don't want surgery. It's time for me to leave. You have given me love. That is enough.*"

That wasn't what I wanted to hear. I phoned my friend, animal communicator Pam Adams. "Billie, I got the same as you," she said. "He came to you for healing. You gave him unconditional love. That's what his soul needed. He doesn't want to live. "

"Pam, let's ask him again. Let's both send him images of what it looks like when he is healed. When he is better."

Valentine was clear. He appreciated the offer of surgery, but that wasn't his soul's journey. Like many animals amongst us, he needed to be touched by love. I'd given him a healing and while it wasn't a cure, it had healed his soul – and that's what he came for. He said he would return some day. That our souls would meet again. But for now, he wanted to leave. And he needed help.

I got it. I have healed many animals in spirit, cleaning their luminous energy fields, resetting their blue prints so they didn't have to experience the same events over and over. Valentine's soul had orchestrated this so he could have that healing. A tear dripped down my cheek. I wiped it away and picked up my rattle. I held Valentine in the sacred space of the Inka tradition, and I did the Death Rites. Moments before the vet gave him the needle of death, Valentine was free. He zoomed around the office, saluting me. From the vet surgery, Andrew reported on the peacefulness of Valentine's passing.

I may not have saved this goat, but I provided healing for his soul. And that's the core teaching of my work today.

The reason I tell these stories is because this is secret animal business at work. Because we were focused on our deadlines, we weren't aware of something more important – an animal in need. The dogs alerted us by their "behaviour" because we weren't listening. It seemed as though every animal on the property "knew" what was going on – except us. And the dogs conspired to get us to help.

Most of the time behaviour isn't "bad". It is just misunderstood.

It is up to us to listen with all our senses and see the world from the symbolic, mystical and spiritual viewpoint of the animals, not just the literal world we've been conditioned to live in.

This is what I mean by having reverence for our animal kin. Honour them and allow yourself to be humbled by them.

Chapter 13:
Animals are Angels

My friend Lee sent me an awesome YouTube video today. It encompassed a lot about what I want to say about animals. Picture if you will, a dog getting hit by a car on a busy multi-lane highway. Not one human stops. The dog is lying there, with cars whizzing on either side. Another dog, coming from who knows where, trots purposefully through the busy traffic, and uses his front legs and paws to carefully drag the injured dog to safety. Amazingly, they are not hit by the cars whizzing by. Truly a miracle. Just as they reach safety, human help arrives and the injured dog is saved, to live his very valuable life.

I was incredibly struck by so many things about this incident. As there are no accidents as we believe them to be, why did this dog get hit? And what were these two dogs doing on this multi lane busy highway? Where did the other dog come from? How did he know to come to another dog's aid? And how did he know how to save him, and to move him without causing more injury? I swear, he looked like a small human in a dog suit. But he was better than a human – he was an angel.

Do you remember a similar scene in the film Michael, about archangel Michael, played by John Travolta? To prove a miracle, Michael takes a small dog and places him in the middle of a highway where the dog, knowing his fate, and with apologies from Michael, waits until he is killed instantly by a passing truck. Michael then brings him back to life. This was to demonstrate the truth of Michael's angel status, and also to give a human belief and trust in miracles. It was an extraordinary moment for me as someone who communes with animals and knows the truth of their existence.

All over the world today, animals make the same sacrifices for humanity. Beaching whales, live export sheep being stranded in the middle of the ocean, racehorses who die on the track, brumbies shot from the air, thousands of innocent faces of dogs and cats killed daily in our pounds and so-called shelters.

As a species, this sort of thing tugs at our heartstrings and opens our heart chakras. The animals make sacrifices of their lives in the most terrible manner, so we can truly awaken to a higher consciousness and start operating from our hearts. True, they have free will, and as a soul, they chose service. But that just makes me feel even more humble and grateful in their presence.

The 2012 Phenomenon (which I discuss more in *Chapter 41:* 2012 and the Fifth Dimension – The New Earth) is affecting sensitive people the world over. They are crying out for change and are working on themselves to create that change. They want to become enlightened humans – human angels.

If your animals are pushing your buttons, thank them. It means they are asking you to look at something. It could be a goat with a broken jaw, or it could be that your house is full of entities. You might need to change your diet, or do something to lift your depression, anxiety or stress.

So recognise when your buttons are pushed, and seek the answers outside the square. Fly high to the perspective of eagle or spirit and see what you can see. The only reason secret animal business is secret is because we humans have only been taught to view the world in a limited way.

My intention is that this book will change that.

Chapter 14:
Enter the Stillness

Part of the reason it seems the doors of that mysterious, magical world of secret animal business are closed is because our human world is so loud.

We live a life of constant noise and distraction. Our Western culture doesn't encourage people to be still, quiet and on their own.

This is why I encourage my students to practise meditation, and to take mindful walks in nature.

Not only can people be loud, abrasive and hard on the nervous system, but also unconscious with drugs and alcohol, which numb the senses still further. Many people also seem to need attention to make them feel good. There's a lot of ego out there in people land. The "hey, look at me" mentality.

Not so the animals. I'll never forget the quiet job my five dogs did of protecting me when I was vulnerable with my daughter Tamsin as a baby. Andrew was away, and so the dogs took over what they considered to be his job. I had builders in the next room banging away at the flooring of Owl Cottage, and I lay down on a futon on the floor to breastfeed. Tamsin and I both dosed off. The dogs were scattered all over the room, with Tala, Suki, and Twylah cuddled close. As I slipped into sleep, I felt Cedar and Louie join us, making a circle of protection around me. When I started waking up, they simply padded off. They didn't want any fanfare. They were just doing their job.

And what struck me about it was their quiet, cohesive, cooperation and communication.

Another example is the wild animals on the road. Ever hit a bird, fox, a wombat or a kangaroo? Well, next time, take pause and understand there are no accidents. What is the animal telling you? Sometimes, unless you get a direct answer, it's hard to unravel the mystery for yourself, but if you keep asking, the answer will come.

I was giving a lecture once, and a woman asked me why birds always crashed into cars.

"I think you might need to look at what they're trying to tell you?" I said. "Because they don't crash into my car."

I then asked the audience to put up their hands if this was a regular occurrence for them. No one did, except the woman who asked the question.

A friend of mine hit a wombat. Easy to do, you might think, especially living in the country among dirt roads and darkness. The roads are littered with road kill.

This was a mangy wombat with baby. Suicide, obviously, and targeted to a human who would do the right thing by the baby and to herself. Wildlife rescue was a heartbeat away and the incident had a sort of happy ending.

But then my friend hit a second wombat. This was serious and he was very shaken. What were the wombats trying to tell him?

My friend was very, very tired and needed a holiday, which he just wouldn't take. Even though he thought he was driving carefully, he was mentally exhausted to the point of disassociation. The wombats were the whispers before the Mack truck – and he took note of the warning and followed it with action.

This brings us to the question of why an animal would kill themselves for us? Good question, and really why we need to be humble and grateful in their presence and for their presence, and why we need to honour their actions by learning about the spiritual and metaphysical world at large.

It's because the animals are angels.

And this is their secret animal business.

I used to have an argument with people about the importance and value of animals in our society. I've been arguing about this all my life. So when Mark said to me: "So Billie, if there was a dog and a baby in the middle of the road with a truck heading toward them, you'd save the dog."

"I would want to save the dog and the baby", I said. "But if I could only save one, then I'd have to save the baby – only because the dog would want me to."

Mind you, that's not an easy thing for me to say, because I value the life of animals highly and consider them far better company than most people. But the truth is, animals sacrifice themselves for us every single day. They give us the gift of their life. And that's a very, very humbling realisation. Like I said – they are truly angels in fur coats.

And now it's time for us to give back.

Chapter 15:
Aho Mitakuye Oyasin

"Save me"

My head snapped up. There was no one else in the room. What was that voice? Who was it? I was standing in the vet surgery, my mind running through the million things I had to do before we moved. Andrew and the vet nurse were somewhere else, sorting the last bill. The voice I heard was so loud it sounded human. Sounded physical. It cut through my mental chatter. I scanned the room.

There. I found the source. A small, sad-eyed black puppy in a cage. I walked over to her. On closer inspection, I could see there was a sign on the cage. "Two Days to Go." I stuck my finger through the bars and touched the fluffy black coat. "Yes," I whispered. "Don't worry, I will."

– Excerpt from Billie's journal, 1991

I had no intention of taking on another dog, but I couldn't let the puppy down. Released from her miserable predicament, she was lively and hungry. She joined us – two humans, two other dogs, three cats and two budgies – squashed in our tiny blue Honda as we headed off to our new home in the mountains.

We tried to find her a family, but she kept coming back. There was something else going here and I'd forgotten to ask her, so she worked it out herself, using her own connection to the Divine.

She barked with the first people, and didn't stop, knowing she would drive the father crazy. I was thrilled to see her again but still didn't get it. We gave her to a woman with another dog – and there the puppy became so hopeless and helpless that the woman couldn't stand to leave her all day when she was at work. I collected her from that country property, my heart on fire. Andrew and I had already bonded with her and I was relieved to have her back. We called her Suki, and she and her irrepressible kelpie spirit made our days richer from that moment on.

It didn't occur to me until much, much, much later that Suki was strongly psychic and needed to be with me – someone who could hear her. And more importantly, that I was in need of a teacher – her.

Suki never fails to remind me that we humans are currently a bit slow on the uptake. *"But it will get better,"* she says. *"Humans just have to climb out of their dead suits and come alive."*

There are no accidents and no coincidences. Suki was what I call a Master Teacher. Through our film Seven Days with Seven Dogs (which she got us to make), she not only taught and touched her human family, she taught and touched thousands of humans around the world. In the greater scheme of things, we needed each other. I was grateful I stretched my comfort zone to embrace dog number three, and that she was patient and smart enough to persevere with me.

Like all animals, Suki needed to be honoured, and I share this story now because so many animals find their way to people who don't think they can take them in. If we all stretch for the ones who find us, the world and life will be much more beautiful. After all, what's more important, designer jeans, plastic knick-knacks, a bottle of wine, a second piece of cheesecake, or the life of a soul in need?

In this book, I focus on the domestic animal – the dogs, cats and horses who touch our hearts and live in our homes and paddocks. But all animals are psychic. All have tremendous sentience. And by our souls, the spark of divinity within, we are all connected.

The indigenous among us call the other animals "little brother" and "little sister". And from the Lakota nation of Native Americans, we have the prayer *Aho Mitakuye Oyasin* – In Honour of All Our Relations. This prayer embraces not just the furry families who live in our homes, but all of life. The Earth we walk upon is our Mother and she is alive, and all the animals and insects and elements are our immediate family, our brothers and sisters.

If you can step into that mindset for a minute, you can understand that we are not alone. We are never alone. And that like human souls, animals choose the "family" they want to live with, and that we are all family no matter who we live with.

A Moment of Meditation

Picture if you will, walking barefoot in the country or a park. It's a beautiful day, with blue sky, a gentle breeze, and green grass under your feet. Above you flies a red robin. You acknowledge his presence with a smile. He says he is with you today to keep your spirits up. You thank him, feeling gratitude in your heart. As you walk you can feel the soft grass and warm earth under your feet. The earth hums. Is that a heartbeat you can hear? You feel nurtured by the Mother and know when you get home to your garden, She will help feed you by helping you grow vegetables in your garden. You feel gratitude that She is there, and that She is also an instrument of healing, helping you ground when you need to, and taking your pain into her belly for mulching and transforming. Your heart opens with gratitude for her. In the distance you see horses galloping and pigrooting with exuberance. Your soul stirs as you laugh with delight. And by your side, two dogs appear, eyes bright with love, as they nudge you into a game of ball or stick throwing.

You thank the dogs and the horses for inviting you to play, and head home, feeling light and tall. You're already vibrating at a much higher frequency. You feel so much more alive, and so grateful to all these family members who appeared in your world to lift you up. The breeze gently caresses the skin on your face. You smile, and tears of gratitude slip down your cheeks. You feel so loved.

Something makes you look up. A great eagle flies on the currents. You nod your acknowledgement. Thank you my sisters and brothers, for helping me think high thoughts. Thank you, Brother Eagle. My thoughts will fly with you today in the realms of the Great Spirit.

You reach your home, and there, basking in the sun, is a big orange cat. You reach out your hand to stroke the soft fur and are immediately met with a loud, contented, rumbling purr. The vibration tones in your own body, and you, too, feel contented. You sit with her for a while, basking in the gentle rays of sunlight. It is good. Life is good. Thank you my sister for helping me understand that it is good for my soul to sit in silence and stillness."

I think the world would be a very different place if all humanity lived with this kind of reverence and understanding of our family members, no matter what they looked like on the outside.

Aho Mitakuye Oyasin is the prayer that I adopted many years ago from my Lakota-Sioux teacher Grandmother Kitty. Traditionally, it is used in ceremony and prayer to honour all our relations, and to invite them to be present at that place, time and moment. But even before Grandmother Kitty, and before I had ever heard of the Lakota prayer, it was the way I walked in the world of animals.

The animals are my true family, as they are yours. And they are indeed our teachers, healers and guides in this merry journey called life. They are here to answer all our questions and to help heal our inner wounds. What they want and need in return is our love and our respect. Indeed, our reverence.

It's time we started thinking about a new way of seeing and interacting with the world around us, and making a conscious effort to lift our game and transform our lives.

I walk a shamanic path of the animals. From their teachings I have learnt to see humans in the light they show me. It's not always a pleasant sight. The animals need us to change, to start seeing the big picture because they are affected by our personal troubles and they are growing tired of it. There is an urgency to their message and mine, for our connection might be psychic and unseen, but it exists. The animals are our mirror and they want to mirror health and happiness, not illness, death, drama and violence.

For the love of animals, start living your life as a prayer, honouring All Our Relations – yourself included.

Chapter 16:
Animals Were the First Tribes

"Never presume to know us and what we are to you. Each one of us is different and all our connections with humans are deeply personal."

– Erin the pony, 2008

Keep Your Mind and Heart Open

Despite my 30 years of working with animals and my lifetime of communicating with them at a deep level, I still would never say, "I know everything about animals". To me this is the greatest arrogance because how can any soul presume to know the depth of another soul – without asking. It would be like saying "I know everything about ET's. I watched Star Trek!"

So to me, it is important that all people who work intimately with animals, even hard core animal behaviourists, people who train, heal, groom, whatever, come to this book with an open mind.

Secret Animal Business

We humans are a flawed species. We see the world through the filters of our wounds. These wounds may have occurred in this lifetime or thousands of years ago, but they are stuck in our blueprint in a repeating loop until we heal them. We create and perceive our world and everything in it from that source of wounding. And this is what we also do to the animals in our lives.

We project our shadow onto the animals we love. If we haven't had enough love, or we've been abused or abandoned, or haven't befriended Death or our emotional nature, then we can project this onto the animals we love.

If the world was a healed place, do you think we would still have Death Row? Would we have the violence that we still hold in our hearts, that seeks revenge, creates war and suffering, and inflicts pain on all species who dwell here? We haven't learnt yet to shine light on our shadow, and this is what we must do. Collectively and individually.

Unless you understand who animals really are and can be open to the weirdest of conversations, you may also end up projecting your own beliefs and thoughts, invalidating what the animals are really trying to say. And let's face it, some of the conversations can appear weird to our limited way of thinking.

That's what my dog Twylah said to me once. *"There's nothing secret about our life,"* she said. *"It's just that we see life in such a different way."*

Western humans often have a "quick fix" mentality. People want to learn how to communicate instantly. And then use that ability so their dog can be a Lassie – perfectly trained and fitting in with the house rules, so they aren't a bother.

It's time to shift that thinking.

Animals are wisdom keepers. They are message bearers. They are shamanic teachers in that they don't let us off easily. It's difficult for us to own our faults and shadows. We now need to go the extra mile to believe what our intuition and heart tells us, and to act accordingly.

To communicate with animals, we must come from a position of humility and respect. We need to understand that we've been conditioned to see animals in a certain, very limited way. They're not just furry pets – cute, cuddly things who are dumb, forgiving and good for the kids.

They are so much more.

The Truth of the First Tribes

All animals, right down to the goldfish or the canary, are complex beings with a host of emotions. Like us, they have past lives. Their senses are different, which means they perceive the world differently (think about an eagle's eyesight or the way a snake smells with her tongue). Plus, they have extra senses, are closer to Source with their instincts, and they have been on this planet for a long, long, long time.

Remember that the animals were here before humans. In truth, they are our spiritual and physical elders. They are the holders of an ancient, indigenous wisdom of their own.

And they weren't thrown out of the Garden of Eden either. Neither were the indigenous peoples around the world.

As an exercise, look up the creation stories from around the world. Many cultures revere the animals, and remind us that at one time we all spoke the same language and lived in harmony.

This is the time I believe will come again.

Many native teachings say we come from the stars – other planets. The Pleiades and the Sirius System get most of the attention. They'll also tell you some of our animal friends come from the stars also.

One text, *Voyagers 11, The Secret of Amenti* by Ashayana Deane, puts forward the thought that beings from other planets called the Christos Founder Races, were the "seed races of the Palaidia Empires." They were animal in origin, but an interesting hybrid blend of the animals and humans.

This might sound like a stretch to some. But I "met" a being with a lion's head and a human body who called himself Christos seven years before I'd heard of this book. He came to me with a group of angels when I was meditating on a hill at home. It was just before we started filming Finding Joy. I accepted the sight and presence of him as a friend on the other side, just as I do all the people and animals there I regularly communicate with.

Egyptian mythology is filled with strange hybrid beings and the reverence for cats. Indeed today, many clients' cats urge their people to remember the Egyptian teachings.

Michael Harner, in his book *The Way of the Shaman*, talks about how animals can appear to humans in human form, according to North and South Native American mythology. And certainly there are tales throughout the indigenous shamanic world of the interconnectedness of humans and animals, as well as the ability to shape shift from one form to another. Sometimes this is done in non-ordinary reality such as the dreamtime or while shamanic journeying. And other times it is in this physical reality. The work of Taliesin the bard is just one ancient text of the Celts which explores this human-to-animal transformation.

Back in the introduction, I quoted Lekota-Lesa, who said, "In the beginning of all things, wisdom and knowledge were with the animals, for Tirawa, the One Above, did not speak to man." But why did Tirawa talk to the animals instead of people? It seems to me that today it is still the case that messages from Spirit come through the animals. Most humans have forgotten to be instinctive. We have forgotten the silent language of the natural world, and we have forgotten the simplicity of answering Spirit's call through our intuition – our gut reactions, our heart songs. Today we are cut off from the essence of who we really are, and we've forgotten that not only are animals our Elders, with wisdom passed down through the ages, but they are messengers from the Otherworlds and need to be listened to, and honoured for the work they do.

We live in an unlimited universe. So let the animals be our guides. Let them out of the box our culture has put them in, and let's get to know the wise ones within the fur, feathers and scales.

Chapter 17:
How Can One Own a Soul?

"This we know. The earth does not belong to man. Man belongs to the earth. All things are united, like the blood that unites us all. Man did not weave the web of life. He is merely a strand in it. Whatever he does to the web, he does to himself."

– Attributed to Chief Seattle of the Suquamish tribe

Okay, so this famous quote did not actually come from Chief Seattle (Google can help you with the somewhat coloured history of it). But even so, I think it is one of the most beautiful and profound environmental statements ever made. Here is another misattribution to Chief Seattle that I also think is great. It holds a high beauty which is poignant and so incredibly relevant to our work and thoughts today.

How can you buy or sell the sky, the warmth of the land?
The idea is strange to us. If we do not own the freshness of
the air and the sparkle of the water, how can you buy them?

Language is a funny thing. It reflects how we see things and how we behave. But it also can determine how we act. Language can hold our thinking in a box, or free us from the same.

Indigenous peoples don't have a concept of land ownership because the land was Mother and they had a different way of viewing the world. In the Quechua language of Peru, for example, there is no verb "to have". Instead, one might say of an animal companion, "This beautiful gift of a dog is with me."

Personally, I love that statement. It is the essence of how I see my world with animals. In that sentence is everything I teach – gratitude for the gift which is dog or cat, bird, bunny or horse, and acknowledgement that they have chosen to be with you.

It's very different from "owning" an animal.

Our society is big on ownership. The more we own, the better off we are seen to be. Our collective self-esteem is wrapped up in the new car, the big home, the designer clothes and lots of things deemed unattainable by the majority of people. This puts lots of pressure on us to conform and work, work, work so we can spend, spend, spend. We are the society with the disposable attitude. If it's not perfect or working properly, chuck it out. Buy a new one.

Sadly, this attitude crosses over to our animal companions. We think because we "own" them, we can do what we like with them – and they need to "obey" us. In the word "own", there is no room for understanding that animals, too, have free will and something to offer. There is no partnership in the concept of ownership.

I believe that in the future we will look back and view our relationships with animals with shame and horror, much as we do with all the dark deeds of humanity, such as oppression of indigenous peoples, the religious inquisition of "witches", human slavery, and the holocaust of Jews and gypsies by the Nazis.

Problem Animals?

Many people, sadly, seem to have little patience or real understanding when it comes to animals. When the animals "don't work" properly – the horses "play up", the dog's bark, the cat's pee, the puppy pulls the washing off the line or digs a hole – they are sent to the pound or sold. These "problem" animals are usually killed, unless they luckily fall into the hands of someone with knowledge and commitment. There are way too many instances of people who chuck out their animals when it is time to go on holidays, only to get a new one on their return. The list of reasons why animals are dumped goes on and on.

Why should an animal die simply because they have been misunderstood, or are sick, aged or bored? What is it in our society that thinks we have the right to treat another species this way?

And most importantly, how can we change it?

I believe we can make a good start by changing our vocabulary. Our language is made of words, and words have power. The following chapter covers words I insist my students never use in relation to animals. By changing the terminology around animals, we can change society's attitudes.

Chapter 18:
Change Your Words and Change Minds!

"Why do men speak so commanding? What gives a man a right to command a dog, if they are not pack?" (Nighteyes the wolf)

"Some men think they are better than beasts. That they have the right to use them or command them in any way they please." (Fitz, the Bastard Witted Son of Prince Chivalry)

– Robin Hobb, Assassin's Quest

I love this excerpt from author Robin Hobb's fantasy novel. It gets to the heart of everything I want to say.

Language, in my opinion, is all about respect. And to communicate with another being, you need to come from that space of respect and humility, to really hear the words, feelings and messages they have for us.

The following are words I ask my students to change in their language and thinking around animals.

- **Owner**. If you can own an animal, you can insist on them behaving a certain way and disposing of them when you tire of them, like a toy, a car, or a pair of jeans. Slaves were owned. But if we start thinking of ourselves as animal carers or kin or guardians, it puts us into a space of loving commitment. I am my animal companion's **guardian**, **kin** or **caretaker**. This means I protect, I care for – always.

    When we take an animal into our protection or care, we make a commitment for life.

- **Pet**. A pet is a toy, a thing which can be used up and thrown away. It's like a cuddly, fluffy stuffed animal. "Pet" gives us permission to abuse our toys, and break them like we were rough children. It does not encourage us to care for them. "Pet" does not equal "conscious, intelligent being with a mind of her own". Perhaps those people who were less caring would not have "pets" if we changed that phrase to **animal companion**, **friend**, **kin**, and **family**. Animal "family" implies long-term commitment, and recognises the individuality of the being in our home or paddock. We may have our different ways and we might disagree sometimes, but they are family and we stick by them.

- **It**. When we call an animal "it", we depersonalise them to things again. It is definitely more polite and respectful to call animals **he**, **she**, **they**, or **them**. I once had a mare in trouble, and the young vet on the phone kept talking about "it" this and "it" that. I knew he had no idea the pain my mare Tessa was in, and that she indeed was family. He soon learned, because every time he used the word "it", I said "she" or "Tessa" until he finally heard me.

- **Creature.** Like "pet", the word "creature" has mucky connotations. A creature is an Other. A creature has been popularised to be something feared and despised, often a monster. They are outside of us, unconnected. Or are we creatures too? After all, we too are animals and this is something humans forget. So let's call animals **friends**, **family** and **companions**.

- **Beast.** This is another word that today has gross connotations and separates animals from us. A beast is biblical. A beast is ugly. A beast is something to be feared. And what we fear, we kill.

- **Stock**. Farmers always talk about their "stock". But most, not all, talk about stock as a commodity, because that's what the animals are to them. The animals are bought and sold to ensure a livelihood. The word "stock" doesn't differentiate **intelligent**, **sentient beings** from things which are slaughtered. Let's call them **cattle**, **sheep**, **pigs**, **hens**, **goats** or whatever species they happen to be.

- **Training**. I dislike the word "training" because it means to me, "You have to do as you are told." It allows no room at all for animal intelligence or independent thought. And believe me, this they have plenty of. **Animal education** is a better phrase because it implies a kind of training that helps animals live safely and comfortably in our world, understanding boundaries and rules, while leaving room for their own intelligence and personality.

Tamsin and Sarah *Sarah and Willow*

Some other thoughts on "education". I once had someone come to be interviewed for the job of Sanctuary sitter. My puppies were all over the place - loud, noisy, jumping up. Their behaviour was unruly. While these dogs are energetic and lively, this was beyond normal.

I observed the behaviour of this woman with my dogs, and went cold when she sat opposite me at my kitchen table and said, "I like dogs to do as they are told." Her mind, body and words all spoke of someone who wanted her world to be in order and would make animals fit into it. She wouldn't listen or bend like a willow. I could tell that my house might become sanitary clean while I was away, but my dogs would be miserable.

My Kelpie puppies are working dogs, full of zest and enthusiasm for life. I was educating them to be partners with me in our work together, not training them to be mindless robots. After Catherine had gone, the dogs told me they didn't want her, and they'd played up to make her show her true colours. They showed me their fine nervous systems and lively spirits, and told me she would have broken them.

So yes, let's think about education, rather than training.

Later, I found someone else, and noticed that when she turned up, the dogs were lively and enthusiastic, but loving towards this woman. They knew they would be fine in her capable hands and told me with both their bodies and heart language.

An educated dog is like Strongheart, the movie star character in *Kinship with All Life* by J. Allen Boone. He had been over trained to obey as a police dog, and then had to be educated to make his own decisions as a movie star.

Our own movie star, Blue Heeler Raffi instinctively knew how to act. When shooting our film *Finding Joy*, working with him was a dream. It helped that I was the director and lead actress, but Raffi looked depressed on cue and always "hit the mark" for the camera. That meant he had to stop at a certain point marked on the ground. Film acting can be very technical, but Raffi – without being trained – was a natural. He also did some neat improvisation. He gave my character a kiss at a poignant moment, and jumped up on my lap. In another scene he improvised refusing to leave my side because the character Peter was about to commit what I consider to be a doggy crime by sticking him on the back of a truck. Raffi used his natural psychic intelligence and made my script a far better one.

When you educate an animal, you prepare them to live in your community. You are giving them room to use their natural intelligence. If a horse doesn't want to perform on a certain day, perhaps he is avoiding an accident. Perhaps he is sore. It's a different way of looking at "training". Be prepared to learn from your animals, and make education time fun and full of positive reinforcement.

Chapter 19:
The Animal Point of View

Animals are souls who come into bodies. They have their own point of view. They don't all think the way we do. They have different ways of relating to the world.

For example, I once had a dog client who had started going to the toilet on a particular rug in the house. The dog didn't do this until a new cat had come into the family. When I asked him what was going on, he told me that where the cat went to the toilet, there was a lot of attention and praise and cleaning up. He couldn't understand why he didn't get the same in his "litter tray."

Here are a few stories which demonstrate the animal point of view:

The Horse Who Attacked a Human

"Billie, you have to come and talk to my newest rescue horse." Grace was one of my students, and she was clearly distressed. "She attacked Kali this morning."

Kali was another student, staying with Grace at the time. She was blonde, beautiful and gentle – and I was immediately curious as to why any horse would want to attack her. Kali didn't have a mean bone in her body.

Grace, Kali and I wandered into the paddock, stopping to say hello to Jay, Grace's rescued gelding. Suddenly, out of the corner of my eyes, I saw a creamy blur heading toward us.

"Watch yourself," I said to Kali, who whirled around in time and flung her arms wide. The mare spooked.

"*Why do you attack this one?*" I asked the mare, who wasn't the slightest bit interested in attacking me or Grace – just Kali.

"*That mare is going to take me away.*"

I glanced at Kali, then back to the horse. *"You see her as horse?"* I asked.

"She is mare."

"She is a human mare," I said.

"Is she?" The horse was genuinely bewildered.

I looked at Kali with my spirit eyes and saw her as the mare saw her. A horse in a human body. Kali was indeed a mare. I could see the imprint of horse in her energy field.

"Kali won't take you away, beloved. This is your forever home. Kali is a friend, who has come to speak with your new person, Grace. You are safe from travels. This is your home now."

The mare snorted and wheeled away. And I wondered privately what had set her off. Had Kali had a moment where she coveted the mare? This is the nature of telepathy. Animals demand us to be honest with ourselves and them. They know our souls. They read our auras and our thoughts.

Daisy the Protector

My puppy Daisy attached herself to me as my protector when she first arrived at the Sanctuary when she was just five weeks old. She was riveted to my side, following me silently everywhere I went, and sitting under my desk as I worked. But when my friend Janice came to visit, Daisy wouldn't stop barking at her.

"What's up Daisy?"

"I was with you when you were stoned to death. I couldn't save you and I was left all alone and it wasn't nice."

"Aah, I see. But Janice isn't going to stone me to death. She's a friend."

Daisy was quiet. I could tell she didn't agree.

One night, we all sat down to watch my one favourite TV program. I'd been working hard and wanted nothing more to do than be entertained. Daisy was quiet, until my friend started chatting during the program, and I felt my irritation rise. Even though I said nothing, Daisy barked at her. It was a big "a-ha" moment. Dogs, being telepathic, are more honest than we are. Daisy was cross with her for me.

The next day, as my friend was leaving, she admitted that she was actually cross with me because I was working on deadlines, with clients, and with the Sanctuary animals, and I wasn't giving her the attention she'd hoped to get from me. She needed me to take time off to be with her, even though she'd stayed with us before and understood the workload.

That's why Daisy barked at her all the time. She knew Janice was cross underneath her calm exterior, and I didn't.

Max, the Escape Artist

Max was an escape artist. He drove his person Penny crazy with her efforts to keep him in her yard. Fences were scaled, dug under, destroyed. And when she left him in the house, he dived through windows and if they weren't open, he smashed them.

When I first tuned into Max, he told me there was a dark man who he was both frightened of and also protecting the house from. Penny and I wondered about the neighbours.

And then I asked Max if this "dark man" was in spirit or in the physical.

Max said he was in spirit.

Apparently the place was being haunted by the earthbound spirit of an Aboriginal man, who had died suddenly when he tripped over a dog when he was drunk. So the spirit wasn't keen on dogs. This was what Max was upset about.

I released the earthbound spirit to the light.

Chapter 20:
Opening Your Mind to the Psychic World of Animals

We live in a complex and intriguing world of spirit. Communing in the silent language of the animals and nature requires an open and flexible mind. To truly listen, you have to understand the sentience and spirituality of animals. People who have set ideas about what an animal is may find themselves invalidating a conversation because they don't believe what the animal says to be true.

For example, many years ago I had a student who only believed in a linear progression of souls that started with "lower" animals, moved through lifetimes to "higher" animals, and ultimately reached the "top" of the soul's journey as humans. She couldn't wrap her head around the possibility that an animal's soul might previously have lived a human lifetime. This presumes you believe in reincarnation in the first place.

Reincarnation

Reincarnation is the belief that the soul is eternal, and that when a body dies, the spirit or soul returns to inhabit a new body, beginning again as a baby. There is a school of thought that says animals don't reincarnate, but I doubt you will find any animal communicator who will agree with that.

My experience is that the soul of the animal in your living room could come from anywhere. I've had dogs who were my children in past lives. I've met animals who claimed they came from the stars. It makes you think twice about treating an animal poorly – you never know, it could be your mum or your grandmother!

Suki and Tusuque

When my dog Suki died, she told me she would be back quickly, as we had "lots more work to do." Suki was the dog responsible for us making the documentary Seven Days with Seven Dogs. That's where we wanted to make every day a jewel for her because she had a large, inoperable mass on her throat. Suki told me she wanted to go on more outings, so we designed a holiday just for her and her six doggie mates. And in what still seems both miraculous and ordinary to me, a week before we set to go, when all the plans were in place, the mass just disappeared.

Suki and Billie

Suki told me before we started shooting that the film would win her lots of fans, and it certainly did – thousands of them. So I was intrigued we had more work to do together. She sent me a picture of a brown kelpie and told me she would be found locally, not in the pound. I got the impression she would be a puppy at the local vet surgery. *"And watch out for the ears,"* she said.

Suki had floppy ears.

We live outside a small town, and when people heard I was looking for a kelpie pup, I was stopped in the street twice. There were three black kelpie pups looking for a home. Hardening my heart, I said "no" to the first person. I was looking for a brown kelpie pup. A second person stopped me and mentioned the same three black pups. But I was resolute. I was looking for Suki.

But when Barry, the pups'

Tusuque

person rang me, I knew this was something I needed to look at. He was the third person to bring them to my attention. I "knew" I'd found Suki. Excitement raced through my body. The pups were black, but their mother was a brown kelpie. And there was a photo of them at the local vet surgery. I needed no other encouragement. This was Suki.

The dates were not quite right. These pups were five weeks old and Suki had only passed away three weeks before. But I understood body swapping and walk-ins, and knew that Suki was a determined little soul. Barry told me the mother had taken a sudden dislike to the little, bright, brown-eyed pup dancing in front of me – and I knew that was exactly what had happened. I grinned. And took her home immediately.

Like Suki, this pup was bubbly, bright and irrepressible. Her new body was strong and athletic, unlike her previous one, which had been challenged. We called her Suki 2 for a while, which soon changed into Tusuque.

As Barry was leaving to go overseas for a year, the other two pups were in danger, as no one else wanted them. I went back the next day and brought them home. The one with the floppy ears like Suki used to have adopted me immediately and I knew her for my dog Tala. Daisy became my companion-protector, just as Tala had been – and Reka before her.

A lot of people ask if their animal companion will reincarnate. I've spoken to a rat who told me he would come back as a camel, horses who want to come back as horses, but to "kind hands", and some animals who aren't coming back to this plane at all.

Most of my current eight dogs are returnees and soul family, as are the cats. I have also seen myself as a horse and see others who have been horses as well. One of my dearest friends carries unicorn energy. These are the people my wild horses recognise and will approach.

Often a domestic animal who is "badly behaved" is simply a soul new to Earth or to that particular species and doesn't know the rules. On the other hand, you might find a dog or a cat who is incredibly familiar with the territory. He knows what to do and exactly how to fit in and behave. He's been here before!

Group Mind and Other Evolutionary Thoughts

There is also a school of thought that animals have a group mind. This is true up to a point. They are connected to the whole, but they are also very capable of independent thought and action. Each is a unique individual.

There is another line of spiritual thought that to become human, we have to first experience life as stones, plants, elementals and animals. And yet another says that once we domesticate an animal, they can go on to become a human in their next life.

I can understand this thinking. If we are on this Earth to learn and experience, it makes sense to experience every life form, not just human. But that form of thinking also can be construed that to be human, must then be superior. And that I don't agree with! In my experience, if you haven't learnt a lesson, or you want to experience something again, then you can, in whatever species that requires. Some souls need to be in animal form to be touched by love. Other souls take animal form to assist in our awakening. Sometimes these souls are one and the same.

I have certainly come across an interesting phenomenon with regards to animals evolving – but it is not automatic. It seems to me that only souls who have experienced love get to step away from previous karma. This is why animals who die naturally, or who are assisted to die with love, are so grateful. I asked Sollie, my soul mate horse, whether or not he wanted assistance to die. He said no because then he would be *"gone forever."* As he now exists outside of time, not in the spirit world of the dead, I can only wonder at the choice he made, and I'm glad I honoured it.

Soul Family

I've met animals who have been with their people friends in different bodies over and over, travelling as soul family. We've all had that experience when you immediately bonded with an animal friend and you may even wonder if that animal friend is a reincarnation of another. He may be part of your soul family, here with you again this life to assist you in climbing the rope ladder to spiritual evolvement. And these lessons might mean bringing discomfort to help you shift, or comfort as you learn. Or both.

Suki says, *"Souls who incarnate as soul family always love you very much, no matter what their lessons."*

Walk-ins

A walk-in is when a soul takes over the body of another soul who wants to leave. The switch is generally done at a point of trauma, near death, or childbirth in humans. The same goes for animals. In humans, the new soul will look the same to the person's friends and family, but may act differently. They may not be able to remember their childhood very well. Some people remember being a walk-in. Others don't.

Here's an example of an animal walk-in.

The Story of Toby

One of the most intriguing clients I ever had was a lost cat named Toby. When I tuned in, it was obvious the cat had died. He showed me a dark, wet road, shining headlights and blackness. I also made sure I asked his twin brother what had happened and was told the lost cat was no longer living. The twin brother cat was heartbroken, and as well as telling me in words, he showed me the same black darkness.

Telling people their animal friend has died is a very difficult thing to do, and they accepted this gracefully. It gave them a sense of completion.

But the next day I got an excited call. Toby had just walked into the house, and apart from an injury which looked like a run-in with a car, Toby was fine.

Stunned, I told them I was delighted for them. I put down the phone and called Toby.

"Why did you tell me you were dead? You surely don't want to hurt my reputation?"

"I'm not Toby. My name is Prenth.

The penny dropped. There had been a swap!

I rang back Toby's people, Melissa and Greg. "Did you notice any strange behaviour or reactions to Toby from the other animals when he came home?" I asked.

"Yes, it was really strange,' Melissa said. "Toby's twin brother Ted hissed and spat at him. This was really odd – they've always been very close. They seem all right now, although Ted's still a bit put out."

Aha, I thought. Prenth definitely is a walk-in.

A year later the cat was dying, and Melissa contacted me again. When I tuned in, I found that Prenth had gone and Toby was back. Toby told me he was deeply bonded to Greg and had a cycle to complete. He wanted nothing more than to curl up with Greg as he said his goodbye.

Toby insisted I explain all this to Melissa and Greg because it was important for their own spiritual growth to understand the psychic nature of animals.

Body Swapping and Doubling

My friend Michelle, a fellow shaman, had a feeling her dog in spirit, Mickey, was trying to return. She asked me to tune in. The spirit was indeed back on this plane, but using other dog's bodies to get to her – kind of like hitchhiking. I saw him jumping into a dog's body and trotting along, experiencing that for a while, and then jumping into another body to get a bit closer to Michelle.

Two souls can inhabit the same body. I wondered what he was going to do when he finally arrived at Michelle's place and when. He told me he had "five years of travelling", and that his "travels would make him a better being." He said he would be an "able partner in the work she would do then." He showed me Michelle's healing and singing gifts – and he was sitting there, close by her, guiding her and the spirits who helped her. He said, "I'm gaining experience for the work we will do", and he told me he would have his "own dog" (body) for that role.

Spells

I once "met" a cat who insisted she was under a spell. Her person, Carmel, had rung to say her cat Lily had gone missing. "There's been a white cat around here the last couple of days," she told me. "I'm convinced Lily has gone off with her."

When I tuned in, I could see that Lily was in the bush. She told me she had been lured out by the white cat to settle an old score when they had been sisters and witches. It was now done.

Carmel wanted to come and get Lily, but Lily said, *"She'll never find me. I'll be home at dark. But tell Carmel she has to ritually cleanse the house, before I can come in."*

I was worried about Lily because she sounded sleepy and drugged. Carmel dutifully cleansed the house and I got a call from her the next day to say that Lily had indeed turned up – with a tick.

Paralysis ticks would make a cat feel very drugged and I marvelled she made it home before things got worse and she died. Carmel reported that Lily survived and they never saw the white cat again.

It was important to do the house cleansing so that Lily could come home without having to endure the darker energies left remnant in the home, something she may not have been able to do in her weakened state.

Star Animals

Not all animal souls come from planet Earth. Some of them are from other star systems. One of my clients was a cat who had just popped in to check things out. There have also been star souls wearing the bodies of horses and dogs who I have met. I'm sure others take other forms. We live in a galaxy with lots of planets with lots of souls who come to Earth to experience life here for whatever reason. The animals I've personally met who have come from the stars have always been very sage.

The Multi-Dimensional Nature of Animals

Just as we are multi-dimensional beings, so are animals. I've personally experienced this in several ways. The first is when an animal takes me back into one or more of their past lives, which they are living at the same time as they are living now. Sometimes they will show me their future lives. And then there is the ability to talk to an animal's soul as well as the animal herself, caught in the limitations of her physical body. So it brings up the question in communication – who is running the show in this moment and how can you tell?

Sometimes I find a soul who is stuck, or who has lost part of their soul in trauma. For these animals, I do a shamanic healing called a Soul Retrieval, bringing back the healed part which fled during the traumatic situation.

As a shamanic healer, I work on the luminous energy field of both human and animal clients. Both always have people or animals in the forms of energetic attachments who need forgiveness, healing, and release. Normally these are beings from their previous lives. But I've also encountered these energetic attachments as the client herself living in a past life at the same time as the present. This is what I mean by multi-dimensional. Different lives happening simultaneously on different planes. These healings heal and free up the multi-dimensional self, creating health and the ability to move forward in life.

I believe the multi-dimensional nature of reality will become more and more apparent as the 2012 Phenomenon unfolds.

Animals as Healers, Sages and Teachers

I was doing an animal consultation one day with a black cat named Merlin who lived in a city hundreds of miles from me. My blue Burmese cat Binah came straight over to me, settling on my lap. Curious, I asked her if she knew Merlin.

"Oh yes, he's a healer cat. Everyone knows Merlin."

Some animals are healers and understand very well the nature of healing and what they need for their own and their person's well-being. Others know nothing about healing.

As animals can mirror our dis-eases, they also become healers in the sense that they reflect back to us what we need for our own healing and return to wholeness.

They also heal through their companionship and touch, by taking us out into nature, and in a host of unexpected and different ways.

Perhaps not surprisingly, many cats lately have been appearing with teachings from Egypt for their people. One cat showed me how he, his person in male form, and another man were all together in Egypt as humans, studying the Mysteries. His job was to help her remember her teachings from that life. "Co-incidentally" (and there are never any co-incidences), she had already planned a trip to Egypt, for a few months later.

All animals are teachers. In almost every animal communication consultation I do, the animals give the gift of sage advice for their people. It seems to me that without fail, if you take an animal into your life, you're signing up for some intense personal training.

Many animals in spirit are also very sage, and usually have something important to say to their people if their people can't stop thinking about them, long after the intense grieving stage is over. I once had a spirit dog client who literally would show up to his people, leaving paw prints and the like, when he had an urgent message for them – usually warnings about his person's heart condition and state of health.

In short, opening the door to animal communication is like opening a door to the greater mysteries. Walk in with an open mind, and discover the riches you find there.

Part 3:
Communicating with Animals

Chapter 21:
About Telepathy

The Ancient Art of Listening

Like four black bullets, my lively kelpie dogs raced around the back hills of my home, chasing birds, and each other. Their delight brought smiles to my advanced students watching them. "They're so happy," said Lisa. "This is how dogs should be."

I smiled as well. My intention for this excursion was a different one. I wanted to demonstrate without a doubt to the students that there is a direct link between animals and ourselves. That idea of oneness and kinship.

We were happy being out in the cold winter sunshine, and so were the dogs.

We came to a resting place half way up the mountain where you can see the sacred Aboriginal woman's mountain in the distance. This place is special. It is a place to call on the earth energies and, if you were sensitive, to feel them. The women settled themselves as I asked them to go within, calling on Mother Earth for peace and wisdom, and the spirit of the mountain for guidance.

The dogs immediately stopped playing and lay down quietly in the shade. "Please notice the dogs," I said quietly. " If there is peace within, there is peace without.

But the next minute bedlam broke out. Sage jumped up all over Deb, one of the students, wagging her feathery black tail, Daisy barked at Tusuque, urging her to play, and Heyoka was in the pounce position, ready for anything. Sage wouldn't leave Deb alone. To anyone else it might have looked like "bad behaviour", but I asked Deb what her thoughts had been. "I *was thinking about wolves," she said, astonished. "And I was calling in the spirit wolves."*

"You also called the dogs Deb," I grinned. "And they're very excited to meet their relatives!! See how easy thought transference is!"

– Excerpt from Billie's journal, 2008

This kind of dialogue is far superior to speech – it is more rapid and conveys far more information. You would call it thought transfer. ...It involves not just a more efficient method of information exchange, but getting to know a person's soul, along with the animal and plant world, and what constitutes creation as a whole.

– Anastasia from Anastasia, by Vladimir Megre.

Telepathy is the forgotten language. It is the universal language of all species. Once the realm of the tribal shaman of indigenous cultures, it is an ability which is growing among sensitive people today. And this is important when you consider that one of the things that will help the planet today is for people to understand that she is animate.

If anyone has any doubts about the nature of telepathy and that speech is possible between all species, in fact, all life, then consider reading scientist Rupert Sheldrake's book *Dogs That Know When Their Owners are Coming Home*.

He says that people have noticed the uncanny abilities of animals for centuries and millions have experienced them personally with their own animal companions. But because of institutional science, many people feel they have to deny them or ignore them. The psychic nature of animals is considered a taboo subject by science, but Sheldrake didn't let that bother him. His book reveals the findings of his research.

His conclusion was that all animals seemed to be incredibly gifted at receiving our thoughts.

Humans, however, were less so.

Sheldrake noted that there is a long tradition of animal communication and shamans in tribal societies. He added that Indian yogis attained the understanding of the language of animals, as did Christian saints like St. Francis of Assisi and St. Cuthbert.

So there is a tradition of communication between species.

This language is telepathic in nature. Telepathy means "distant feeling". If you break down the word it is from two Greek roots – *tele,* as in telephone and television, and *pathe*, as in sympathy and empathy.

While Sheldrake admitted to animal communication being attainable in our society, both he and American animal communicator and teacher Penelope Smith echo my own concern regarding people who project their unhealed shadow onto their communications. People coming from ego, who have their own agendas, judgements, or emotional stuff, can muddy the waters of their telepathic communications.

This is not good for the animals and why both this book and my classes are now "transformational", in that they are geared to helping people shift consciousness and increase self-awareness. My goal is to create human angels for animals who communicate from a place of purity without projecting their shadow and unhealed self onto the animals. I have seen this happen over and over again, and it just causes heartbreak and also gives animal communicators a bad reputation.

The whole goal of *Secret Animal Business* is to share with others some understandings of animals and their behaviour so that animals get a better deal. I want to see a world where animals are treated better, where their voice is heard, where they are nourished and tended well and they are more understood. I want to see happy, healthy, long-lived animals – and I believe that you do too. This book attempts to give you the tools to do this.

While I believe you can learn to pick up the subtle whisperings of the language of silence, and I really feel every animal-loving human needs to, it has to go hand in hand with the type of spiritual work that I talk about in this book.

It's about going the extra mile for our animal companions, and doing our personal work to shift, change, be aware of our shadow, and drop the stories which bind us. No more blaming others for our situation. No more looking at animals and their "voice" through the filters of your own inner suffering, stories and upbringing. It's lifting ourselves up from any misery of our everyday thoughts and learning to understand that every thought creates a reaction, every thought goes out into the universe and is heard, and every thought lands on our beloved animal companions.

Such is the nature of telepathy that you cannot hide your true and authentic self from an animal. You cannot lie. You cannot think or speak abusive thoughts, for example, without them understanding exactly what you mean. They feel everything you feel – in their own bodies. More on this later.

So you might as well have good thoughts, learning to live with daily gratitude, making an effort to be happy and study the universal Law of Attraction, which essentially says that what you focus on expands. If you want to put your focus on misery, you'll get more of it. But if you want to put your focus on how happy and grateful you are for the animal in your life, for the food on your table, the blue sky overhead, the friends you have and the clothes you wear, your being will begin to attract more of what you want, because it is resonating at a higher level.

And believe me, your animals want this.

For me, telepathy and the whole secret animal business is not just about how Fluffy needs a softer bed. It's about humans understanding that Fluffy is an incredible being and deserves to be living not just with humans who love him, but humans who insist on being the best they can be – for him and for themselves.

It is in this way that the animals in our lives help us raise our consciousness and contribute to the Great Shift we are currently experiencing. Believe me, the animals are longing for us to become the human angels we can be.

Learning telepathy is an incredible journey and an important one. I believe in the future we will all be highly telepathic and the world will be a better place to live.

Examples of Animals "Knowing" Thoughts

Once when I was staying on a friend's property, I got lost riding. The only thing I could do was drop the reins and let the horse know I was lost and ask him to take me home. I knew without a doubt that he would succeed and trusted him completely. And to the homestead he took me.

Now this is nothing unusual. We've all heard of the extra sensory perceptions of animals – how they know when natural disasters are coming, how they know when their people are coming home, how they can appear ready for a walk when we've only just thought of it.

The language of silence is the whispers on the wind. It is the language of the heart and the soul. It belongs to the realm of the intuition; it is of the realm of the imagination – not as we know that word, but as "mage in action".

The animals call our speech the "language of the tongue." Many of them are frustrated that we don't listen with our spirit ears, with our bodies, our souls or with our hearts.

Many animals, simply given the opportunity to be heard, change their behaviour and their state of health.

The language of animals and nature is a soul-to-soul and heart-to-heart communication. It is thought transference, it is intuitive, and it comes from deep connection, respect and high regard for animals and nature. It's listening with the rusty extra senses we're given but don't use. It's about being sensitive to the world around us and coming from a place of humility and love.

Chapter 22:
The Wider Ramifications of Learning the Silent Language

In my experience, everything has consciousness and everything talks. Often loudly and definitely when they need you to hear them. And if you don't listen, that's when you get into trouble. And it's not only about listening. It's about honouring what you hear, and acting on it.

Shamans speak with all of life. In fact Michael Harner in *The Way of the Shaman* says, "It is only the shaman, or the person with shamanistic tendencies, who is able to resume the lost ability to communicate with the (other) animals."

However today, more and more people are waking up to their rusty extra senses. As we are all telepathic, and so are the animals, then we must be able to engage in two-way dialogue if we have the heart and desire to do so.

Not only do animals have a voice, everything does. Over two decades ago, I met and studied under a Hawaiian shaman, or *kahuna,* who told us all that he was hired by corporations to fix computers – by speaking to them.

I'm still saddened by a pair of shoes I left in Greenwich Village twenty years ago, who beseeched me not to leave them. At home, even my daughter knows when a piece of wood doesn't wish to be burnt in the fireplace. This gets back to a human attribute that sadly has gone missing for centuries, one of deep respect – to each other as well as to the world we interface with.

The shamanic viewpoint that everything is alive is very relevant to today's global crisis.

Being able to listen to the world of nature falls into the same category as the importance of being intuitive. This isn't stuff taught in schools. And it should be!

Listening is vital. There's that old catch phrase that if you don't listen to the whispers, you'll hear the screams of a Mack truck. Today these Mack trucks usually look like illness, accidents, income failures, even death. And if we don't start listening to the voice of the planet, we face oblivion. Our freeloading holiday on Earth is over. We're past the Use By date. We're in the red.

On a smaller scale, listening to the wisdom of your animal companions will help keep you healthy and on the right track. On a larger scale, if humans shifted their thoughts and saw a world where everything has meaning and is alive, they would begin to operate on the planet as less of a human pestilence and more of an organic whole.

You might have noticed that Mother Earth is cranky right now. Some people are putting it down to climate change – global warming. But there is a world of thought out there which says that what we do, and how we are in the world, directly affects the climate as well, because nature is alive. It's not just burning fossil fuels. It's our emotions and thoughts that are contributing to what the indigenous people call the Earth Changes.

For instance, I tuned into the rain spirits during Australia's long and severe drought. These feminine spirits were very upset. Humans were cranky, fearful and abusive about the drought, and this energy was being flung at the rain spirits. In my online newsletter Animal Whispers, I asked people to join in a rain experiment. We needed 100 people to praise rain, to be grateful for rain, to thank rain, to dance rain and to become rain. We got well over 100 people and we got rain. A year later, the drought changed and we got years of increased rain and the water table began to stabilise. One psychic on my list shared with me an Aboriginal women's ritual to help with rain and said the Aboriginal Elders also knew rain as feminine.

And it makes sense. The great feminine is the nurturer, the one who makes seeds grow. This is water. This is life. To honour, respect and be grateful for water surely must be one of the first things we teach each other and our children.

Alberto Villoldo PhD, in his book *The Four Insights* tells the story of the shaman who was asked by a drought-stricken village to make it rain. The shaman went into a tent and four days later came out. Sure enough, there were clouds followed by rain. The shaman explained to Alberto that he prayed rain and that he had to first correct the imbalances of the village by correcting the imbalance in himself. Alberto thought he was poking fun and said, "You prayed *for* rain." "No," said his mentor. "I prayed rain, and rain came."

And then there is the work of Masaru Emoto, and his book *The Hidden Messages in Water*, which says: "intense energy will bring natural disasters, but we need to realise that these are not evil events. If we consider the enormous amount of evil energy being blown away, perhaps we should actually be appreciative of lightning and storms."

We are all connected. Our animal companions are giant mirrors for us, frustrated by their lack of the "language of the tongue" to get their message across. And in a world which can always do with more love, our many calls for love are reflected by the illnesses and behaviours of our furry family.

I've had many other experiences where listening to animals and nature has literally put me into a state of grace instead of falling headlong into disaster. And the animals of my clients nearly always give advice and guidance as to how their people can travel on the path of life lighter and better, whether it is a warning to stop drinking alcohol, to turn off the television, to run on the beach, to start writing or taking up art – our animal friends can read us like books and often have a good understanding of where our future is headed.

How many times have you heard of the dog who is on the same medication as his person, whether it be heart, arthritis, or cancer? The animals in your home absorb energies like a sponge and it is up to us to take care of ourselves in new and better ways so we and our animal companions can live healthier and happier lives.

When my daughter's pony Little Tam was dying, she wanted to warn me about burnout, something I was on the brink of, if not already there. *"You need to nurture yourself and not see my dying as a personal failure,"* she told me. *"It is simply my time and I'm grateful for the loving kindness I have received."*

I could tell her heart was full and she seemed happy and at peace. It really helped me nurse her. But I wondered how I could nurture myself more when every part of my being was trying to take care of her around the clock.

The animals noticed I took care of them, and not myself. If I didn't heed the whispers, there would be a Mack truck. I chose the whispers. But it wasn't an easy shift for me. I forced myself to breath, calm, and accept that Tammy was leaving; to tend her lightly and lovingly, and still take care of myself.

Secret Animal Business

Listening to the world of nature and the animals helps us to walk in the world more softly and teaches us the art of mindfulness and awareness. It enriches our kinship with our animal companions and nature a thousandfold. There's joy, love and mutual respect aplenty. And once you learn to talk the language of silence, you realise you are never alone, for the world is whispering all the time.

In his book *Kinship with All Life,* J. Allen Boone calls the secret language of the animals and nature, "the voice of Existence", and that there was a time when the whole planet was of one language. This was a time when humans and animals lived in sacred harmony, as they will do again, in an enlightened age of peace, love, joy and oneness.

Chapter 23:
The Right Mental Space for Communication

If one is to communicate and communicate well, one must see animals as equal to us in consciousness. You won't get anywhere if you consider yourself superior. You'll make giant leaps if you see animals as teachers and healers, and honestly desire in yourself to help them, and to learn their wisdom.

So set aside your intellect and practise both humility and patience. The silent language of the heart with its whispers and feelings, flashes and insights, is one which unites all of life and truly helps us understand that the animals and all of nature are our brothers and sisters.

I really don't consider this a psychic ability. I think it is an ability we all have, but it's a rusty and needs oiling and use. It takes practice.

Further, I think in the future, we all will use this ability with both animals and each other, and the world will become a more honest, sincere and better place.

Benefits of Learning the Silent Language

Increased awareness

Better connection with nature and animals

Better able to understand animals

Able to receive guidance

More joy and aliveness

More magic

Chapter 24:
The Art of Telepathic Listening

Sollie and I cantered towards the dam, in harmony as usual with our thoughts. Later I wondered if I had actually thought about where I was going. My thoughts were simply on riding – being with my friend Sollie. It was Sollie who wanted to go to the dam. He told me we were going by sending me an image of the dam, and I had said yes. And with my heart, hands and feet, we turned and cantered there, as Sollie had wanted.

– Excerpt from Billie's journal

The language I often refer to as "whispers in the silence" is just that. It is a subtle brush of one mind on another - whispers of thoughts, images, feelings, words, and intuitive knowing. We all do it on a daily basis. It's just that no one has trained us to know what it is.

This telepathic connection happens for mothers when they "just know" their baby is in trouble or needs feeding. The pre-verbal child uses the language of silence to make her needs known. Many children born today are being labelled incorrectly as autistic. Instead, they are highly telepathic and operating differently. We are changing as a species, evolving into a more peaceful, Earth-loving telepathic people.

We use this faculty when we pick up the phone, knowing who is calling. Or we call a friend who says, "Oh, I was just thinking about you." In thinking about you, they were connecting with you, and you picked up on it enough to want to contact them.

Couples will finish each other's sentences. Parents will know when their child is thinking of them. My daughter Tamsin and I will often be ringing each other at the same time and not be able to get through! Andrew and I often bring up the same subject at the same time, or name a tune we're both hearing. Or I'll look out the office window for Andrew, just in time to see our blue van pulling up at the front gate.

So it's not such a stretch to go from human connection to animal connection. If you find yourself thinking of a particular animal, that animal is probably thinking of you. And it's often more than thinking – it's their way of calling you. If a thought runs across your mind that your lost cat is in the laundry, you will probably find he is. If you fleetingly think you need to feed the dog dinner, you are definitely receiving a clear communication!

Know that you are already telepathic. The only reason you don't understand the language of animals is because we have never been taught how to recognise and interpret what we are experiencing. The silent language is subtle and requires awareness. Many of my animal-loving students realise they have been communing psychically with their animal companions for years, but just didn't know what it was until I explained it.

Try This
Read *Kinship with All Life*, by J. Allen Boone. The thing I love about Boone's book is his emphasis on humility. The arrogance of human superiority has long been a barrier to human-animal relations.

Understanding the Subtle Nature of the Silent Language

It was raining and cold, and suddenly the thought of cat entered my mind. I also vaguely thought of the veranda. Understanding the nature of telepathy, I thought I'd better check the veranda to see if there was a cat there. Sure enough, Red was ready to come in.

– Excerpt from Billie's journal

Secret Animal Business

Many years ago I found myself in a disreputable horse dealer's yard. The horses were harshly treated and poorly fed on stale white bread. I cast out my senses and asked who wanted to come home with me. As usual I wanted to save them all, but as the fellow was asking $600 per horse, I couldn't. Surprisingly, I found many of the horses knew their own destiny and didn't want to come with me.

The first horse I came across was a beautiful skewbald mare who was very put out that I wanted to even look at someone else. *"What's wrong with me?"* she sent, with a wave of sadness and loss. A small, bay pony danced and jumped around, determined to catch my eye. She physically collapsed in on herself and stopped dancing when I walked passed her, disappointment radiating from every pore. A rangy, appaloosa mare was so skinny she didn't care what happened to her. I took her home first.

I went back for the bay pony, whom I couldn't stop thinking about, and I took the skewbald too, because she insisted. The way she insisted was to just stay in my thoughts, like the bay did, for days. Unlike other animals I have rescued, she didn't say "save me". She just let it be known that she was thinking of me. A bond had been formed and a bridge to my mind and my heart. She also leaned on the man who ran the yards, because he personally rang me and asked me to take her. When I discovered she'd been at the yards for over six months, I didn't hesitate. I wasn't going to let her stay there a moment longer, despite the cost.

I named her Sequoia and she became a horse everyone was drawn to for their own healing. The bay, Saraid, became a heart partner for Sebastian, a very mature grey pony I had had for many years. Sadly he outlived her, and then Bastie fortunately, eventually lost his heart to Sequoia. The appaloosa, Montana, became a riding horse for me for a while. At the time of writing she is still here at Ballyoncree, now one of our special needs who get regular feeds, supplements and attention.

Another example of a subtle communication was Jaffah. Jaffah was a striking red bay who I had never met. Her person needed to let her and her paddock mate Maverick go to a new home, as she could no longer afford to keep them. At the time we couldn't either, but Saraid had just died and I was taking a peek at older ponies who might bond with Sebastian, to help him heal his broken heart. I was certain that Jaffah was not this horse.

Jaffah intruded on my thoughts. There was an urgent push to her communication. She didn't say anything, but she let a picture of herself lean on my mind and imagination. I remember standing in the office telling Andrew that I didn't know why, but we had to take Jaffah and Maverick and as soon as possible. Andrew, sitting at his desk, didn't question it. He simply sighed and nodded. Who knows the way of Spirit, and of course when Spirit calls, a shaman always answers.

Jaffah

So we collected Jaffah and Maverick from Nikki, their person. They were two very pleasant and well-loved horses and they settled into a paddock where they appeared very happy and relaxed.

Three days later, Canberra exploded into the worst firestorm the city has ever experienced. At home, over a hundred kilometres away, our skies went dark and soot and ash fell in dark clumps everywhere. It was terrifying.

When the worst was over, we got a shaky call from Nikki, saying we had saved the horses' lives. "A fireball went right through their paddock," she said. "There was no way I would have been able to save them as I was struggling with my house and two toddlers."

I looked at Jaffah eating contentedly in the paddock and my mouth went dry. I sent her a silent thanks, and one to Spirit for sparing them. So many Canberra horses and other animals had died.

Jaffah became a horse who helped people heal their fear of horses. She absolutely insisted on staying with the special needs herd and not running with the thoroughbreds. Both she and Maverick were a wonderful addition to our family for far too short a time. Sadly, they have now passed and I miss them with an ache in my heart which never seems to leave. It seems to me such a little thing to give shelter for a time to the souls who require it. The rhymes and reasons often aren't ours to figure out. But it is said in shaman lore that no meeting of souls is ever coincidental.

Try This

Our mind is filled with a million thoughts at any one time, so practise mindfulness. Meditation is a wonderful training for telepathic communication. It helps you still the restless chattering and clattering of thoughts in our head, and find the space where you can concentrate on the small voices from animals and nature.

Meditation is also a practice for peace, which you need as you embark on a journey with animal communication. Hearing the silent language is so much harder when you are stressed or a jangle of nerves. This is often why my clients and students ring me when their animal companion is in crisis. All their faculties for listening to the subtle language of the heart and intuition close down.

My CD "Time of the Drum" was made especially to help people get into the right mental attitude for communication. The guided meditations help you get into a peaceful, centred and receptive state for listening with your inner or Spirit ears.

When practising with my CD, always write down what you get in your animal communication journal.

Chapter 25:
Learning the Silent Language

If you talk to the animals, they will talk with you and you will know each other. If you do not talk to them you will not know them and what you do not know, you will fear. What one fears, one destroys.

– Chief Dan George

Many people think that animal communication is like Dr. Dolittle and become easily discouraged when all they get back from their dog, cat, horse or guinea pig is a stare or a snore.

But don't be discouraged, because often behind that stare or snore is a wealth of information waiting to be unleashed on your unsuspecting spirit ears. You just have to allow it to happen.

In my classes, I've noticed the people who sometimes have the most difficulty in understanding the silent language are those who work in left-brained fields. They can set up more hurdles for themselves because often they don't recognise the intuitive faculty in play. That's why I always start with lots of improvisation games and paired exercises to help people open up to the communication of the soul.

People in right-brained work like healers and artists are already using their intuition in their work, and it's simply a matter of helping them see the similarities.

And always, it's just a matter of confidence through validation.

One of my students was an angel intuitive already. She spoke with angels with no problem at all. But she couldn't speak with her dog.

"All I get is a feeling in my solar plexus," she said.

I confirmed for her that was the communication, and suddenly she got it. Light bulbs went off and she quickly went from feelings to words and images. Once she understood her particular way of receiving information (feelings), she was able to move forward.

So let's get away from the thought that when you speak to an animal you will get back something which sounds like the spoken English. You may get a flash of insight, a feeling in a part of your body like the heart or solar plexus, or an image. Or you might get words. Silent words, as the voice of Spirit talks to us.

People in our society have been taught that the imagination is not real. Many education techniques work to actively destroy the imagination, as people are encouraged to conform to the norm. Artists are largely discouraged, being told they should get a "proper job". And we're told as children that the fairies we played with are "just our imagination" and that "dreaming is for losers". "Stop your day-dreaming!"

What are children doing when daydreaming? They're watching the action in their minds – the cinema screens of their imagination. They could be having a full-blown conversation with someone in the silent realms!

Imagination is simply inner images. And if you dissect it still further, you might see the word as inner mage in action! Magic!

Einstein once said, "Imagination is more important than knowledge."

The shamanic viewpoint is that the imagination is knowledge. Through accessing the imagination, we part the curtains of illusion to enter an animate world where the invisible becomes visible, everything becomes conscious, and all of life has a voice.

The four basic telepathic techniques are:

- Meditation – inner stillness. Learning to switch off the mental chatter.

- Learning not to think – going with the first thing which comes to mind.

- Listening with and being aware of the whole body when in silent communication.

- Keeping a communication journal.

Try This
Imagine right now you are sucking on a lemon. Feel the way your salivary glands automatically go into action! That's the power of imagination!

Meditation
When you communicate with animals, you retreat inside to the place of stillness, to the place of quiet, where the mental chatter doesn't intrude.

Meditation is the primary practice then, to help you get to a place of stillness so you can experience the whispers in the silence.

Again, try my meditation CD "Time of the Drum", which is designed for animal communication.

Games to Increase Telepathy
To prepare people for their journey into the world of telepathy I'll ask them to practise at home, playing games with themselves or their partners or children. How many messages are on the answering machine? When the phone rings, guess who it is. Guess what song is in your partner's mind right now?

One of the tricks to success in these sorts of games is the basic rule of improvised comedy: Don't think. Go with the first thing in your mind.

As soon as we start thinking, we're open to that part of our ego which says, "That's not right. You could do better". In our creative writing classes, Andrew and I gave this part of ourselves a name – "Mrs Crotchety". She's the one who tells us we're not good enough, that we could think of something better. She sits on our shoulders with a stick and let's us have it! If Robin Williams hadn't already made the name famous, I'd call her Mrs Doubtfire – she fires up our self-doubt!

And it's the same with telepathy. Did I really hear that? It sounds just like me. I made it up, I'm sure I did.

So let's do some exercises to warm up that right brain and get into the flow:

Journal Exercises for Solo Work

1. Find a magazine with great pictures of scenery in it. Write as fast as you can a story about a fairy who lives in the scenery. Start it with, "Once upon a time there was a fairy..."

   Don't think. This isn't anything anyone is going to see, so it doesn't have to be prose. Give yourself permission to write the worst prose in the world. The object of the exercise is to write quickly and whatever comes into your mind. Don't think. Don't censor.

2. Now take a different picture and put yourself in the scene. Start with, "Once upon a time, I..."

   Now add, "Suddenly, X (your favourite animal, celebrity, hero, lightworker, or politician) walks into the scene." What happens next?

3. Write 10 completely unrelated sentences in a list. Now create a story from your favourite of these sentences.

3b. Take one sentence for the beginning of a story and end the story with another.

4. Open any fiction book on your shelf, take the first five words of the first sentence and write three paragraphs of a completely new story.

5. Choose any occupation and choose 10 verbs to do with that profession. For instance the profession baker would have verbs like knead, twist, bake, sprinkle, ice, cut, slice, roll, pound, taste. Now choose 10 random nouns, like house, dog, liver, planet, fence, cake, file, newspaper, hair, and tissue.

   Now take one noun and one verb from your lists and create a sentence which somehow makes sense. The cake twisted in Johnny's stomach. The house sprinkled its feeling of comfort upon all who entered. The tissue tasted Paul's illness and knew he was not long for this world.

5b. Use your favourite sentence as the beginning of a story.

Improvisation Games for One and More than One

Ball Toss

Imagine you hold a ball. First it's a tennis ball. Now it's a soccer ball. Now it's a football. Now it's hot. Now it's made of gravy. Now it's made of slime. Now it's really heavy. Now it's honey and it's all over you!

In a group you could throw this changing ball to each other. If you're on your own you could – juggle with the ball! Or you could just read it and imagine the ball!

The Present Game

This is a good game to play in pairs or a small circle.

Person A hands person B a make-believe object. Person A has no previous thought as to what that object might be. It's up to B to go with the first thing in her mind to say what the object is. No thinking!

If Andrew hands me a long object it could be a snake, or a lamp stand, or a tree. If he hands me a small object it could be a mouse, a grain of sand, a flower...

The object of the game is to Not Think! Go with the first idea that comes up. And have fun letting your imagination come up with answers for you.

One of the tricks of this kind of improvisation is that you always go for something new – no thinking – but no copying either. Here you find you can release your inner genius.

The catchcry for Theatresports when Andrew and I played it was, "A brilliant mind in panic is a wonderful thing to see."

The truth is, when you are in the flow of Non-Thinking and Inner Stillness, you access your higher self, that which is connected to Source. So there is no need to panic, and no need to think, doubt or be in fear.

I learnt the hard way - on stage. My experience was that when I tried to be funny, I failed. But when I opened my mouth and let the first thing that came into my head out – the audience roared with laughter.

In my classes, we have a lot of fun with these sorts of games in a supportive setting.

Word at a Time Story

Here we tell a story one word at a time, alternative words with your partner. Make up a three-word title of a story. For example – The Red Painting.

And you start – A: Harriet. B: loved. A: red. B: and. A: painting.

And let the story take itself wherever it goes.

The beauty of this exercise is learning just how much you want to control the conversation or story. As a society, we are really into control, and control is not what we want to do when we get into a telepathic state with our animal friends. What we want to do is *listen*.

Prop Montage

Take any object like, for example, a hat. Think how many things this hat can be. Perhaps you can steer with it like a steering wheel. Perhaps it is a party hat, perhaps it is a horse to ride, perhaps it's a soup bowl, or a megaphone.

Be creative and use your imagination!!

Drawing

Another technique I offer my students is to invite them to draw their animal companions. By drawing, we focus and are still in our minds. Many people find this a helpful precursor to communication.

Becoming an Animal

This is a useful exercise from sacred drama to help you feel what it feels like to be a particular animal, and create more empathy and understanding for him. Choose an animal you would like to explore and act out being that animal. How do you see the world? What does it feel like to be that animal? How do you see people?

When I was studying TTEAM (the Tellington Touch Equine Awareness Method) with Robin Hood, she would make us wear a dog's choke chain. It was horrible. Imagine wearing a bridle that has a bit with a gag action. Try it on. Is this what you want for your friend? Or can you find it in your heart to look for kinder and more enlightened ways of being in true partnership.

Write It Down in a Journal

I always write down my conversations with animals and I encourage my students to this as well. Allow the conversations to flow like automatic writing. Write down what you feel, see and hear. Don't listen to Mrs Crotchety!! Initially you may think you're making it up. But later you will realise some of the words and terms used, you don't use yourself! And you will start to get confidence in your ability.

Coming from a Place of Respect

This is just a reminder about respect and asking permission before you begin a consultation with an animal. More on that in the next chapter.

Chapter 26:
Being Polite with the Animals You Speak With

"The worst sin towards our fellow creatures is not to hate them, but to be indifferent to them. That's the essence of inhumanity."

– George Bernard Shaw

Before we learn to speak with an animal, there are protocols which I like to instil into my students.

Asking Permission

Animals have the right to say no. Because people don't understand their language, they believe they can make decisions for them. I drill it into my students that before every communication, simply request permission. If it is not a good time for a chat, let it be. Come back later. Personally I have never had an animal say "no" to a request for communication, but it is polite to ask.

I did however have to prove myself to a horse once, before she would deign to speak with me. Her person was a powerful and popular shaman, and ordinary people were not this horse's cup of tea. I was relieved when she recognised me as worthy.

Asking permission is an indigenous protocol which has been lost by a culture which believes it is superior and has the right to do anything it wants. In my teaching, not only do students need to remember to ask permission of animals before communicating, but also before doing any healing, and definitely in regards to euthanasia. (There's more on that in *Part Six:* Death, Dying and Euthanasia.)

I don't do anything without a being's permission, and that includes picking vegetables to eat, picking grass for the budgies, digging a dam, taking water from the creek. I definitely respect wood which doesn't want to be burnt and stones who do not want to be moved. If you understand that everything is alive and has consciousness, then you can understand that asking permission is simply manners and great respect.

Mother Earth and the animals and plants, need humans to regain their respect for them now. Respect is important for proper or right relations, that subtle flow of energy which keeps us in sacred harmony.

Being Grateful, Thankful and Humble

Like asking permission, it is also respectful and polite to be grateful, thankful and humble. One cannot demand a communication with another being. Come from a space of humility. Honour the animal as an intelligent, conscious life force and you will be amazed at how much incredible information you receive. See them as "dumb animals" and you won't hear a thing.

Walk and work from that place of humility and gratitude. After you have finished a communication, thank your animal friends! After you have picked vegetables for your meal, thank them. As you chop wood, garden, wash the dog, or clean the cat litter tray, thank them for being your teachers, for allowing you to be in service. As we delve further into the Secret Animal Business of animals, you'll begin to understand how thankful we need to be.

The Practice of Service

I was up early, as usual, making up breakfasts for our special needs horses. Something made me look up. It was Maverick, Jaffah's friend, walking up the lane way across the creek to our yards. Just looking at him I knew that despite his bright eyes, all was not completely well with him. "Andrew, another one for breakfast," I called out, and went down to see how else I could be of service to this horse.

– Excerpt from Billie's journal, 2005

Many people make jokes about being "owned" by their animals. They think that the feeding, caring for, cleaning up after, opening the door for, and exercising of their animals is what service is all about.

And so it is. On one level.

In the path of the Earthkeeper, that more enlightened, human angel state of being with animals, the practice of service is a shift in perception and consciousness.

It is said that when humans rise above the chains of the personal stories that bind them, they are free to be of service. This is the place of the sage. This is the place of Walking in Beauty. With this understanding you can see how animals are already sages who walk in beauty, because their lives are one of service – to us.

So for me, if my animals are my master teachers, then it is an honour to do service for them. *For in the very act of serving them, I serve my own soul's growth.*

And it is also an honour to serve those souls who in this lifetime may not yet be sage, because in that, we both grow. And who is to say a troubled animal may not simply be a sage in disguise, and teach you your greatest lessons?

When you consider your life with animals to be of service in this way, it changes the way you view your animal relationships and the way you approach them.

Always approach an animal with that mindset of "How can I be of service today?" and you will be rewarded by an open and clear communication, and with many wonderful lessons for your life's journey.

You can feel how the shift of perception immediately makes you respectful of an animal. This is what we need for inter-species communication.

The mindset of service is also one which filters into the daily routines of our lives. It makes the mundane a spiritual path.

To serve we take care of our animal friend's needs – food, water, shelter, love, companionship and play. They are in service to us by holding a mirror to our state of being. If we listen to them, they will give us great advice and wisdom, and free us from the shackles of humanity. They will help us embody some of the wild within which has been suppressed through cultural conditioning. They will help us find freedom, joy and ultimately help us Walk in Beauty.

Our service is to listen, respect and honour. Take off the filters through which we see dog, horse, or cat. Instead, see with your spirit eyes. See magnificent soul dressed in a suit of fur or feathers, or scales. They are not just here to help us. We are to help them. Animals will often give me a message for their people during their final transition process that says, "Thank them for the love they gave me, for it healed me and helped me evolve to a new level."

Further, our society is in a mess partly because we are so isolated from each other, and when someone is depressed, they don't know what to do aside from taking medication. But if you do something spontaneously for someone else, it gives you a "feel good' hit. It takes you out of yourself. And when you do service with love, it raises your vibration.

So while some people can help the old lady next door by doing her weeding, mowing her lawn or chopping her wood, animal angels might take up dog walking at the local shelter, volunteering at an animal sanctuary, or fostering an animal in need.

The very act of taking in another living being in need can indeed transform your life. You might start taking more of an interest in what that dog, cat or horse, for example, likes to do, and that way you might become involved with other people who like to do the same things. Suddenly your life is full and rich with meaning. The service you did became a service to you as well.

(Not) Using Communication to Demand a Certain Behaviour

Sometimes I get calls from people who want their animals to behave a certain way. They want me to tell their animals what to do. This is not what the art of the silent language is all about. It's about respectfully asking the animal, just as you would a human.

If an animal is displaying a behaviour that you don't like, simply ask the animal why? Perhaps there is a reason for this behaviour that the animal is trying to get across his message to you. Perhaps he is in pain. Perhaps he is hungry. Perhaps he is trying to teach you something. Perhaps there is something about you which is causing him to act that way.

Horses are a prime example. When someone says they can't catch their horse, I'm always suspicious of their horsemanship. Why doesn't the horse want to be caught? What does he think is going to happen to him, if he does get caught? Does the saddle fit, does his mouth hurt, or does his person ride badly according to horse?

Many horses don't want to do what their person wants them to do. I had one client whose young horse wanted the freedom to play and have fun, not settle into the rigours of dressage. The client didn't like hearing that, but clearly the horse wasn't ready and wasn't suited to do what she wanted to do.

Much better and respectful is to ask, negotiate and try to work things out together.

And now we'll learn how!

Chapter 27:
The Practise of Telepathy

Communicating with animals can be so subtle that you can miss it when you try too hard. It's about stepping out of your left-brain mind chatter and getting into the stream of stillness in your right brain. There you can switch on your other senses and understand the meaning of the wind caressing your face, and speak to the spirits of the fire, the trees and plants in your garden, animals everywhere and Mother Earth herself.

Sometimes I liken my animal communication consultations as going into a light trance. At other times I experience regular two-way communication, just as I would with a human.

There are two ways to communicate with animals. The first, obviously, is in their presence, and the second is from a distance. And this includes animals anywhere – on the planet, elsewhere in the universe, and in spirit.

Telepathy is instant. Sometimes you get responses as you are formulating the question. It may comes to you in the form of words, feelings which you feel in your own body, images and intuitive knowing. Some people are strongly empathetic, and they can feel in their own body the animal's pain or emotional responses. Others are visual. They see a lot of images. Others see a flicker of an image. Others hear words.

Just like you wouldn't expect to learn French, German or Latin in a day, neither can you expect to be proficient in the silent language from a weekend workshop or from one reading of a book. You need to practise, practise, practise. One of the best ways is to get into a routine of practising at least once a day. You also need to write down your sessions in a journal. This way, when you write something that feels like it is just coming from your imagination, you can see, when you look back, that perhaps the speech rhythms or words used aren't yours. And neither were the thoughts your usual thoughts.

It helps build your confidence.

I always ask the students at my study retreats to practise with each other's animals outside class, and to be really honest in the feedback. Of course when people are just beginning, be gentle with each other. I'm always tougher with my advanced students because it is imperative they get a clear communication. But you especially want to encourage a beginner because with interspecies communication, confidence with humility is a key!

One of the questions I often get is how do I exist in a world when I can hear everyone talking at once. While it can be quite painful to be as sensitive as I am, it's not that I live in a loud universe full of whisperings. Often animals in need will catch my attention, as I have to catch theirs when I want to speak with them. Usually I have to ask for a conversation, and yes, there are many, many times when communications will just happen. To me, this is just part of life and where I put my awareness. I often have conversations with animals and trees and plants and stones, just like I do with people.

My wise pony Sebastian was a terrific example. Once when we were just learning natural horsemanship, Bastie asked what we were doing.

"Learning a language," I replied as I wiggled ropes at him and made loud gestures with my body language.

"How primitive," snorted Bastie. I had to laugh.

Another time, a natural horsemanship instructor was asking my stubborn pony to walk backwards. Bastie resisted, and I had my heart in my mouth as the instructor insisted, as he could see Bastie knew what to do and was physically able. As soon as Bastie took one step back, he stopped asking and let Bastie rest and digest.

Sebastian

"A true horseman," Bastie said loudly to me. And I could feel his respect for the young man.

Bastie of course, had no need to learn a language. But I did – even though we already communed perfectly well.

Another time, when we lived in the mountains, a lady drove into our fence when she fell asleep at the wheel. On my way back from sorting out the mess, Bastie swung around and faced me, curiosity on his snowy face.

"What happened," he asked.

I showed him pictures of the red car in a ditch.

"Are they all right?"

'Yes, I said. "Shaken, but having a cup of tea at the café."

And then he shut off, and went back to grazing, his curiosity and concern satisfied.

I live in the country and often see cattle and sheep trucks going off to the abattoir. This reduces me to spontaneous tears, as I get a wave of misery, distress, discomfort and fear from the animals on the trucks. I don't hear them all yelling at me, but I definitely feel them just as acutely.

The pounds are different. I'll hear many silent voices crying out for help, and be hit by the emotions of distress, resignation, fear both dull and sharp and pure misery. The pounds smell of death and the animals know it. I smell it too. Some animals will see you as a beacon of hope, and get very excited.

Sadly, most animals are so used to human beings not being able to hear them that they don't bother to engage with us. And when they discover one who remembers how to speak, they are delighted and relieved. Some are suspicious. Some are big talkers, and some are animals of few words – just like some people. Some have wisdom to share, and others are still exploring the confines and viewpoints of the body they have chosen to be in.

Exercises in Telepathic Communication

Telepathy is thought transference. To do it we have a brief merging of the energy field around our bodies. This is why respect is important. When we are sitting next to our dog or looking at a photo of our cat, mentally push away the mental chatter and sit in a state of peace and stillness. You can even imagine pushing the mental energy body away from you about a foot to help bring the stillness. What can you feel as you look at them? You need to relax and trust you can do it.

1. Settle yourself. Take time to breathe some deep breaths. Relax. If you are new to it, perhaps listen to the Grandfather meditation on "Time of the Drum".

2. Push away your mental chatter and turn your attention to the animal in front of you. Drop down into stillness, and really open and allow your being to receive transference of thoughts, feelings, images and "knowing". Be fully present to this exchange.

3. The silent language is light and subtle. If you try too hard, you'll miss it. So just relax and close your eyes. Think of your animal friend. Put your awareness onto him or her.

4. Get his attention by calling his name. You might "see" the animal's energy body come into the room, or sense it.

5. Ask permission to speak. *"May I speak with you?"*

6. When permission is granted, speak in your mind with your attention firmly on the picture of the animal in your mind.

   "Hello, are you well today. I'm learning how to speak your language. Can you help me?"

   "Do you have a message for me today?"

   "Is there anything I can do for your well-being and happiness today?"

7. Write it down as it comes. Don't censor, doubt or think. Just honour everything your body and mind is showing you. If you want to feel what's happening in the tummy, think of the animal's tummy and sense it in your own. The important thing here is to be clear what your own tummy feels like first. Write down those fleeting images, words, thoughts, sensations, and feelings...

The information may come at you in bits until you get better at learning what it is you are receiving. What are you hearing? What are you feeling? What are you seeing?

8. Practise placing your consciousness, awareness or attention on different parts of the animal's body. Practise listening with your whole body. Can you feel anything different? If you keep your eyes closed for a minute you might receive a picture, or a feeling. Stay open.

9. As you mentally step in to an animal's energy field and ask them how they are you might be surprised by the answer. Your animal may look okay to you, but how are they really? Maybe they feel excited. Maybe they feel anxious. Maybe you are stronger in clairvoyance and see a fleeting image. Maybe you hear words.

10. Move your consciousness to his tummy and see how it feels. So many dogs fed on commercial dog food feel heavy and toxic inside. That's how I can tell what sort of diet they're being fed. Often I'll receive an image of some unidentifiable mess in a bowl. Definitely canned food! Sometimes cats on dried food will feel dry inside. Move your consciousness to the hips, to the bladder, to the heart. Stay open. Ask if there is something you are supposed to feel or see or know about your animal companion? Be guided by them, by that small, intuitive, subtle voice of spirit in your heart.

11. In your journal, write the first things which come to mind. Don't censor and don't think. Don't let Mrs Crotchety get in the way of two-way communication with your animal companion!

12. Practise! Practise! Practise!

It takes a lot of practice! Telepathy is like a muscle and the more you use it, the better it gets.

Raffi

Raffi the Blue Heeler stands waiting at the door. His whole body radiates purposefulness. He's ready to work.

"I am needed", he says to me.

"Yes, you are indeed." I open the cottage door and he rushes over to our old blue van.

Raffi knows without me telling him that today he is going to be working with my students.

My students all oooh and aah over Raffi as he struts in the door, taking his measure of them. They miss their own animals at home and let's face it, Raffi is a small dog with a big personality. Like an actor on the stage he owns the room. He goes over to each student, lapping up their smiles, pats and cuddles.

I smile. Inside I am grateful for this opportunity to give my dog friend a sense of importance. Raffi is a dog who needs a job. He knows as well as I do, that he is already working his multi-faceted magic.

– Excerpt from Billie's journal, 2007

Raffi the Blue Heeler loves to work. He has a twinkle in his eye and knows what to do instinctively. He is very people-friendly and says he is here to help people understand the silent language and raise people's understanding of what it is to be dog. He loves an audience whether this is in front of the camera, the students or a film audience when we screen his movies.

Wise Words from Raffi

Here's an example of a Grade One class communicating with Raffi.

"We're not just dogs, we are your eyes and ears," Raffi says.

Raffi sits on the floor and opens himself up to receive the student's psychic probing. He looks like he is sleeping.

Rose:

"I get a fluttering in my heart and a tingling energy in my eyes," she says.

And she says she heard Raffi say: *"I like to work, helping, guiding and taking care of others. I like coming here, it's fun. I get to show off how special I am."*

Sarah:

"He likes to walk alongside when you are doing the chores. He likes to "see" things in order. He likes to watch the horses. He loves to help and doesn't miss a thing. Life is so exciting and "site", (not sight) is important."

"His message to me was not to grieve. And he also said the birds were a bit arrogant but fun to watch."

And in a class when, asked for words of wisdom, Raffi told Lee:

"Listen to the animals. We have much to teach you. Listen to us. We're very wise beings. You [humans], most of you, don't know this yet, and don't accept it, but it's important that you do. Humans are off track. We need you to help the world. You are very important. You're doing very important work. We [animals] have the knowledge; most humans have forgotten it, a long, long time ago. We need you to help us help them remember."

Difficulty? Another Step to Animal Communication and Other Tips

If you are having difficulty with animal communication, there's an extra step you can take. Understand that the animal you wish to communicate with has a luminous energy field just like you do. Pretend that you can "see" this, merging a little bit with yours so that you can feel the other being's body, and see it more clearly. You can also hear the animal's "voice" more clearly.

I see it as becoming one with that animal. I feel their pain in my body as we merge and can tell what's happening inside them.

Don't forget to ask permission because it could be seen as an invasion – that's why we have to invite the animals to communicate by calling them in by their name.

Finally don't forget to disengage and thank them for their cooperation.

A Word of Caution – Reading Body Language Instead of the Silent Language

Generally speaking, you and the animal are not looking at each other as we do in our conversations. Animals, especially cats and dogs, who are ready to speak may look as if they are asleep. Sometimes you have to wait until they have calmed down, and so have you.

Some people look at an animal and read their body language instead of really hearing the inner voice of the heart. There is definitely a difference. When I look at a body, I'll track for vitality, energies and colours which tell me the health of the animal. I can run my hand over their body and seek out cold and hot spots which also tell me the truth of their physical state. I step inside their body, merging their energy field with mine, to feel their pain, tightness or upset.

Body language is only part of the physical communication, and it can often be deceptive.

A dog who is ill or feeling off, for example, might still be enthusiastic for a ball game. The stomachs of every dog on tinned food, feels heavy and yuck. They might wolf down the stuff, but it doesn't feel great inside. Believe me, I've been in there!

Similarly, horses may be feeling sore but still perform for you. I can tell you that there are very few performance horses that I tune into who don't need a massage. Their bodies are tight and sore from saddles and people's bad and tight positions on their backs. They get tight from anxiety, stress, nerves and work.

At an Expo once, I mentioned to a woman whose horse stand I was perusing that her horse (whose picture was on the wall) was the first horse in a long time who didn't need a massage. His body felt good. "That's because I gave him a massage just before I came," she said smiling.

Animals in their last years can look like they're sleeping a lot and not enjoying a quality of life. But a deeper inspection can find them out of their body, having fun with their astral travels and explorations of other dimensions.

Once, when I gave a class in a woman's home, there was a lot of talk among the students and the hostess about her mature dog, Sami, who "talked" a lot. They all thought he was very engaging and sweet.

In the middle of the class, Sami walked in, looked at me, started "talking" and lay down in front of me. His "talking" was groans of pain. I immediately ran my hands over his energy field to ascertain where the pain was and felt it in his hips. His person saw me doing that and realised, in horror, what she had missed. Fortunately for Sami, we were able to communicate with him, to find the source of his emotional pain, and give him natural pain relief for his joints and hips.

Tips for Calming Both You and the Animals for Good Communication Results

The best way you can prepare to listen to an animal in person is to get into a relaxed state. When I visit animals in people's homes, I'll bring myself into a place of stillness and relaxation before communicating.

- Shake off whatever traffic you had or the emotional state you are in. Go to your point of stillness, and anchor it in. Note that when you are calm and still inside, so too will the animal be. I call it "dropping down."

- Come into rapport with the animal by synching your breathing. First match their breathing, and then slow down yours, so they match yours and become calm.

- Sometimes it's appropriate to do some Reiki. But it depends on the health condition of the animal. Some energy work can actually cause more problems, worsening instead of healing the condition. Cancer for example is something you need to be very careful of.

Things Which Interfere with Clear Communication

To be the best, I ask that my students be the clearest, cleanest channel they can be. Personally I have been a vegetarian for over 30 years and don't drink, smoke, or take drugs of any kind. I've heard that many medications interfere with your ability to hear the silent language, but I can't verify it because I don't take them. You need to also get enough sleep, be well hydrated, and have confidence in your ability stemming from lots of validation and a thorough understanding of animals. Their spiritual selves especially.

One of the biggest challenges is emotional stress. This usually happens when you are on the spot or it is one of your own animal family members in crisis. It's hard to be objective, and you begin to doubt your own ability.

The good news is that through the web you can have access to animal communicators in an instant. Also, you can learn to deal with the emotional stress which stands in the way of you and your friend communicating clearly.

I was amazed I was able to communicate so clearly when my beloved horse Sollie was dying, as I was an emotional wreck. Similarly, when our horse Sebastian was 44, he gave me one last lesson in trusting myself.

Bastie was in terrible pain and the vet concluded that his stomach had stopped working and he needed euthanasia. I wanted to be clear that this is what Bastie wanted and that it was his time for sure. So I asked for more time from the vet and Bastie was given a painkiller which made him feel really good. *"If this is heaven, I'm in it,"* he reported.

I was in shock that my beloved Bastie was leaving me so suddenly after such a long time. I sent the vet in for a cup of tea, and decided I'd better check in with my animal communicator friends to see what Bastie said to them. No deal. No one answered the phone. I knew immediately that this was Spirit's way of making sure I did this on my own. I took a deep and shaky breath and used all the skill I had to calm myself, throwing on a mantel of determination. I picked up my journal and went outside to sit with Andrew and Sebastian.

With my mind resolved and quiet, I realised that Sebastian's friends in spirit were hanging around him. Sollie was there, Bastie's girl friend Saraid, and Andrew's horse Monty. This was a sure sign it was Bastie's time.

"*We had some good times,*" he said. "*Had to push you!*"

He talked some more and then finally told me to "*get on with it.*" Just at that moment, the vet walked out of the kitchen. I took the "co-incidence" as a sign. It *was* time. After that, I realised I could always rely on myself and thanked Sebastian for his last and very important lesson.

So the lesson here is throw on a mantel of determination. And know you can always master your emotions in times of need.

The Importance of Writing Down Everything You Experience

I was in the middle of a consultation when a silent male voice entered the discussion. I felt the presence of my horse Sollie around me, until I heard the voice say: "I am not your friend." I stopped writing, and wondered who the intruder was. Truth be known, I was a tiny bit shaken. Who was interrupting me to tell me they weren't my friend?

I still felt Sollie's presence, so I blanked my mind to all other thoughts and put pen to paper. "I am not your friend," he repeated. "I am your soul-mate."

Sollie left, as tears rolled down my cheeks. I was so glad I had continued to listen, because this indeed was vital information for my soul.

– Excerpt from Billie's journal

When you are communicating, it is important to open yourself up wide and receive every bit of information coming at you. It might take time to develop the skill and you might begin by hearing only a word or two, or perhaps a feeling, or perhaps a fleeting image. But you will, in time, experience thought transference in its fullness.

It's vital that you record everything you are experiencing and if you are helping a friend or a client, then its exceptionally important you deliver everything you receive because the animal is sending them the information through you. And you may not recognise things that they will.

I almost forgot this important piece of teaching myself when I was teaching a class. A student had handed me a photograph of her late horse to read. The thoughts and images were flying as I repeated them to her.

"He says celebrate his passing," I said. She stared at me dull-eyed and even as my mind was registering that, I was already telling her the word which came before "celebrate."

"Salute."

At the word "salute", my student burst into tears and told me how the other animals had come to salute her horse when she took him for his final journey in the horse trailer.

I nearly made the mistake of leaving out a word with a vital meaning for her, in my desire to get his fuller message, which was to celebrate his passing. Without the word "salute", his message meant nothing. With it, she was able to hear and feel his desire for her to move on.

Other Things You Can Do to Improve Communication

Get Validation

Even though I'd been communicating all my life with animals and nature, it was just something I did. I never doubted what I received, and would get wonderful validation from animals like Suki, for example, when we were selling our house. I would sometimes leave her at home when the agents came over with potential buyers so she could let me know how things were going.

One day Andrew, and I were driving home and I sent a thought out to her asking if all was well. *"People at the gate,"* she said. She then sent me a picture of a man and added: *"The house is charming."*

As we drove up to our home, there were indeed people at the gate, and I had a message from the real estate agent telling me his prospective buyers thought the house was charming. The exact words which Suki used.

Tools

When I first started communicating with other people's animals, I was nervous and really wanted to get it right. So I would use a quartz crystal in my left hand to amplify what I was hearing. This particular crystal was gifted to me by a Native American elder so I felt it was purposefully suited to the task. And so did the crystal.

Another tool you can use is a pendulum to help if you are stuck.

Reiki II, Theta healing and shamanic studies can all help you enhance your connection to the voice of the silent language.

To Enhance Communication
1. Use a quartz crystal.
2. Use a pendulum for yes/no answers.
3. Learn the healing skills Reiki II, Shamanic Healing, Theta Healing.
4. Develop your intuition and other psychic skills, like clairvoyance or clairaudience.
5. Practise intuitive readings with tarot cards, runes or other oracles.

Chapter 28:
Distance Communication with Photographs

Adrienne dropped the photo of the cat she was holding. "It's hot," she looked at me, shaken. I picked it up, closed my eyes and ran my hand over the picture. I could feel the heat. It was anger. When I looked with my spirit eyes, I could see the dark energy running over the photo. The cats were in danger of losing their home because of their person's need to blame them, instead of looking inside herself. They asked me to help them, to work on the woman and help her see that bad things were happening to her because of the energy she created, not because of them. "She is trying to separate us, and without us, the energy cannot be held."

The cats were friends. They didn't want to be separated. They definitely didn't want to be given away to strangers. And despite it all, they loved their human friend.

I turned to Sue and spoke as gently as I could, explaining what the cats had talked about. It took some time, and the help of the other students – and finally Sue shifted. Tears rolled down her face as she realised what she had put the cats through. Her heart chakra opened with love.

I looked at the picture of the cats which I still held in my hand. It was cool now and the dark shadows had lifted. The cats looked happy. And they were. I gave the photo back to Adrienne. "Feel it now," I encouraged her to take it.

Adrienne took it apprehensively but when she did she threw me a look of pure astonishment. " It's changed! It's cool now."

Then Sally called me over to look at the picture of her dog. As I looked, a river of black energy went from Sally to her dog. "No," I said sharply, out loud to the dog. You don't have to do that."

Although Sally didn't see the energy, she was a student and

understood exactly what was going on. "He's not going to take on my stuff," she said through tears. "Tell him I promise I'll work on myself."

And I smiled knowing that here was another who couldn't move forward for herself, but she could for her dog. I thanked him silently.

– Excerpt from Billie's journal

The nature of telepathy is beyond time and space. You can communicate with anyone anywhere on this planet, another galaxy, or beyond the veil of death. It's all the same.

When I do distant readings, usually all I need is the animal's name. This is all I need to call them to me and to get their attention. Really, just because they are in my thoughts is enough, and I'll usually find them ready and waiting as soon as I turn my attention to them.

These days I do all my work over the Internet. The photographs of the animals are all online. It's just the same. You aren't really reading the picture, although you can. If the picture is a recent one, I'll scan it for health and emotional issues, but again, by calling the energy body to me, I have all that information anyway.

Photographs, however, make the animal client come alive for me. I like to see their beauty and "meet" them this way. Most of the time that has nothing to do with telepathy or healing but sometimes I use the photograph to anchor my attention. Having a photograph is a useful tool for students developing their confidence.

So, take a photograph and focus your intention on the animal, silently calling their name.

Open yourself to receive the information they send you, by putting aside your left-brain and your mental chattering. If you have a problem, visualise putting your mental self in a box!

Ask permission to converse.

Ask a question and write in your journal everything you hear, feel and see.

I get my students to practise this method with their friends' animals so they can get validation from their friends or fellow students.

Chapter 29:
Communicating with "Pests" and Wild Animals

Let's think about the word "pest'. As I've said before, our society tends to kill everything we consider to be in our way. And we don't think about the bigger perspective of the web of life and the way we are all connected, or the possible karmic repercussions of the way we interact with the rest of the world. So here is an opportunity to work more holistically.

Think about it this way. Just the way a "weed" is a plant in the "wrong" place, a "pest" is an animal in the "wrong" place. But you have to keep your different perspectives in mind. The "pest" probably thinks you are the pest for exactly the same reason.

When students and clients ask me about dealing with pests, I ask them why they think the being is a pest. If the being irritates you, or you fear them, what is that saying about you? What is the message for you? Do you need to raise your vibration? Do you need to create a cleaner environment? Or is the pest alerting you to something else you need to be aware of.

It was the late Australian animal healer Jackie Fitzgerald, who changed my thinking about fleas, for example, when she mentioned they would go to the weakest part of the body and stimulate it like acupuncture needles.

I realised that the "pests" like fleas, lice and bot flies, were telling me volumes about the immune system of the animals in my care. If I boosted the immune system, I was less likely to get pests and parasites causing a problem. After all, like cancer cells, we live with these beings all the time and it's only when we're out of balance, that they become a threat to our health. This is why the healer strives for homoeostasis, or balance. So instead of taking a predatory approach, I took a more co-operative approach, and also used the Law of Attraction, the power of gratitude, and the practice of right relations or sacred harmony.

"Thank you, thank you, thank you for pointing out this problem with my horse, dog or cat. Thank you for leaving them alone, now that you have done your work. My animals now, have healthy immune systems, and are filled with vitality and energy."

I visualise the animals as healthy and well, as well as supplementing them with the products which best served their needs – like garlic.

And I do my own personal work to make sure I am in right relations with the world. Because we are all connected.

Anne Wigmore, the woman who discovered the health benefits of wheat grass, always used to say that healthy dogs and cats didn't attract fleas and she attributed this to a healthy, raw food diet.

Once, during a drought, our property was being ravaged by wild pigs. It was very distressing. The farmers around us were shooting them. And we were under pressure to do the same. But to a couple who rescue ants from a burning log, shooting pigs just wasn't an option we were willing to take. So we tried something different. I called in the leader of the pigs and asked permission to communicate.

Permission was granted, and I explained that I was concerned about the land being dug up, and my need to feed my horses.

"This is our home too and we are hungry."

I was immediately struck with compassion. Of course they were hungry. It was drought. They had families. I didn't "own" the land we all lived on. They had as much right as I did to find food and shelter.

"Okay," I said, *"I understand. But please be careful of other humans. Best you stay within our boundaries."* I sent him a mental map, knowing that it was his choice whether or not he decided to agree, and his risk if he didn't.

The Pig Leader set Andrew and I thinking. Was the land really being torn up? We ended up buying grass seed and on our walks with the dogs, we'd throw seeds in the disturbed land. We were buying hay for the horses anyway. What little food there was in the paddocks, I was happy for the wildlife to have. Eventually better times came, and we saw no more evidence of ripped up land or the pigs, our land hadn't suffered from housing the pigs, and we felt good about being able to solve a problem without resorting to the predatory patriarchal ways of violence and death.

Secret Animal Business

There are countless stories of people who have been able to communicate with animals and insects and asked them to change their behaviour or habits, when they came from that space of humility and respect.

J. Allen Boone in *Kinship with All Life* talks about how ants were eating him out of house and home, and how he nearly came to dealing with them by poison. Instead he chose to talk to them. At first he reprimanded them. Nothing happened. And then he remembered how every living being loves to be acknowledged and appreciated. So he began heaping on the praise for everything he sincerely felt were the ant's positive attributes.

At first it appeared not to be working, but later, after he returned home that night from the theatre, all the ants had disappeared and at the time of writing he hadn't had a visitation, save a scout ant, anywhere in his home or when he was away.

To me this is a wonderful example of a man in right relations with the world. In the same book, Boone also talks about his relationship with a fly named Freddy who was a wonderful philosopher and teacher.

In *Talking with Nature*, Michael J. Roads tells of his experience with wallabies. Michael was successful on his first attempt at making an agreement with the wallabies who were eating his pasture. He, at first, held the thoughts in his mind and sent them to the animals silently, and then he spoke out loud to the empty paddock.

He made an agreement with the wallabies that in return for not eating his pasture, he would ensure nobody shot them again. He also said he recognised his need to share the land with them and asked them to graze the outside of the paddock for no more than 20 yards.

To his surprise, the wallabies kept their side of the bargain, although on average it seemed they grazed about 40 yards into the paddock. However the pasture grew lush and he was able to graze 90 cows and calves.

Wouldn't it be great if everyone recognised an animal's "divine right to life" and understood the potential of cooperating with nature, instead of simply being a predator.

If the Australian Government had the same attitude, we could stop the shocking and violent culling of kangaroos and brumbies. Michael wrote his book in 1985. Perhaps it's time all farmers took a page from it.

Speaking of kangaroos and wallabies, we have left 100 acres of native land for them on our property. This is also where we run the dogs in the morning and when Sage was a young dog, she took off after an enormous old man kangaroo. Now kangaroos can kill a dog, and will do so by drowning them. So my heart was in my mouth, but luckily the kangaroo felt my distress. We were standing in a paddock, feeling tense and worried, when suddenly the roo jumped back into the paddock with us, Sage at his heels.

"Take the dog, will you," he said to me, standing there, quite still, towering over us all. I called her to safety and bowed to him. "Thank you for returning her safely, I said. "I'm sure we've learnt many lessons today."

The kangaroo merely looked at me and hopped away.

Recently we were cleaning out the old kitchen in our place, which was where we stored our herbs and other tools of healing. Andrew opened a drawer which hadn't been used for years to find it occupied by baby rats. Their little furry faces looked at me, and I felt a wave of love and compassion. As the dogs came rushing in to investigate, I quickly closed the drawer and ushered the dogs outside the room.

"You guys are going to have to find a place to live outside," I sent, *"because we're moving this entire cabinet to the tip. "*

As Andrew and I focused on other work, I fretted how I was going to get the rats out of the drawer and into a home outside without them leaping out of the drawer as soon as I moved it.

And then Tamsin heard about them and pulled open the drawer to check them out. "Mum, there's nothing here," she said. And sure enough, the rats had all vacated outside as I had asked.

There are many, many stories about this kind of heart communication with all kinds of animals from rats to a flock of King parrots who were destroying a woman's home. With love, appreciation, humility and an open heart chakra we can come into harmony with every living being.

Animals and insects all share the same spark of divinity that we have. Raise your vibration and come into right relations with the world and you will find yourself living in sacred harmony with all life.

If you come across a spider in the house and this bothers you, ask the spider if you can help him outside. Always tell the insects what you are going to do, ask permission, make agreements – and keep them. Always look for ways to be in polite and right relations with the world.

Communicating with Wild Animals

Telepathy works with every living being, domesticated or wild. If you are out in nature, you can send thoughts to the animals there. If you want to speak to a particular group of animals, ask for their leader or just make a general announcement.

If an animal crosses your path, then they are trying to get your attention. So engage by putting your attention onto that animal, pushing your left, chattering brain away, and dropping into silence. Ask them the question, "Do you have a message for me?"

If you just want to randomly communicate with a wild animal, cast out the net of your awareness and ask permission of the particular species you want to communicate with. Or you could ask for the leader of the pack or herd. Someone will answer.

Always be respectful, always ask permission and always thank them for their time and wisdom.

Part 4:
The Secret to Harmonious Animal Relations and Secrets the Animals Want You to Know

My Vision

Now that you have an understanding that it is possible to communicate with animals and that they have a point of view and a secret, psychic life that goes way beyond what we once considered animals to be, I'd like to share with you my vision for a future world and invite you to join me in making it happen.

We are in a very exciting time in human history, a time when love and compassion are coming to the fore, as they have never done before.

I'm not religious, but I am deeply spiritual and may I suggest here that the future could be everything Jesus was attempting to teach 2,000 years ago – a life of peace, love, unity and miracles.

May I suggest that life could be as it once was on Earth, when indigenous people lived in harmony with Mother Earth and all the animals.

What if there was a world without predators?

What if there was a world without suffering?

The animals have been telling me for some time they have had enough of being misunderstood by their human carers, that they can't stand the food they are being forced to eat, that they are over the misery of the pound system and the suffering and even the supposed suffering of humanity – because they have to deal with that too.

In short, they want humanity to evolve to a new and better species, so they can be free from their suffering.

Imagine that.

There is a prophecy around the end date of the Mayan Calender for December 21, 2012. Already there is a lot of fear around that time. But as a shaman, I have travelled the timelines and seen a beautiful, possible future. It is a future where people act like angels, with dignity, reverence for all life, love and compassion and where miracles are everyday occurrences.

To get this beautiful, possible future, there are some things we need to change. The following sections in this book outline a deeper understanding of the animals, better ways of dealing with them and steps to become the human angels they need us to be.

Please join me in creating a better world for people, animals and Mother Earth.

Chapter 30:
Animal Care as a Spiritual Art Form

Animals are so loved in our society and yet there is so much dis-ease, death, suffering and animal abuse. So what gives? Why are there so many animals surrendered to pounds? Why do some people have such trouble with the animal-human relationship? Why aren't animals honoured and revered? After all, they are in some cultures, so why not ours?

I would say it's because we humans are dis-connected from the natural world, and that world includes animals. The way most of us live, with constant stress, depression, despair and time-challenges, isn't conducive to taking the time it takes to invite another being into our lives and allowing them to teach us.

On the other hand, there are so many benefits when we do.

I call animals "shamanic teachers" because they teach us by allowing us to come into understanding and realisations through our own experience. They don't lecture to us and they don't give it to us straight. Rather, they put us into situations where we will either pass or fail. Sadly, because this concept is so little understood, many humans fail, and their animal teachers sadly fail as well.

To understand the shamanic nature of animal companions, you have to understand their secret animal business. They are here to receive love for themselves and to haul us up the ladder of enlightenment with their teachings. So if we view animals as more than fluffy beings to pet and pamper, we realise we have an awesome opportunity for personal and spiritual growth sitting in our living rooms and paddocks.

I ask my students to see all the challenges in their life as spiritual tests. So instead of complaining about their lot, I encourage them to figure out how they created it with their thoughts (that's basic Law of Attraction) and how they can change it to be better.

Sometimes those thoughts are subconscious, so it takes a bit of work to unravel the threads that keep you bound. But if you consider everything in your life as a projection of your thoughts – a great big, old mirror reflecting back at you the lessons you have to get, it kind of makes sense.

And it gives you the power to change things.

So, if you are going to have an animal in your life, then perhaps you could consider looking at their welfare as an art form, or initiations, or tests into higher consciousness. This is why I call my students human angels and spiritual or enlightened warriors. I ask them to think very differently about the animals in their care. Animals are teachers and healers who will engage you in the dance of life and ask you to be the best you can be.

All over the world we see people and animals co-existing. Sadly the animals are the ones who are carrying the burden from people's inability to see the truth of the relationship. So let's change that now and open your eyes to the truth of secret animal business.

I see a world where animals and people co-exist together in mutual harmony and sacred partnership for the greater good of both. All species need love, and that lies at the bottom or the core of everything. How you deal with the challenges or tests set by the animals for you determines your path into spiritual evolvement.

Chapter 31:
Understanding Animal Behaviour

In the many, many years I've had with animals, I've learnt some important things. One is to always give respect and to understand that when an animal presents with a challenge, to never give up until you've found a solution. Further, being calm and confident is a key to having them respect you, and talking with them is the greatest key of all.

Dealing with Frustrations

The first thing I want to discuss is that even though an animal may be exhibiting a behaviour you don't like, like going to the toilet inside, incessant barking, jumping up, growling, pigrooting, bolting and so on, one thing we humans have to remember is that our furry friends only have so many ways to communicate with us, especially before we understand their silent whispers.

So instead of swearing, yelling and losing patience, take a step back. It's okay to feel frustrated, but the way you deal with it makes the world of difference and it is one of the big lessons our animal friends want us to get. Do you deal with your companions in a loving and constructive way, or in a way you'd rather the neighbours didn't see? Or hear?

These beloveds are trying to communicate something. And if you look closely at the situation from the point of view of needing to learn something, you might find a wonderful lesson for you. Or a hard one.

I hope some of the work here will help you understand your animal companion better and help you learn to think outside the square for constructive ways of dealing with your animal's behaviour, and passing the spiritual tests that have been set for your soul's journey.

Soul Journey

Probably the most important thing to remember is that an animal, like us, is a light-filled soul in a body. And just like us, animals have a soul journey. They are a soul who has chosen a furry or other body to adopt certain attributes of that particular species' viewpoint or behaviour. They are here to learn lessons, to be of service, to explore a different viewpoint – there are all kinds of wonderful and mysterious reasons. They are also here to give and experience love. And ultimately, this is the most important reason of all.

It breaks my heart sometimes when I think of the service these wonderful beings offer humanity that goes so unrecognised. When I look at humans from the animal's viewpoint, I see how slow we've been and how sad that is. On the other hand, more and more people are awakening to compassion and love, and are willing and ready to care for their animal companions in a high way. This, I'm sure, is a profound relief to the animal kingdom.

I've already talked about the way animals are shamanic teachers, helping us learn and grow through our actions and deeds, and through using our intelligence to ferret out new ways of dealing with the challenges they present. They are doing Spirit's work when they come to us.

And despite this enormous gift to humanity, too many animals who behave "badly" wind up in pounds, abattoirs and in new homes. Too many are surrendered to pounds and killed within two days, subjected to the misery of smelling death in the air and the horrors of behavioural assessment testing. And for what?

Often this bad behaviour isn't bad at all. It's simply a misunderstanding. It's often boredom. Sometimes it's deeply emotional. And always it is a challenge for us not to ignore, but to grow from.

Ann adopted Huey, a Rottweiler cross, because his person had Chronic Fatigue Syndrome and couldn't take care of him properly. And Huey had killed a chicken.

At Ann's house, Huey went into kill mode and all of Ann's assorted animal friends, from a baby goat to her chickens, were in danger. Ann decided she didn't want to be one of those people who didn't understand. She wasn't going to fob him off to the pound, no matter how much easier this might have been. She wasn't going to absolve her responsibility to this new member of her family.

Fortunately, the local dog "trainer" was an educator – of people as well as animals. She explained to Ann that Huey had been kicked out of his pack and emotionally this was affecting his behaviour. She advised Ann to be friendly with Huey's former person so it was a less rude transition for him. Now he wasn't kicked out of the pack, he was being cared for by a friend. Ann took the time to understand the psychology behind Huey's behaviour – and six weeks later he was a calm and increasingly mature, "well behaved" dog. And the chickens were safe!!

Ann, too, had been on a journey and learnt from it. It gave her a deep satisfaction that she hadn't given up on her dog, and that was something vitally important for both their souls.

Sometimes though, an animal behaviourist or educator will miss something vitally important in understanding an animal's behaviour, especially if they don't understand soul journey. This is where animal communication can really help by going to the source of the problem and eliminating any judgements or guesswork.

I once had a dog trainer tell me that my rescue dog Tala would "never become right". As a young dog, Tala had nipped her on the back of the calf. The woman didn't ask why – just assumed it was a terrible behaviour and tried to put into my consciousness and Tala's that it would never go away. In effect, she projected her shadow onto my dog. Fortunately I was able to intervene and I didn't take the advice of "authority" on board.

In Tala's fourteen years with me, she only nipped one other person, and her thinking behind it was interesting.

Our dog Kai had been abused as a pup and was wary of people. Many people don't really understand dog psychology and would look him in the eye and try and pat him, despite us saying not to. We'd try to explain that they were challenging him and threatening him with this behaviour.

"Oh but I'm good with dogs," they'd say, trying to force the issue. Kai felt he would have to nip them to stop them "attacking" him. It was never nasty. Just a warning nip or growl.

One day, Robert showed up at our place and was determined to prove that he could pat Kai. I had Kai by the collar and was telling Robert not to try. I could feel Kai's growing tension. It made me tense too. But Robert wouldn't stop. Suddenly, Tala appeared and grabbed Robert by the arm. Robert let go of hassling Kai, immediately wounded that Tala had nipped him. "*Why did you do that?*" I asked Tala. "*Well you weren't doing anything,*" she said.

And she was right. My attempts to protect Kai were polite and useless. Tala had simply been direct and effective. Later she went up to Robert, looked at him to get his attention and said: "*I'm sorry, I didn't mean to scare you.*"

The thing I found fascinating about Kai, who was sweet, sensitive and frightened, was how men reacted when he barked, growled or nipped at them. They immediately became aggressive and wanted to punch him. Women would be soft and understanding, turning their back on him and tickling him under the chin – which he loved. But men would take it personally. And want revenge. I found it a disturbing reflection of our society.

Kai did end up healing his trauma and his fear of people when we took him to a TTEAM workshop with Robin Hood. But with his healing, his purpose for being here was completed. He contracted an osteo-sarcoma and died the following year.

There's also the story of Skidboot, a "naughty" dog who was about to get the boot, when his male person decided to teach him a few tricks. He showed Skidboot how to do things and was amazed at how quickly the dog picked it up. Skidboot wasn't naughty, he was highly intelligent and simply needed something to do. He'd been bored. He ended up travelling the USA with his person, entertaining and showing others, the intelligence and the beauty of dog. You can see Skidboot videos posted on our Ballyoncree blog (see www.ballyoncree.com) and on YouTube.

Understanding the Deeper Meaning of Animal Behaviour

The dog who counter surfs, won't sit on command, hogs your favourite sofa and reduces your pillow to shredded mozzarella may be trying to get your attention. Perhaps he has a message for you. Perhaps he's trying to teach you a lesson in laughter or letting go. Or perhaps you are sending him mixed messages and he's trying to teach you to get it right.

The cat who sprays all over the house may be upset by a new addition to the family or the block. She might be seeing ghosts, and trying to protect you. Or she might have cystitis, urinary stones or kidney problems.

The horse who threw you in front of the hunky guy in jodhpurs, doesn't deserve to be scolded. Perhaps her back hurts or the saddle doesn't fit right. Perhaps you're sitting the wrong way or hurting her mouth. Her teeth might be sharp. Or perhaps the hunky guy in jodhpurs isn't for you.

One of my special needs dogs told me that she had special needs because it was would teach me about healing.

Two of my horses told me they played up because I needed to be more assertive. And I needed to learn from natural horse masters like Pat Parelli and Robin Hood. If things had kept going swimmingly, I would never have discovered that pathway, and then wouldn't have been able to help my clients or my wild brumbies, for example.

Everything happens for a reason and we may not be able to see the big picture at the time. But we have to trust and follow the soul's calling.

Jaffah, one of our rescue horses, knew more about her physical condition than I did. She knew she had to be close by us, so she injured herself every time we tried to put her into the herd. Instead, she became a "special needs" horse, living around the house paddock. Jaffah ended up having repeating colic, which, because we were on the spot, we were able to treat naturally and quickly.

One serious bout of colic came just as we were leaving for a break. Jaffah told me she didn't like the young woman we'd hired for the job of looking after them. We got a young man instead, and Jaffah was fine. Mind you, we postponed our break to take care of her, and even that worked out even better.

Taliesin the wild brumby, cut his leg to the bone so I would give him the attention he needed, and recognise him for the soul family he was. We told him he didn't have to go to such drastic measures to get our attention. But it worked, we bonded deeply and I have always been surprised and pleased at the trust this horse has given me.

Instead of forcing an animal to do something, honour what they are trying to tell you. It really doesn't suit our paddock management to have Taliesin and his two girls around the house paddocks all the time. But when we tried to move them across the creek, Taliesin got tangled in the fence – twice. We got the message, and around the house paddocks he stays. Our job is to discover the deeper message behind the behaviour, honour his current needs, and find creative ways of finding a win-win solution.

Peeing In The House

Chris's cat Maisie was peeing in the house. Chris was convinced Maisie no longer loved her. But when I contacted Maisie, she was terribly embarrassed and in pain. *'I can't help myself,"* she said. *"I am so ashamed."* I recognised the burning symptoms I felt from her immediately – Maisie had cystitis.

I was sad to hear an Australian animal communicator call a cat spiteful because he peed in the house. In all my life I have never met a spiteful animal, and my feeling was that this was the communicator's projection.

In my experience, cats are extremely clean animals and pee in the house for many reasons – one of them being discomfort and problems with their bladder and kidneys. I'll never forget an animal worker coming to my home and show me her brand new, animal education program. I was enjoying the positivity of it until she suddenly threw a wad of paper at my mature cat Rhodri. Shocked, I asked her why she did that.

"He was peeing inappropriately", she said in way of explanation. "This is the way we stop that."

Rhodri is a very sensitive cat and he didn't appreciate anything being thrown at him. I stooped down to pick him up, soothing him in my mind.

"He's got urinary problems," I explained, cuddling Rhodri. "He's showing me he's not 100 percent yet. As soon as he's better, he'll go back to his normal behaviour."

Rhodri had a history of all kinds of kidney and urinary problems but whenever he was healthy, he would pee in his box or better still, outside. When he had a problem, I'd always know because he would start peeing in the house. Instead of yelling at him, we would thank him for letting us know how he was doing, and take action to heal him.

Rhodri

Cats also pee to mark their territory – you might have rat or mice visitors, other cats or even spirits. I've had many clients who have complained about their cat's spraying in the house, only to find that some spirit had to be asked to leave. When the house was clear, the spraying stopped.

One woman in a class was complaining about all the things that were wrong in her life. "And to top it off," she said, "the two cats started peeing everywhere, so I had to get rid of them." One thing that must be clear in every person's mind is that whatever is happening in our outer world is a reflection of our inner one. The two cats were reflecting this woman's inner turmoil. Not only did they suffer in the home, but they also lost their home because their actions weren't understood. Their person didn't take one hundred percent responsibility, and she wasn't in right relations.

Aggression

Casey the poodle had suddenly become very aggressive to visitors, and in fact, to anyone who came down the drive. Her people contacted me to see if I could help.

I sat down at my desk and called Casey's etheric body to me.

"What has happened, beloved? Did something frighten you?"

"It's my duty, but I am afraid," she said. *"I am the guard dog."*

The picture she sent me was of a male Great Dane. He was a guard dog and was shot and killed in the line of duty. It was a life time or so ago.

Casey had been badly frightened by a car back firing outside her house, and it had triggered the past life memory. She told me she was afraid because of her new small body. She didn't feel up to the task of guard dog – and besides, in her worldview, guard dogs get killed.

Through counselling Casey, I was able to help her realise she wasn't a guard dog in this life. I asked her to simply "sound the alarm" when visitors came and leave the rest to the people of the house.

There are many reasons behind aggression. All animals read fear in humans and it makes them frightened too. There is nothing better than a human who is calm and confident to make an animal feel safe.

Often the aggression can be triggered by emotional reasons, by surgery, by vaccinations, by chemicals in the diet, by a past life memory, by an entity attachment. Often it is a learned behaviour because of the way they are treated.

Animals need to be treated kindly and with confidence and compassion. The best kind of dog education focuses on positive reinforcement of good behaviour. Let the dog know what you want by praising him when he does well. Fear begets fear, and aggression begets aggression.

The same goes for horses. I've known many horses belonging to women who become "dangerous". They're not really dangerous, they're misunderstood. The women haven't given them the leadership that's been needed. The women have been soft and gentle, but not strong. And this is what a horse looks for. They need a different kind of human relationship with a different kind of human – one who is calm, strong, confident – and soft and gentle. All of this. Most of the time these horses are very intelligent and sensitive. They're desperate for a human who will help them feel safe. They don't want someone aggressive, but they don't want a doormat either.

We're lucky at home to have herds of horses in our care and I've watched the way the herd leaders carry themselves – like royalty. Andrew's horse Dakota is a herd leader and he hasn't a mean bone in his body. But he is strong, gentle, decisive and intelligent. When he became "uncle" to two newly weaned wild colts, he took his job seriously and they told me he made them feel safe and secure.

This is where horses become such excellent teachers for humans. I've had the privilege of watching some of the best natural horse people work with horses – and all of them were grounded, easy, firm, gentle, and strong inside – and best of all they really understood horse. None of them were aggressive and they had all mastered their emotions.

Horses are prey animals and humans are predators. Horses read our emotions from miles away and teach us to master them. If you are upset, frustrated, or cranky, walk away from your horse friend. They demand from us love, inner strength, courtesy and respect.

Andrew and I had an interesting experience with one of the horses in Sanctuary here at home. Rupert was a racehorse destined for dog meat who had been scooped up by a series of incidents and landed with a lovely young woman for dressage. Rupert hated the city, hated everything about agistment, the tiny yards and the way he was treated by others, and got a reputation for going "ballistic". When his person became ill, the advice she got was to kill her seven-year-old horse because no one would want him and he was no use to anyone.

He ended up here and we saw no sign of "ballistic" behaviour save the moment he got off the horse float. Once he realised he was in the country and there was Andrew's horse Dakota waiting to welcome him, Rupert calmed right down.

In big paddocks, roaming in a herd of eight to ten horses, Rupert was very, very happy. Then he presented with mild colic and I brought him in, forgetting his background, and put him in the yard by the house we use for observing and treating any horse with colic. There were horses all around and plenty of hay and water – but in the morning, Rupert didn't have colic, he looked demented.

Immediately I realised that the small yard had triggered memories of the city and obvious terror. I also realised, as the previous women in his life had been ineffective and downright aggressive, this horse needed a calm man to handle him for quickest results. I took him over to Andrew. Rupert was clearly somewhere else in his mind, but I watched as he calmed down as Andrew instinctively took control of the situation.

Andrew was calm, efficient, and best of all, he talked to Rupert and told him exactly what was going on in detailed chunks – including the big picture that he was going back to his own herd. "I'm going to take off your coat now," he told the horse. "And you're going to look this way and watch as I unbuckle the strap." Rupert did. "Now the other one." Rupert did. The big thoroughbred listened to every word Andrew said, and was like a lamb in his care. He walked back to the herd as good as gold.

Please note that at no time was this horse hit to "make him stand up", as I've seen many people do. He was able to calm and get himself together because his leader, Andrew, was calm. And because his leader respected him enough to explain exactly what was going on.

Later I suspected he had put himself in this situation to remind us of the importance of these two basic principles of horse care. I sent him a big hug of gratitude.

Matching breathing is another technique you can use in situations like this. You can aid a frightened animal by getting into rapport with them with the breath, and letting this breath get slower and slower. Instilling confidence in an animal is the goal, through being confident and trustworthy yourself.

Another aggressive horse story came from Pat Parelli. He was asked to find the most troubled horse he could find, and see what could be done. Mossy was duly found, a race horse who was kept off the race course because "nothing could be done for him." His people insisted they were "real horse people", but when it came time for Mossy and Pat's demonstration, they were seen with a syringe full of horse tranquilliser – their way of dealing with Mossy. It was the only way to handle him, they insisted.

Instead of drugs, Pat simply used his energy, unflappable calm, and consummate horse skills to have the horse following him around in less than 20 minutes. "He's just super sensitive," Pat explained. Sadly, his people refused to learn the lesson and Mossy was left to his fate, despite offers to buy him.

I've found being with animals teaches humans how to be the best humans – if we listen to and understand the animals we're learning from.

Dog Attacks

In life there are no accidents or co-incidences. How then, do some dogs and cats get attacked by others, while others never do?

There are no victims, there are only volunteers. If we can fly to the perspective of Great Spirit, we can see that perhaps an attack is simply a call for help for release. Sadly in our society, we kill the dogs who respond to that call.

One example of this was Ralph, a big dog who attacked a small dog. The situation from the outside was very frightening. Here was a big dog attacking a tiny dog, the people freaking out, and the tiny dog having to go to the vet surgery for emergency care. The dog lived and Ralph was put in the category of dangerous dog and his life hung in the balance.

But let's look at the situation more closely. The small dog had just lost his beloved person, the husband of the woman who was walking him that day. From a dog's perspective, waves of grief were coming from the pair of them. Who knows what the woman was thinking, but clearly the small dog was her husband's friend and not as bonded to her. Did his dog want to go on living? Did they both need a wake up call? Did the woman need something to help her focus on what she nearly lost so the dog was valued more?

Did Ralph merely respond to a call for help?

Ralph is not a dangerous dog. He plays with other dogs and children extremely well. He's actually a big softie. So what was going on that day? And what were the thoughts going on in everybody's heads that nobody else was privy to? Except Ralph.

Another example was a woman who had bad health and a lot of animals to take care of. One of those animals was a wolf. She had been wondering for some time how this wolf was going to go when his time came, as he wouldn't allow a vet to give him care, much less a needle. It had been bothering her because she loved the wolf and didn't want him to suffer. She also had other animals and was finding the care of them too much with her health challenges.

So along came a pack of dogs. Her wishes were their command. She came home one day to find a blood bath. Her valiant wolf friend had died in the fight, and several of her other animals had been killed quickly and cleanly.

Despite all her wishes being granted, the woman was (understandably) upset. But instead of understanding and honouring what had happened, she reacted and took revenge on the pack of dogs, who were subsequently killed.

Personally I don't believe in revenge. I believe in taking 100 percent responsibility.

My point is, we have to be so incredibly careful of our thoughts, and take responsibility for them.

Everything is connected. Everything. All thoughts are creative and go on into infinity forever. This is what waking up is all about. It's about being alert and aware of what we are putting out in the universe.

Each situation of animal attack is different and unique. But rest assured there is more going on than what meets the eye, and it has everything to do with a matrix of thoughts, feelings and extra senses that we can't even begin to fathom with our current limitations. So if there is an "aggressive" animal, please don't reach for the needle or the gun. Consider looking at the situation with your spirit eyes and ears. There will always be something else going on. And it might even be coming from you.

What To Do If Your Animal Is Mirroring Your Aggression

There are many paths to wholeness, but doing work to dissolve your anger is a really good idea, and this might be exactly what your animal shamanic teacher is trying to get you to do.

There are all kinds of healing modalities such as meditation, yoga, Shamanic healing, The Journey, body work – ask for a sign and be guided by Spirit to the "right" practitioner.

But the one thing you can do right now is to practise forgiveness. Forgive others, and forgive yourself. Try it and use your "aggressive" animal to see how well you are doing. The more peace you have within, the more peace will be mirrored in your external world.

I can't stress this enough.

Here's another interesting example of dog aggression with a different root cause.

Milo

Milo was a small dog, a cross of what his people thought might be, Jack Russell, daschund and Chihuahua. His people came to me because he didn't like children or other dogs. At home he was deeply loved and a pampered pooch, but his people couldn't quite work him out.

The first thing Milo told me was *"I am not a doll."* He said he was small *"this time around"*, and people see him differently to *"who I really am."*

Milo was living multiple lives. In the past, he was a wolf who roamed the forest alone, embittered and old, cast out of the pack because of his age. He said he felt awkward in *"this little body"* but *"there are many images placed upon me that have nothing to do with the real me inside."*

"The real me is used to padding along a quiet forest trail and sensing with all of my senses the entire forest within and without. The real me inside is the one who was wolf and lived in harmony with the other wolves and with the forest.

"Inside I am a big animal who carries wisdom and yes, also bitterness. I disliked getting old."

Inside, Milo was still his wolf self, angry, embittered, elderly and walking the trail alone. When the children all pat and tease him, it is confirmation that he is living in his own private hell.

To help Milo, I had to teach him the power of his thoughts, and how by changing his perception of life, he could be happier. I showed him the path not taken – the elder wolf walking the trail alone but instead of feeling bitter, feeling dignified and bestowing his wisdom and love on all he meets. I showed him meeting a lone human and the two of them bonding in mutual companionship and sharing of knowledge and wisdom. The human prepares food, so the wolf doesn't have to hunt. And the wolf keeps her warm, protected and is a good friend.

This appealed to Milo and the bitterness within disappeared with a trail of tears. It was a big moment for him. He likes the idea of finding another pack. I tell him that the children and other dogs might not recognise him at first, but given a chance, they would. He needed to radiate the greatest wisdom of all – love.

I did a shamanic healing on Milo and integrated his lives so he could move into the world with happiness and ease. He asked that his person Rebecca understood that *"when you walk me, you walk with a wolf at your side and in your heart. Connect through me to the wilderness within. I may be cute but I am also very wise and unlike most dogs, I remember the source from which I came."*

He had lots more to say to Rebecca and according to her, the next day when she took him for a walk he was "much less aggressive to a big dog, and tolerated another one." Milo would go on to integrate his session, and Rebecca was thrilled with the insights into her dog, as well as the path to spiritual enrichment he had shown her.

The Terrible Twos

The majority of dogs in pounds are that age between gangly and mature – the teen years. A dog's troubled years might start when they are a few months old and not end until they are four or five. Most of the time what is really needed is not a new home or a trip to the pound, it is love, patience, understanding and exercise. I repeat, exercise.

They also need companionship and a job – something to do.

I'm always quite shocked when I see young dogs in pounds lined up for their death sentence because their only crime was pulling clothes off the washing line (read: very bored), or digging a hole (read: very bored) or not matching the sofa (read: sad human).

Dogs going through the terrible twos are also vying for their place in the pack and most humans don't realise that they are pack to dogs. Dogs need packs as much as horses need herds. Even if that pack or herd is only one other, or you.

I once spoke to a woman who had one two-year-old dog who was kept in a cage at the bottom of their yard. When I asked why the dog didn't sleep in the house, she said he stank. I dragged her into my house where seven dogs slept in my bedroom and there's no smell. The difference, I explained to her, is diet. Our dogs are fed a natural, raw food diet. Hers was fed on processed food.

Fortunately for this sad and lonely bundle of two-year-old dog, his people found him a new home where he could run and interact with another dog – his pack.

The Need for Exercise

Does your dog destroy your furniture, dig up your back yard, rip your washing off the line, bark incessantly, or dig into the garbage? It could be that he's sad, lonely, bored and desperately needing a morning work out – just like you do.

To a dog, that daily or twice daily walk, run or swim not only provides a channel for his energy, it feeds his mind. This is the way he gets to catch up with the neighbourhood news. A walk is like reading the newspaper. Watching the world go by from a window or through the fence is like watching the TV. Both give him something to do, and believe me he needs it. A walk is stimulating and satisfying on so many levels, but best of all it is his way of getting you to connect with nature. And no matter how stressful your day or your job, spending time outdoors in the park, on the beach or strolling through the bushland is definitely the best medicine for the human psyche.

Health and fitness benefits aside, a morning walk will set you up for a day of right relations, especially when you do it with gratitude, and in mindfulness. From this mindset, everything goes right and the Universe gives you green lights. It's a recipe for success on every level and in every aspect of your life – and your dog knows this. Which is why he behaves so poorly when he and you miss out on this vital activity.

Dogs need daily exercise. People do too.

So many people tell me they don't have time to walk their dogs, and sometimes, yes, life happens. But our society is wrong about so many things and it might be time for a shift in priorities. The reason we have so many problems in today's world is because we are disconnected from nature. When we don't get our daily nature fix, the human body starts to run like a back-firing car. We are so removed from what is natural in our society that we don't realise that something is wrong. We just grab another cup of coffee.

Dogs are much closer to our wild, instinctual selves, and they know the importance of feeling Mother Earth under their feet, a daily dose of oxygen infusing their blood, and a chance to commune with the neighbourhood. They want you to experience it as well.

When I lived in Sydney, I'd take Reka for a run every morning. After she had had a chance to burn off her early morning energy, I'd take a few moments for daily meditation. There is something purely magical about sitting in stillness and silence in nature. It renews the spirit. I'd also take her for a walk in the afternoon after a day's work, and I found that the best de-stresser in the world.

This is still my habit today, two decades later. I found if I didn't run my dogs, they would take themselves for a walk and an explore, and here in sheep and kangaroo country, I really don't want them doing that.

When I run every day I'm fitter, leaner, toned, and my mind is clear. I get great ideas and thoughts and have energy for the day. And my day is my own. Their needs satisfied, my dogs curl up under the desk or sprawl on the bed and are quiet. That is, until it's time to do the evening chores, which is more playtime for them. And it's a time we all enjoy.

If I'm really pressed for time, I bundle the dogs into the car, drive them up the hill and let them run home. They race each other the whole way. bright-eyed and panting, that pent up energy out of their system. The other thing we'll do is play a vigorous game of ball.

A couple of my senior dogs developed some phobias about walking where the horses grazed, one because of his nervous system and the other because of his compromised eyesight. I make a point of taking them for outings in the car, which they love, and letting them out at the front gate. If they're worried, one of us will walk home with them. But normally, running along the dirt road through the paddocks to the house is the magic medicine that makes their day. To see tails up and eyes shining is a reward in itself for making a small extra effort.

Perhaps dogs in the city don't have the benefits of hills or a long country driveway, but there are other things you can do when you are short of time – like a vigorous ball game or a brisk walk around the block.

So many young dogs end up in the pound because they have so much life and energy. This is their only crime – a crime which for so many ends in death. It's so incredibly wrong.

Most dogs can't take themselves for a walk or they end up in trouble with the dog catcher. They need us to understand that a daily walk or run is part of the bargain we signed up for when we took them in. For us to be back in balance with the planet, it's essential we spend time in nature. So it's a bit of a no brainer to have your furry personal trainer take you for a walk. It will nourish and replenish you both.

Take your dog for a run. It just might save your life, and it will certainly save his.

Human Babies, Dogs and Cats

In my experience, there is a lot of hoo-hah about bringing home new babies and not letting the dogs and cats near them. Can you imagine what it must be like for a dog or cat to suddenly be booted out of their home, and maybe into the pound, just because a baby has come along? The trick, again, is to communicate. You embrace the animals and ask them to embrace the newcomer.

When my daughter Tamsin was born, I showed the tiny bundle to my then five curious dogs. "Look what I have," I said. "A new human puppy."

Dogs are not dumb. They are incredibly sensitive. I set the intention that my dogs would embrace Tamsin as a younger sibling. She slept in the bed with us and they continued sleeping in the bedroom as well. One happy family. Nothing changed. I made sure I continued to give the dogs the same love, affection and attention I always had. And so did Andrew.

My dogs surpassed themselves. Suki took it upon herself to be Tamsin's protector. I have photos of Suki sitting on the end of the bed where Tamsin was, and on the blanket when Tam was outside.

We used to leave Tamsin in the backpack asleep while we played with the horses, and one day the dogs came around us quietly distressed. I looked up to see Dakota, Andrew's horse, curiously checking out the baby. The dogs were concerned he would eat her! It was very subtle and quiet – in the way of the animals. They knew they couldn't bark, because the horses would spook and Tamsin might be trampled. They were watching out for their younger sibling!

When Tamsin came along, we also had an elderly cat. Binah decided she liked the stroller and soft blankets Tamsin had, and would vie for position with the baby. So we found an old stroller and made it just as cosy. Binah was very content to have one of her own.

Animals are not spiteful or mean, but they can feel upset, jealous, insecure, miserable and fearful about their situation when a human baby comes along. Their survival depends on you. Trouble happens when their situation is changed. Many dogs and cats go from being the coveted baby substitute to being locked out and ignored in favour of the new human baby. This is what causes the problems.

As with human relationships, to get the best out of your animal relationships, treat them as you would like to be treated – with respect and understanding.

And as usual, talk with them and explain what is going on. This is simply common courtesy.

One of my clients is a midwife and dog lover. Penny sees her job including saving as many dogs as possible from the fate of being homeless by counselling families and insisting that a baby does not replace a dog in the family. The baby is quite simply another member of the pack.

"I am very clear to emphasise that the dogs must *never* be displaced when the baby arrives. The dogs' life ought to continue as was, inclusive of and involved with another family member," she says. "Predictably the responses vary from absolute shock, horror and disbelief to a grateful, soft sigh of recognised permission."

Lost Animals

Most of the time, lost animals are not lost. They are simply not in sight. You have to ask yourself why an animal is lost when they have excellent extra senses to draw on. If you can understand that nothing is ever lost, then you have to ask yourself why this particular animal is not in the place the humans expect him or her to be.

There are plenty of reasons. Many animals run off because they want more attention or to bring attention to someone or something. There are often emotions or spiritual lessons involved. Dogs often run off because they can't stand the diet they're on. I've had more than one lost dog client who has requested fresh meat, not canned food, before he will be found. Some are under-exercised. Others have been slighted by someone who has offended them. Still others run off because of a visiting animal or an animal who has invaded their space, and no human discussed it with them.

And still others think it is time to move in with someone else.

I believe that if an animal is meant to be with you, they will be, barring accident and human interference. But then, in life there are no accidents, so perhaps it is all as it should be.

Many animals are trying to teach their people spiritual lessons by running off. Eve had a missing cat who she loved desperately and she was in an emotional state. But Missy the cat wasn't coming home until Eve had learnt the powerful spiritual lesson of letting go. Despite counselling her, Eve didn't understand. "I love her, I'll never let her go.

"You wouldn't be letting her go. You're letting go the attachment and the need," I explained. "You're allowing her the freedom to return without any psychic force."

Eve didn't get it, even after hours of counselling and explaining. Missy found someone else who did get it, where she felt more comfortable.

When an animal has been stolen, that's a whole different matter. These are very difficult situations, especially when the animal is not happy about his new people.

Brad had his dog at work with him, when she suddenly disappeared. I could sense her when I tuned in, but she was a dark ball of misery. We were all worried because dog fighting was big in the area, and we kept holding Angel in the light and affirming she was fine and safe. I checked in with her every day and was frustrated that I couldn't get more for Brad who was on a mission of his own. One day Angel came through excited and glowing – "*I'm going home!*"

Later that day I got a call from Brad telling me that a man had come in talking about the reward for the dog and he intuitively knew that this was the kidnapper. Following the man like a sleuth in a TV show, Brad stole Angel back!!

But she knew hours before what the outcome would be! And he was empowered by the situation.

Horses also can predict the future. I once tracked a stolen horse for three weeks. She was in a bush paddock and not far from where she disappeared. She told me she was well treated, but not with the understanding and care from her own people. Her people even hired a plane for the search and had posters everywhere. One Saturday morning I tuned into the horse who said excitedly "*I'm going home.*" And sure enough, that very afternoon Judy rang to tell me her horse had been found wandering on the road. She'd been released and someone who had seen the posters spotted the mare, and took care of her until Judy could collect her.

What to Do When an Animal is Lost

When an animal is lost, take a deep breath and still your mind. Push away the left-brain mental chatter and clear a space for receiving thought transference.

Call the animal to you, making a note of how they seem emotionally. Do they need help coming home? Are they stuck somewhere? Is there an emotional reason why they aren't at home? Does something need to be done before they return home?

Ask them to show you where they are. Are there any landmarks? Are there people involved? What can you see? What can you hear? Traffic, sirens, trains? What's the weather like? Are they hungry? Are they in their body or in spirit? Are they with people? Are they alone? Understand that animals see the world from a different point of view, so I don't expect them to say, "I'm at 123 Maple Street."

I once had a cat show me a purple jacaranda tree on a suburban street with gardens out the front. My friend Carla said there were only two jacaranda trees in the street where she lived and was able to go looking for her cat. The cat however, came home by himself. Carla had just taken on a new kitten, and the cat wanted to remind my friend that he was still top cat in her heart.

If animals are just on secret animal business, remind them that their people are fretting and love them, and would like to know what time they will be home.

I always ask their person to hold a firm picture in their mind of being reunited with their animal companion. You hold the intention that the animal will return, and unless it goes counter to their own will, they will come home.

Of course, if your animal is missing from home, don't forget to do the important work of putting up posters and flyers alerting your community that if they see your animal kin, he is family and wanted back home. If you suspect she was stolen, then your poster should include emotional phrases which talk about how much you miss her, and how distraught your children are. Sometimes these emotional appeals can shift the situation. But you still have to visualise the outcome you want "for the highest good of all concerned".

Sometimes I ask people to mentally illuminate the path home with lots of light by imagining the home radiating light and a light-filled path leading toward it.

One lost puppy was frantically running around the streets of a busy city suburb for 10 days. He was new to the area and couldn't seem to get home. People would call his person saying they had seen him, but no one was able to catch him. I asked for a map of the area and held that in my mind for the dog to follow at the same time as I asked the woman to do the above exercise. That night he found his way home to a joyful reunion.

As there are no accidents in life, you have to ask yourself and your animal friend what the lesson is. In the case of the missing puppy, did he just want his person to understand the power of her mind? Did she need to believe in the paranormal more? Was he a lesson in love to all the community, touching the heartstrings of all who saw him and making his person feel part of a community which cared? Or did he successfully do all of the above and more?

Rex the indoor cat was missing, and his people all thought he had come to a terrible end. No one could sense him and he had been gone for a week. Plus there were these "horrible drug dealers" in the same street. I was called and immediately sensed the mesh of fear and judgement. Rex was quiet when I called him and said nothing. I wasn't even sure he was alive. But a little voice suggested there was a major lesson going on here and it had everything to do with fear and judgement. I suggested that Rex's people lift their thoughts and see only good and love in the world, and to mentally turn back the clock of time to when Rex first left. They were very open to trying, and Rex came home the next morning.

Lost animals who insist they are alive and home when they aren't home, may be in spirit and not know it. Or they may not know if they are in their bodies or not. If they don't know, generally they aren't. These animals may be earthbound and gently need releasing to the Light.

Separation Anxiety

I rushed out of the house, jumped in the car, and heard every one of my seven dogs howling. A splendid symphony of dog. Uh, oh. I turned the car around and raced back inside to talk with them.

"Sorry guys, I'm dashing into town to pick up Tamsin, and then we're having a meal with Ally, and we'll be home at 9 PM-ish, OK? Take care of the house for me! I'd take you with me except there are dogs everywhere and I have to pick up loads of horse feed. I'll make sure you all get an outing very soon."

The dogs had a job and knew what was going on. They immediately settled.

Another time my four young kelpies were in the car as we dashed off to catch Tamsin's flute recital. The dogs were very upset and unsettled, so I rushed back and told them that the recital would last two hours and they were to guard the car. Sage gave me a psychic nod and immediately settled in the front seat. The pups took their cue from her. And all was quiet.

Another time the dogs were in the car, and Tamsin and I headed off to breakfast after dropping Andrew at the train. I heard their howling several shops away. Again, I dashed back to the car, apologised profusely, and told them we weren't disappearing, only getting something to eat and would be back in about an hour. They instantly settled.

I have used this technique with tremendous results to help hundreds of clients with dogs suffering separation anxiety. Tell the dogs out loud where you are going, why, and what time they expect to be home. The dogs are family to be considered just like you would another human.

If the problem persists, many of my clients have put in dog doors to let their dogs access the house. Being able to go into their den when their pack members go away gives the dogs added security. It also gives them access to the outside again if they need to go to the toilet.

All animals like to know what's happening and be included in conversations. Just speak to them as you would another person. This might seem daft, but they understand more than you think they do, and as you speak you are also sending images and feelings which they also understand.

Company

Animals tend not to like being on their own. It's a lonely life being stuck in a backyard with nothing to do and no one to play with. Horses definitely need another companion, being very strong herd animals. If you can't be that herd, or for a dog, pack, then you need to consider a companion for the animal.

My own dog Reka was an only dog for eight years. For most of that eight years I was a freelance photojournalist and actress. She spent almost all of her time with me. But when I got busy, I realised she was spending more time on her own, so we got Kai. When Kai arrived as a little bundle of black fluff, Reka mothered him fiercely. She would growl at him and put him in his place and tell him off for sleeping on her furniture and her toys. But he adored her, and after a while she got used to him, and they became excellent friends.

Having the two dogs also affected us, as we felt they were protection and company for each other in the car. So not only did Reka gain a companion, she got to go out even more.

Horses really don't thrive in lone animal situation. One of my first horse rescues was a gorgeous, ancient black trotter who had been rescued in Sydney and dumped on a property near us. Andrew and I were out riding one day and came across him standing in a paddock with only the kangaroos for company. He was quite literally dying of loneliness and a broken heart. His well-meaning person had little understanding of horses, and visited him once a year when the family came to the property for their annual holiday.

I told the man about the horse's condition and suggested I take him to live with my horses. The man resisted at first, but his 15-year-old daughter saw the sense of it. Jamaica came home with us and our horses, and quickly settled in.

Horses get the sense of where they are and who they're with from the resident members of the herd. Jamaica went from being half wild and "crazy" to calm. He settled literally overnight. His previous people couldn't believe it when they saw their "crazy" horse standing relaxed in the sun, as we brushed his matted mane and coat into shining glory. Jamaica died ten months later. But he died having been loved, and having been happy. That made all the difference to his soul.

What It's Like To Be Sold, Dumped Or Moved When You Are An Animal

Like us, animals suffer from stress and feel emotions. These emotions play a huge part in their health, vitality, and behaviour. It's vital when you are moving house to consider your animal family by telling them exactly what is going on – and that you are taking them with you.

I'll never forget the relief of my German Shepherd Reka when we arrived at our new property in the mountains having sold our Sydney home and moved all our stuff from our previous farm, including the animals. She'd been subdued on the last drive, squashed in the car with the two other dogs and the last of our possessions. When I drove the car through the front gate, she asked, *"Is this our new home?"* When I said yes, she leapt out of the car with such enthusiasm that I felt abashed that I hadn't explained it to her properly before.

The most important thing you can do with your animal friend is to talk to them all the time and explain exactly what is going on.

Horses form deep relationships with both people and other horses, yet they are often sold on and on and on. Wrenched from their previous home and herd, they are expected to immediately perform for a person they have no relationship with.

Some horses are lucky and end up in homes better suited to them, but I can tell you that grief from torn past bonds comes up in many of my horse healing sessions. This can be helped with emotional essences like

Bach or Bush Flower Essences.

Lady M, one of the horses here in sanctuary, told us during her hospice care that she missed the tiny hands of a small boy who would pet her and really wanted our daughter Tamsin to stroke her face like he had. Tamsin was happy to stroke her face, feed her carrots, and do anything else she could do to fill the gap in Lady's big, soft heart.

Dumped animals often go through their own dark night of the soul, unless they are blessed with future sight which helps them know where they will end up next.

Some animals who have been fostered need a settling in time. Being moved from home to home makes them anxious, and they only know they don't want to go back to the pound. There is huge fear there. They sometimes view every new person they see as someone who could potentially take them to a different environment. And sometimes they just want to stay where they are to recover from their trauma. These animals only settle once they are reassured they are in a home for life, and that they won't go back to the pound.

If you are fostering, make it clear that the animal will stay there until their true person comes, and that they will always be safe. Animals just need to be talked to. That's what it comes down to really.

Rescue remedies can help here.

New Arrivals

When we get a new horse here at the sanctuary, we leave them overnight in the yards or in a small paddock with another horse, so they can "speak" to our other horses without having the stress of being sorted out in the herd hierarchy.

We never ask anything of these horses. We never immediately work them as if they were a new car. We give them plenty of time to get used to us and our ways. We let them settle in completely. We tend them and serve them with fresh water and hay, and we leave them alone. Often they feel traumatised from their past experiences with humans, and our objective is to let them learn from direct experience that we want nothing from them, only their trust. They get that experience by us keeping our promises.

Hanging out with other happy horses and having regular food and no stress goes a long way to healing them. Eventually the new horse comes to trust us and we can begin to handle them. And you can always tell when a horse is ready to trust because that's when they approach you.

Always give a horse time to learn about his new environment. Just because you paid money for him doesn't mean you own him. It means he's in your care and you need to respect his emotional and physical needs.

Some horses take longer than others to settle in. It might be weeks, months, and for some, years. Horses don't forget their pain, but they can also be quick to learn new habits if they are treated right.

Saraid was a great example of this. A little bay rescue pony, she kicked out at us and tried to bite if we came near. We ignored her behaviour and continued to feed her and brush her and take care of her. She calmed down. I knew she'd been very badly handled. She wasn't a nasty pony at all. I haven't met one of those – ever. She simply was a horse who was clear she didn't want to be handled that way again.

She healed, and it was a few years later that I asked her to take Tamsin for a ride. We chunked down the saddling, so it was polite, gentle and respectful at all times. When Andrew drew in the girth Saraid turned around to nip him, only to find he'd finished and the girth was still loose. We walked her around a bit and then did it up another notch. This time she looked really surprised. We walked her around again and she realised we weren't going to cause her any pain at all, and she relaxed and allowed our then five year old daughter to have a pony ride.

It was a real healing for Saraid, and a lesson for us, as I could see the manner with which she had been treated previously, including the energetic imprint of the man who had hurt her.

Saraid

The same goes for new dogs and cats in the family. Everything is strange and they may be pleased with their new home or overwhelmed. Try to make their first day and night quiet, relaxed and easy. You both have to get to know each other. And don't forget dogs especially are pack animals and to them, shutting them away on their lonesome in the laundry is just plain miserable. If your house is too nice for a dog to be in it, then don't have a dog.

All our dog new arrivals are given a cosy bed inside, normally close to us so we can bond and they can feel safe. Some of the cats we've taken in have needed their own little space – especially Tab who had been traumatised by dogs and came into a house with five dogs at the time.

We once took in four young cats who had been locked in a cage for a year. They lived in our old kitchen area with the bottom part of the stable door closed to give them a feeling of enclosure, while the top stayed open so they could learn to be part of the family and get to know us. This continued until they grew comfortable enough to venture into the house, and finally outside.

The other thing we do here at home is talk to the other animals about bringing in any new ones. We let them know what's going on and ask if anyone has any objections. When the new animal comes, we'll introduce them. And if the new animal is a dog, we make the introductions on a walk outside, away from the pack's territory. Once the walk is finished the new animal has been accepted into the pack without drama.

Animals may come with names which don't suit them, and you may need to change them to true heart name. They also may need a job. I've had many animal clients who have wanted and needed a job, like welcoming people into the house or shop, or "looking after the humans." Some have told me they are healers or teachers, and some have wanted me to show them pictures of what a "companion" does. So I've shown them mental images of playing ball with children, lolling in the garden with a person, curled up in front of the fire, walking with a person, and explained that companion means friend, mate, or pack.

Education

We've already established the word "training" has the connotation of obeying like a robot without considering an animal's needs, deep wisdom or natural intelligence. That's why I make a distinction between education and training. It's a different way of looking at things. When I educate my animals, I am considering who they really are.

In the education of animals, always keep in mind that you want your beloved to experience success. So never set up your animals to fail. Figure out how to make them right.

I had a lesson from my irrepressible kelpie puppy Tusuque, who thinks her job is to tell the horses what to do. I was feeding horses one night when she nearly drove all the horses into me. "Tusuque, watch what you're doing!" I bellowed, reacting from fright. But then I saw Tusuque dancing in front of me, every pore radiating an apology, and I had another major lesson in humility.

"I'm sorry sweetie,"' I said, dropping to my knees, inviting her to come to me. I realised in an instant I hadn't told her what I expected her to do. I hadn't taken the time it took to educate her. I thanked her for the lesson. "OK, let's start again." And this time I specifically asked her to stay outside the stable and yards while I fed out. She did it beautifully, and I praised her with lots of enthusiasm. My reward was incident-free horse handling, and a very happy dog.

Tusuque and her sisters have never been 'trained." The first thing I do for new animals is spend time talking to them so they learn English. I tell them what everything is and what we are doing. And normally I will tell them what I expect them to do. For example, "This is the car." "This is the bed." "This is your mat." "Let's go outside to go to the toilet." I praise them when I catch them doing any behaviour I want to encourage, even if they do it inadvertently.

We build our mutual partnership and education on top of that.

An educated horse is a partner, and as it is with all animals, this goes two ways. Horses are expected to obey whether they have sore backs or stomach aches. Many people use horses not as partners but as a way to further their ego and win blue ribbons. I'll never forget Pat Parelli talking about an Olympics where he gave a bridleless, saddleless dressage demonstration on a mule. Yet the "top" riders had horses with blood on their mouths after competing. The big learning I got from Pat and his wife Linda, were play, politeness and partnership. Consider the needs of your horse, and make your education fun, always finding ways to help them be right.

Take The Pressure Off Your Relationship

In our society, there's a lot of pressure on people to "do" something with animals. And some of it is fun for the animal and the human, and some of it is definitely not. It completely depends on the motive and personality of the human, and the personality and make up of the animal.

The reason I enjoyed Pat Parelli's Natural Horsemanship program so much when we were involved with it was because I could have fun with Sollie – by myself. We developed a partnership and there was no competition – except a desire within me to be the best I could be as a horse companion.

(Pat did encourage advanced students to take their naturally educated horses into competition to spread the word that fear and intimidation didn't have to be the only way. In fact, it was not the way, because he and his students got better results from their horses by being a leader, and being polite, playful and respectful.)

One of my favourite things to do with my animals is to read to them. My daily routine with Sollie included reading out loud to him for at least 20 minutes every afternoon, sitting on his bare back, with no bridle or halter, while he grazed and listened to the story.

Tamsin is good at reading to horses making their transition. Her favourite book to read to them is the *Hollywell Stables* series by Samantha Alexander. This is set in an animal sanctuary in England where animals live out their lives in peace, as they do here.

I've noticed my dogs can be very restless at night when the TV is on because the drama on it creates so much tension. If we turn it off, the psychic irritation immediately ceases and they all settle in relief. We read out loud as a family for years and I noticed they would curl up and appear peacefully asleep. Their favourite was *The Famous Five* by Enid Blyton. Even reading Harry Potter out loud was preferable to the television which says a lot about the nature of television.

Likewise our animals can't stand heavy metal or raucous rock and roll. It tears at their sensitive nervous systems and makes them uncomfortable.

Ask your animals what they want to do, and give them special days where it's their turn to call the shots. They might want a walk in the park, go to the outdoor dog café, go swimming, lie in the sun – whatever it is, spend some time being in their world instead of always asking them to be in yours.

Asking your animals what they want to do extends beyond outings. You can talk to them about their role in life, especially if you have particular ideas. You'll remember the story of Bliss, the young mare who's person asked me what she wanted to do. In her case, she was young and didn't yet know, although she was clear that she didn't want to be alone. She appreciated being asked and was open to exploring possibilities.

Other animals are very clear about what they have come here for, what they are good at, and what they want and need to do. So it is important to ask. There are horses who don't want to do dressage or race, and horses who do. Some dogs want to go into service for humans, and some want to be companions and spiritual teachers. There are cats who want to be office or hospital workers, and others who want to sit in the sun and guard their spiritual and physical territories.

Breeding, Spaying and Neutering

Many people ask me about spaying and neutering, but I can tell you that all the male dogs who I have spoken to were actually relieved to be less driven by their sexual urges. It caused them a great deal of frustration and they realised that in our society, it didn't help them. You'll remember the story of Sinjin, the stud dog who was given to running off and enjoying the scents of freedom. He begged me to tell his person to "cut off his balls". Those were his words, not mine.

Even though this is a common reaction, it's always respectful to ask first. Who knows the soul journey of that animal and their offspring?

Likewise with breeding. Not all animals want to be bred. Some are natural mothers. Some want birth but don't want to lose their offspring. Some don't want it at all and view it as rape. Some understand that they will be separated from their offspring and would prefer not to go through that.

It's time we stopped assuming what the animals want and need, and started asking them instead.

Here at Ballyoncree, we realised we had to get the wild brumbies gelded and explained to them that we weren't in the business of breeding horses. This was a forever home. The two colts told me they had no desire to be "king", and the stallion said he was just plain tired and would welcome his change. And indeed he was well behaved for the vet who came, letting him near when he let no one else.

But I was worried because I'd heard on the psychic grapevine that another soul needed to be born so I was fully prepared to honour that and not let the gelding happen if no one wanted it.

They were all gelded.

And months later Spirit was born to one of the wild mares anyway. She was already pregnant when the boys were gelded – so I'd heard right!

Pointing – Your Hands As a Weapon!

Spirit with his mum

In our society, we've been taught to point the finger at people and animals when we are making a point or when we are angry. Sadly, this is a form of sorcery which cuts through the luminous energy field around us and can cause harm. I wasn't surprised when a woman told me that she had given her horse "a talking to", and he'd turned around and bolted. The woman had been sending bolts of energy as she also talked with her hands, pointing at him with a finger as a loaded weapon. Believe me, this hurts!

If I want to make a point now, I'll point with a soft finger or hand, my intention always mindful of not sending energy in the direction of the person or animal. It is something we all need to be aware of, and we need to be clear with our intention and ethics.

Vibration

Currently, many animals are at a higher frequency or vibration than humans. They are more highly attuned to the world around them. This makes them extra sensitive to nuances we are barely aware of. They respond well to our own personal stillness and the direction of energy through body language and thought. They also work hard to lift up our vibration or frequency. If you've ever been delighted, amused, enthralled, or in awe of an animal – this is them raising your frequency.

The Power and Importance of Words

After a long day teaching, I was approached by a student in the kitchen as I made myself a cup of tea. My dogs, Tala, Twylah, Suki and Raffi, were with me, quietly watching and staying close by, unphased by the number of people and the work they had to do.

"You speak to your dogs like they were equals," said Nancy. "And it shows. I speak to mine like they were children, and so they act like it."

– Excerpt from Billie's journal, 2002

Words are swords. They can harm or heal. They can cut deep, causing wounds. In shamanism, when a sword is used this way, it is called sorcery, that is, the use of words with the intent to harm. Name-calling, put-down humour, gossip – those are all sorcery.

When words are used without mindfulness, the wounds they cause can create negative beliefs in people and animals alike. When people and animals operate from these negative beliefs, health and behavioural problems can follow.

Never underestimate the importance and power of words. The spoken word goes out into the universe like an arrow. Words can hurt the innocent. Be careful of your words, and use them instead to heal. Be mindful. Use words to uplift and inspire, to help both people and animals shine. Encourage them. Lift them to greater heights.

There's a huge misconception among some animal-loving people that animals don't understand a word we say. This is just plain wrong. Animals are telepathic. They understand a lot more than we think they do.

My client's horse told me that she was threatening to sell him as "dog meat". The woman was most embarrassed. "I only said that on the phone," she stuttered. She might have only said that on the phone, but I bet she thought it as well. And then wondered why the poor animal didn't "behave" as she wanted him to.

Telepathy makes us honest.

I had a student once who was having problems with her horse. She admitted several times that she would tell this horse he was going to the knackery, if he didn't behave. She said that she said it as a joke and that he knew it was a joke, but she was also thinking of selling him.

It wasn't a joke and she knew it. I see sorcery done to animals constantly by well meaning people calling them all the names under the sun in a voice meant to deceive them. Animals are not deceived. They are telepathic and they read our hearts.

The student finally got it, and promised to shift her attitude towards her horse in an effort to shift his attitude to her. Only then could they move forward toward having the kind of relationship she, and he, really wanted.

Words have power. We live in a world where we speak all day and don't stop to think that with our words and thoughts we create our world. Pause, take stock of what you are about to say, and speak words which are considered, for with our words we create our world. The odds are good that you have heard of the Law of Attraction, due mainly to the success of The Secret. What we have to realise is that it doesn't just apply to our dreams, health and desires. It affects everything. **Everything is a result of what we say and think.** If you want a better life or a better relationship with animals, set your intention to create that.

Life is Simply a Series of Self-Fulfilling Prophecies

So let's consider how the animals in your home are treated? What names do you call them? What words do you fling about in anger? Do you bind them into poor behaviour by your thoughts and words? Do you condemn them with your thoughts and words?

Or do you free them with the words that help them shine and be all they can be?

Expect the best from your animal friends. Just because your dog has counter surfed today, doesn't make him a "greedy" dog or a counter surfer forever. Perhaps he was just hungry. Don't bind them with your thoughts.

There's an old story about a guy trying to "train" his dog to sit. The dog kept running away, because the picture in the guy's mind was of the dog running away. So even though his voice said, "Sit", the dog saw the mental image of "running away". And being a brilliant dog, he did just that. But instead of being praised for that brilliance, he was punished. How confusing for the dog.

Animals, given a chance, will try to work with us. But we have to understand the messages we send them.

I'm always amused when people think of themselves as greater than animals, and yet behave like a pack of dogs attacking prey towards someone weaker than themselves. Someone once said to me, "It's all about the top dog. People will tread on others and put them down if they can raise themselves higher in someone else's eyes."

Not quite impeccable human angel behaviour, is it?

Words are affirmations. Labels are words, and affirmations.

For example, how many times have you heard people call their animal companions stupid, lazy, dumb, grumpy, crazy, cranky, old, sick, nasty, fat, and so on. Try it on. Get someone to call you those names and feel what it does to your body. And your spirit.

When I've corrected people for using these kinds of words, I get, "Oh, but, Billie, he is stupid. He is cranky." I have to explain that unless they change their words, so it will always be. Words have that kind of power.

In the beginning was the word.

Words are all-powerful, and in our society we are not taught to watch our words. From the book *In Beauty May I Walk*, we learn that the Navajo have a saying, *"Be careful when speaking. You create the world around you with your words."*

And let's face it, even Doctor Who understands the power of words. Look how he got back at Prime Minister Harriet Jones when she killed the Sycorax. "I can bring down your government with six words," he says, and destroys her career by asking her assistant, "Don't you think she looks tired?"

So how do you turn around the cranky, stubborn, dumb animals in your home? First, understand that by calling them names you are projecting. So who is cranky, stubborn and dumb? You! Consider that for a moment!

Second, try giving your animal the unconditional love he deserves. Come from that place of the heart chakra. Every time you blame, swear at, jab your finger at, make jokes at the expense of, and name call, you commit sorcery. Energetically you are belittling another and sending the denser energies their way. That's not what you want to do to your beloved animal family. In our culture, we are not taught the important things. We don't understand the power of words.

But you do now.

So turn it around. Your dogs are lively and intelligent, your horses gentle and very sensitive, and your cats are wisdom keepers and healers.

By projecting and affirming beautiful attributes to your animals, you help them become so and free them from sorcery and limiting beliefs. You get them out of a box which holds them, and set them free to grow their wings and step into their becoming, as you step into yours.

Names

A name is a word, and as we've just discussed, words have power and meaning. Names are daily affirmations, and they carry an energetic vibration.

So when a dog is Butch or Bruiser, or a horse is Satan or Demon, don't expect a saint. One person gave a rescued wild horse the name Jezebel, which she hated. Every time people speak the name, all the thoughts and energy associated with the name are transferred to the animal. Yuck.

Instead, give your animal companion the gift of a beautiful name which speaks to his highest vibration. Many of my animals ask for their names to be changed so they don't carry the vibration or trauma of the past, and some want it to be changed because they know the name they request matches the vibration of who they will become.

My wild brumbies, for example, spoke to me of wind in their manes, and earth under their feet. They spoke of whispering trees, and spirit lights. When I called our wild stallion Finn, the other colts recognised the name as "magical" and wanted the same.

Holly and Gemma were two rescue dogs I took from foster care. Holly was a Kelpie/German shepherd/something cross and Gemma was a sleek bundle of Kelpie energy. Their names were fine. But not suited to their highest vibration.

After they had been with us a short time, new names came bubbling up. Gemma became Sage, after the wise one, and the healing herb. She was smart and a healing presence in the house, both in her actions and her manner with the other dogs and us. Further, we would often call her Dr Sage.

Holly on the other hand was a laidback sweetie, and I was surprised when she kept insisting on the name Heyoka. Heyoka, in Native American mythology, is the sacred clown – a vital member of the tribe who would turn everything upside down. This person's job was to make people laugh and see something from a different perspective. I honoured her, thinking this was very strange for a dog like her. As soon as we named her, she started to act differently. She made us laugh with her antics. I realised there was a lot more to our Heyoka than met the eye.

And it was much later on that I realised she was giving me an important message. As they are our mirrors, she was holding up one to me, saying use humour to make people laugh and help them see a different perspective!

We got one of our cats from a cattery. He was a retired stud with the name Sergeant Plod, and overweight and ploddy he was. I was reading a book on white magic at the time and renamed him Chockmah. The difference was amazing. He brightened up, lost weight and became cheerful, lithe, active and happy.

When our dog Willie came along, we suddenly had a Willie, a Billie and a goat named Millie. Someone's name had to change because when Andrew called any of us, we'd all show up! Willie was a beautiful, majestic German Shorthaired Pointer and Willie just didn't suit him. We changed it to Louie and he grew even more majestic.

Chapter 32:
Love, Acknowledgement and Seeing the Good in All

"I was walking in the mountain forest minding my own business when I became aware that on a ledge above me was a mountain lion. And she was looking at me as if I was dinner. I stopped. "My you're a pretty cat," I said when I'd steadied myself. "I'll bet you're a beautiful mother – a really good mother – and I bet your babies are the best. I bet you look after them so well...

"I kept this up for what seemed like 20 minutes but was probably a lot less. The big cat started purring and walked away."

– Grandmother Kitty, Lakota Sioux elder, 1992

A couple of years after Gran Kitty told me about her experience with the mountain lion, I had the opportunity to put the teachings into practice. I was reading quietly on the veranda with the dogs when a brown snake suddenly appeared in front of us, and, shocked to see us, reared up ready to strike.

Australian brown snakes are highly poisonous and have been known to chase people. I was alone except for the animals, and the snake was positioned between me and the door. I called the dogs to me and instructed them to be very still.

"The dogs are going to be really still now. Because we respect the snakes", I said out loud in as calm a voice I could muster. "We do. And you are a beautiful snake, and I bet you're surprised to see us here, and if you want to go, may I suggest that you could go over there towards the tree and then down that way. I bet you're a great mother and that you're really smart. We all really respect snakes. "

I kept this up until I relaxed myself. As I relaxed and began to believe my words sincerely, the snake relaxed and wandered off in the direction I had suggested she go. I raced inside and collapsed on the bed, shaking. But as I made myself a cup of tea I thought, "What a lesson." And why hadn't I thought she might be trying to communicate with me.

I immediately called her spirit and asked if she had a message for me. *"Boondocks"*, she said. " *I'm going to the boondocks."*

"What does that mean, beloved"?

"Today it means that you are blessed."

Snake carries much meaning throughout many indigenous cultures. For example, in Native American animal medicine, the presence of snake across your path heralds transmutation. The snake of South American shamanism sheds her skin, as we shed our old stories which no longer bind us. And truly the incident affected me on many different levels, and made me see some things with new clarity.

The first lesson was how fear begets fear. Second was how much every living being reacts to love and acknowledgement. Third was how we are all interconnected and how, in my fear, I had missed the opportunity to learn from the snake's mouth.

It wasn't long after the incident that the bush around us was ravaged by bushfires. We were indeed blessed, because our house and horse paddocks were safe, even as the fire licked the edges. In fact a fireball dropped in the horse paddock and simply went out.

How we interact and communicate with our animal companions affects them and their behaviour. I'm a big believer in the art of gratitude, acknowledgement, appreciation, praising with enthusiasm, seeing the good in all, and saying it out aloud.

This is not simply a pleasant or polite way of behaving. It's essential when striving for sacred harmony and sacred partnerships and relationships with animals and people. By acknowledging the good in others, we lift their vibration. And everybody benefits from that.

This is important in human relationships as well. Andrew, Tamsin and I are in the habit of thanking each other for everything, like washing up, cooking, cleaning the cat litter, or shovelling the manure. We also try not to miss an opportunity to give compliments, helping others see themselves in the light of beauty. Acknowledgement and compliments are important to make both people and animals feel not only appreciated, but seen. It helps their light grow and glow, and this is vital.

We also try to acknowledge and praise the animals when they do something we want them to do, like good sitting and waiting for dinner, standing still quietly while we treat them, or even good herding. It's important to catch people and animals doing the right thing, and praising them so they know to do more of it.

Finally, we continually tell all those around us, including each other, how beautiful they are, what they're good at, and how much we love them and appreciate them. To raise another's vibration is the job of a spiritual warrior – someone who acts to make a difference in the world – not with their swords, but with their words and deeds.

Exercise

- *How many people can you shift today, with your smile and gracious words of gratitude and acknowledgement?*
- *How many animals can you shift today, with your smile, and gracious words of gratitude, acknowledgement and praise?*

Secret Animal Business

Part 5:
Animal Health And Healing

Chapter 33:
A Holistic Approach

As an animal shaman, I take a very holistic view of animal care. This means I look at animals spiritually, physically and emotionally, and I use a range of healing modalities to bring balance to the body.

Sometimes conventional medicine is needed for surgery, pain relieving drugs, emergency care and diagnosis. This is where veterinary care really shines. But when the vets run out of answers, many supposedly hopeless health challenges can be helped with alternative therapies. My motto is, "Where there's life, there's hope", and I don't stop trying to find an answer.

This is something you can do, too. When your beloved animal friend needs help, keep searching. There are some brilliant healing techniques and products on the market, and more coming all the time.

One of our horses, Gingko, split his hoof in half once and was in danger of losing it altogether. Even our farrier was shaking his head. He never thought we could save the horse. But he put a shoe on Gingko to act like a splint for the hoof, while I gave Gingko internal and external herbal care. It took 12 months to heal. But today his hoof is strong, and the most important thing is he is still alive and well.

Always go the extra mile for your animal companion's health. There may be things you need to learn in the journey. As companion animals tend to mirror our own state of health, what works for them might also repair your health or save your life.

I can't count how many times people have listened to healing suggestions I've given them for their animals, and asked me if it would work for them too.

As I live two hours from my wonderful vets and have so many animals under my care, natural healing, with its emphasis on preventing illness, is important. Diet, nutrition, supplements, fresh water and exercise are the keys, while love and right thinking complete the picture. My animals are healthiest when we are in right relations and keep our vibration high.

As a shamanic practitioner, a tool I use to help bring balance and harmony to our land and animals is an Andean prayer bundle known as a *despacho*. When you bring yourself and your world into right relations, what the Inka call *ayni*, the Universe supports you. This is the same technique used by the Andean medicine people to bring health to their llama herds.

We live in interesting times, and more and more people seek alternative medicine for conditions like cancer, arthritis, wounds, skin problems, and injuries. There is a time and a place for allopathy, and there is certainly a time and a place for alternative medicine, as many people worry about the toxicity and long-term side effects of many allopathic drugs.

When caring for animals, consider the whole range of healing modalities at your disposal. This includes allopathic medicine as well as diet, herbs, homeopathy, acupuncture, Bowen, kinesiology, Equine Touch, massage, TTEAM, EFT, shamanic healing, Body Talk, Reiki, Theta, Bio Energetic Medicine, pure vibrational essences... The list is too long to even just mention everything, and it is growing all the time.

I believe in an ultimate future where we and our animals won't get diseased at all, and until then we will see a progression of therapies which will have a lighter and lighter vibration to match our changing bodies. Already at Ballyoncree I'm finding that I work more and more at the level of the energetic with the animals, with tremendous results. Further, there are already cases of instant healing from practitioners around the world, and I believe this will become more commonplace.

People are also working with the power of prayer, vision and intent – "seeing" a vision of the person or animal as healthy to help them become so, if that is their will. This, again, is the Law of Attraction. Increasingly, practitioners work with plant medicine spirits to affect healing.

I call this Fifth Dimensional healing. It is the healing of the Golden Age and is already happening. It will happen more and more as magic and miracles once again grace our planet as the norm.

I mention this because it is important in animal care to broaden your mind and believe in hope and possibility. Of course, it is vital to take your animal to your health care practitioner when necessary. But if your vet has run out of answers, it may not be a death sentence for your beloved. It may mean you have to look further afield.

As an animal's chief carer, we hold a lot of power and responsibility. It is up to us to take care of their needs, as well as our own, to keep disease at bay. Because they are so influenced by our energy fields, they pick up things from us which are still in our own etheric body. Arthritis, heart disease, and cancer are prime examples.

When and if illness comes, we have to be careful of our thoughts, guard our animal kin from the insensitivity of others, and provide the best environment for healing. For example, telling an animal they can get better is so much better than pouring worry into the wound. Our red heeler Cedar was often injured as a young dog, as she ran crazily around in what we call "brain switched off mode". We'd patch her up and make her feel safe in her own little healing room. She would look at me in a worried way. I'd tell her, "Don't worry, this is nothing. It'll be healed soon. You're a good healer. You're young and healthy. You'll be fine." A look of relief would pass over her face, her body would relax and I could tell that true healing could begin.

I would also look at Cedar's "accidents" and consider my own life. Was I racing through life and not being mindful? Was there something I needed to be more mindful of?

If your animal behaves oddly or is ill, please take a moment to ascertain what this might be reflecting back to you. The animals in our lives, like our children, are mirrors, and what we ultimately want are happy, healthy humans and their furry companions. Animals often come into our lives to help us learn certain lessons, and health is one of them. So listen, observe, reflect, and show your gratitude. This is a short cut to spiritual growth. And it also may just save your life.

Here are some things to consider for health and healing.

- **Diet**. Nothing is more important than the food you give your animals. Please don't give them commercial canned or dried food. This might be an easy way to feed, but it is completely counter to good health.

- **Chemicals** such as vaccines, flea washes and wormers need serious thought, as many have disastrous side effects. Personally I use homoeopathic and herbal substitutes with excellent results.

- Our **thoughts**, our emotions, and the **emotions** of our animals.

Chapter 34:
Diet for Dogs and Cats

My eight dogs' coats glisten in the sun. They are soft to touch. Silky. I love burying my face in their fur. They smell like the earth. They smell like heaven. My four cats are the same – soft, silky, sweet.

They weren't always like that. Dusty's coat was orange-tinged and rough to touch. He didn't smell good. But now it's the colour of deep chocolate brown. The difference is astounding. Now he has the colour of health. Heyoka and the kelpie puppies had black coats like straw. Now they are silky to touch. The only thing I've done is feed them a natural diet. That's a simple home made diet without a can in sight or a bag of kibble. It's amazing what you can do for a dog and a cat with a raw food diet.

The best example of a dog I've turned around was Louie the German Shorthaired Pointer, who'd been abandoned and left to fend for himself in the cold winter of the mountains where I lived. He and Cedar lived outside the house their person used to live in. Louie had a reputation for being bad tempered, growled all the time, and was smelly, itchy, dirty, and chased the local ducks. He was riddled with eczema. Nobody wanted him and nobody liked him.

Louie

Fortunately for him, I was called in the day before he was due to go to the pound. I took one look at him and knew he would never be re-homed in the condition he was in. He would have been killed there and then.

When I drove my car up to the house where they lived, the two dogs came rushing at me. *"Will you take us home with you?"*

They were desperate. And hungry. Louie jumped through the open window of my car to eat an entire apple pie I'd bought at the markets that morning.

I already had three dogs and didn't need any more fur family, but I wasn't going to turn my back on these two. We might have found a home for the pup, but they didn't want to be separated. So they came home. And stayed.

Louie's table manners were terrible. He was so hungry he would tremble before a meal. We worked on inner health and within two weeks he was a different dog – his coat took on a shine, he began to settle, and he stopped itching. He'd only growled at people because he was so cold and miserable. So he stopped growling. Underneath the grime and unhappiness was a wonderful, affectionate, intelligent dog. A month after his rescue he looked so magnificent we had people stopping us in the street to ask us where we got him from.

All it took was good, nourishing, real, raw food.

One of my early mentors was the late Australian animal healer Jackie Fitzgerald. She started off life as a groomer and could tell a healthy dog just by their coat. I'm shocked at how many of the dogs out there have grungy coats, and are smelly and revolting to touch. They look at me with desperation in their eyes, imploring me to help them. They're the dogs on tinned food and kibble.

I don't care what the vets say, if the food comes out of a packet or a tin, it doesn't have a life force and doesn't promote health. And if you knew what was in the tin, you'd be worried about giving it to your dog and cat as well.

We are killing our animal friends with the diet we give them. Quite frankly, we're killing ourselves as well, but that's another story. There's an old saying, "You are what you eat." The same applies to our animal companions. Many animal clients, during the course of a consultation, will thrust a picture at me of a gooey-looking mess – canned animal food. Invariably this is followed with "I want *green*".

The "green" comes from their need for high quality chlorophyll like barley, wheat grass, or marine phytoplankton. This builds and cleanses the blood and provides a host of nutrients in an easily accessible form.

No dog or cat I have ever communicated with has ever requested canned or dried food. Instead they tell their people it is addictive and unhealthy. It might look like they are enjoying it. But they're not. Believe me, when you check into their tummies, they feel heavy and disgusting. I can always tell an animal who is on processed food. Yuck.

All our animals are highly supplemented with a range of products, including "green", to keep them as healthy and long-lived as possible. As with humans, it's difficult to get all the nutrients the body requires from today's food.

You can buy a prepared nutritional supplement for your cats and dogs, or make sure you have things like rice bran oil, kelp (seaweed meal), one of the green powders mentioned above, nutritional yeast, vitamin C, slippery elm powder, yoghurt and other food products on hand. And if you feed meat, make it raw and organic.

Our dogs enjoy a varied diet including fruit, and pulped raw vegetables. They smell as sweet as Mother Earth and are lovely to the touch. The coat of a commercial food fed animal is dry, harsh and lacking in sparkle. They smell anything but sweet and their stools are chalky. By introducing fresh, raw foods, this can be quickly changed.

Cats also need a natural diet.

Remember Omar the missing cat who liked omelette and chives? When we spoke, he listed off foods he wanted, including fresh chicken and fish, soft white cheese, and of course the omelettes. That's a good start for a natural cat diet.

Personally, I am a vegan and was a vegetarian for 30 years. As an animal communicator, I won't and can't eat the beings I talk with. I'm even careful with the plants I grow in our garden. I'll ask permission to pick them and request that they withdraw their energy before I do.

In my 30 or so adult years of caring for animals, I have never fed canned food to my four-legged friends. To me that's a one-way ticket to degenerative diseases and skin conditions.

I'll say it again. If you knew what was in commercial animal food, you'd probably turn green. It is *not* healthy. Ann N. Martin did a lot of research into it when her own dog got sick. The result was her book *Food Pets Die For: Shocking Facts About Pet Food*.

Inside those cans are generally too much cereal, as well as meat from sick cattle and sheep. Horses, young and old are also in that can. Unhappy endings for a life of service. I "see" them, milling around an abattoir, terrified by the smell of death, wondering if this is their fate when they are still so young, and tried so hard. I see older horses, heads bowed. Resigned.

Rendering plants produce the "by-products" found in commercial animal food. This is where the pounds send their dead puppies, kittens, dogs and cats – filled with the sodium pentobarbital used for euthanasia. There are dead bodies from vet surgeries, complete with body bags and flea collars, diseased livestock, and all kinds of plastics and wastes. The list continues. All this is boiled up together to make a toxic cocktail for our four-legged companions.

Ethoxyquin, originally a rubber stabilizer, is a synthetic antioxidant found in so-called high quality imported dog and cat food, and reportedly produces an alarming array of health problems. And when it goes back into the rendering vat or slaughterhouse, it enters the companion animal food chain unlisted.

Allergies, eczema, arthritis, cancer, poor immune function, bloat, pancreatitis – I could go on listing all the degenerative diseases and health issues caused by the ingestion of these substances. So please be aware of what it is you are feeding your beloved. Kibble and canned food get a big "no" in our family.

In more recent years we've seen a lot of "pet food" recalls. When you understand what's in them, you can understand why.

My first animal care mentor was Juliette de Bairacli Levy, a woman who studied vet science for four years and gave it up, claiming it didn't promote true healing. Instead, she learnt about animal health mainly from the gypsy people and got a reputation for her herbal cures and natural diet. Thanks to her, my dogs and cats have always enjoyed good health from a healthy, varied, raw diet including fruit and vegetables like bananas, apples, carrots, avocado, spinach, grapes, parsley, celery and so on. She also fed her dogs rolled oats and barley, fresh goat's milk and eggs.

As she points out, the animals in the wild will eat the ripe fruit on the ground, and the partly digested stomach contents of their prey are the first to be consumed.

Animals also don't run around with can openers and cooking pots. We're the only ones who do that. When you cook food, you destroy the all-important enzymes needed for essential assimilation.

In the good old bygone days, people fed their dogs and cats meat, bones and table scraps. Their animal companions thrived. Tinned food and kibble, with its poisonous cocktail of cooked cereals, by-products and preservatives, is what is killing our animals today.

As a vegan concerned with peace on the planet and the suffering of farm and domestic animals, I think it is time we and the animals in our home changed our thinking about a meat-based diet. These animals no longer live in the wild and are under our guardianship. They still have a say in the matter, but by providing them with high quality, nourishing food which meets all their nutritional requirements, we are doing not only them but all the world a service.

This is a quote I found on a vegan web site that sums up my personal views – and shapes my vision for the future.

> *The demand for vegetarian food will increase our production of the right kind of plant foods. We shall cease to breed pigs and other animals for food, thereby ceasing to be responsible for the horror of the slaughterhouses where millions of creatures cry in agony and in vain because of man's selfishness. If such concentration camps for slaughtering continue, can peace ever come to earth? Peace cannot come where peace is not given.*
>
> *– Rukmini Devi Arundale*

Chapter 35:
Considering Vegetarian and Vegan Diets for Dogs, Cats and Humans - a Pathway to Peace and the New Earth

The wolf and the lamb shall feed together, and the lion shall eat straw like the bullock.

Isaiah 65: 25

A search on Google today reveals a growing trend towards a kinder diet for our animal companions. More and more people feel they cannot be involved in the death industries, and want to feed their animal companions meat-free meals. While I personally promote this for peace on the planet, there are problems with people being misinformed or not informed, regarding the dietary needs of their animal friends.

There was the RSPCA-reported case of the animal activist's dog in South Australia, who was so badly malnourished he nearly died. He was fed on bread and peanut butter. Sorry, this is not a healthy diet.

Just like people need certain nutrients to be well, so do our animal companions. While dogs can get away with an omnivorous diet, cats need a bit more thought. The interesting thing about the research done on vegetarian and vegan dogs and cats is that it tends to make them less aggressive. If the diet is done well, it promotes health and well-being. But please note, I said well done and that takes thought and work. Well, it needs this today, in this place and time.

Pioneers in this field are people like Americans Anne Wigmore, Barbara Lynn Peden and James Peden, and the Australian Sandy Anderson. Their recipes, suggestions and products have brought health to animals and peace of mind to their people.

Yes, cats are carnivores, but their dietary and nutritional needs can be met on a vegan diet – with supplements. The supplements are important, especially taurine and L-carnitine. But again, it has to be done very carefully, and it should be monitored to make sure it suits the individual cat. Mature cats might have more problems accepting a radical change of diet, and any changes should be introduced slowly and gradually.

In *Vegetarian Cats and Dogs*, James Peden also takes a philosophic bent and cites the 1940s lioness sensation Little Tyke who made world news for refusing to eat meat.

Exceptionally healthy and exceptionally gentle, Little Tyke grew up on Hidden Valley Ranch, Seattle and grazed with her herbivore friends, including a lamb named Becky who would cuddle up to her at rest time. As they were at first concerned for her health, Little Tyke's people, Georges and Margaret Westbeau, offered $1,000 for someone who could get their beloved big cat to eat meat. But no amount of trickery would entice her to eat meat or even a drop of blood.

Instead she lived on eggs, various grains and milk – and grazed in the field. Little Tyke was an inspiration to millions of Americans and sadly it was during one of her many travelling stints to inspire these humans that she contracted viral pneumonia and died. According to Chinese medicine, pneumonia is stuck grief in the lungs and I've wondered if Little Tyke would have preferred to stay at the farm with her herbivore friends.

Like humans, every animal is unique and the best thing to do, of course, is ask them what they need. You can also ascertain by muscle testing them with different nutrients and foods.

The other thing to remember is body requirements change at different times of life, and different animals at different times may need different supplements. Mature dogs may need extra digestive enzymes, slippery elm or probiotics, for example. Or they may not. Depends on the dog. Or he may need it for a short time. Things like omegas, (rice bran oil or linseed or chia seeds), green powders, anti-inflammatories like turmeric, and antioxidants like goji berries would be other basics to consider daily.

I often like to throw in carob powder for the dogs only, which is up to 8% protein and contains vitamins A, B, B2, B3 and D. It is also high in calcium, phosphorus, potassium and magnesium and contains iron, manganese, barium, copper and nickel. Coconut milk is something else I like to give – not daily, but regularly.

The big thing to remember is that a cat's pH needs to be acid, while dogs, like us, need to be alkaline. Cats who go alkaline might end up with urinary stones. Cats also have a low threshold for magnesium and they have a higher requirement for protein. Dogs who are too acidic can, like us, get arthritis and cancer. Research has shown that cancer cells don't thrive in an alkaline body state, so raw food is a great medicine and preventive.

There are different types of vitamin C. In our house, we give the cats ascorbic acid, which is more acid, while the dogs get sodium ascorbate which is non-acidic. Brewer's or torula yeast is also important to both. When I got some torula yeast powder after some time of not having it, the cats jumped up on the bench, tore the plastic bag it was in, and helped themselves. Until they were back in balance we left a saucer full in their feeding area, and made sure we supplemented all their meals.

For elderly cats who are frail, we'll grow a pot of wheat grass for them to nibble on as their medicine. This is a good idea for people who keep indoor cats.

We also noticed our cat Rhodri helping himself to the parsley in our garden when he was feeling challenged with his kidneys.

Animals know what they need, but it is up to us to provide it for them so they can self-medicate.

Once we planted a chaff bag full of organic garlic, split into individual cloves, out in a paddock. Our goal was to grow garlic that the horses could enjoy if they wanted it. It was still underground when the horses came in, dug it up, and ate it. I'd never seen anything like that, but it showed me how keen they were to get that particular nutrition. A good way of supplementing outdoor animals like horses, geese, sheep, goats and cows is to have a covered feed trailer with different supplements in it in trays. A friend of mine has one of these for his cattle which he moves around as he moves them. When the cattle see him coming with it, they all bustle around it, taking the supplements they need, in the quantities they need. He just leaves it in the paddock and refills the trays as needed.

We've done a similar thing with our horses, leaving them out trays of kelp powder, garlic, minerals, and selenium licks. Australian soils are notoriously deficient in iodine and selenium. Sometimes I'll put a dropper full of iodine in the water troughs to correct imbalances, reduce worm loads and improve health. Silver colloid in the water also helps with internal health, as do garlic and apple cider vinegar. The horses always tell me what they need. And you can tell by observing how they take to the supplements. When I first put garlic and apple cider vinegar in the water, the horses gobbled it down. And once they were more balanced internally, they needed less of it.

Most of the time, however, I prefer to provide them with what they need and allow them to self-select.

It's important to do your research for your animal friends so that you can provide well for them. And it's also important to be considerate to the needs of your animal friends and don't impose your thoughts and values on them.

It is kinder to explain your thoughts regarding handling the dead flesh of other animals, and the suffering it causes those animals. Ask your companions how they feel about it. Perhaps they are ready to make the switch. Perhaps they've been waiting for you to get it. Perhaps they need easing into it. Perhaps they are in the home of an enlightened soul, because they too are enlightened souls.

Perhaps they will tolerate, at this time, *some* vegan and vegetarian meals, supplementing organic raw meat, bones and chicken wings. Juliette de Bairacli-Levy also encouraged a fast day a week to give the digestion a rest. She suggested a meal of goat's milk and honey and maybe some slippery elm powder on these days. You could use hemp milk or coconut milk. She also suggests a meat-free day of cottage cheese, vegetables and fruit for example. Or rolled oats and honey – if that suited your dog.

So consider giving your dog a fast day and a couple of meat-free days to begin with.

Right now, both the animals and humans are subject to "energy shifts" or "ascension symptoms'. In a nutshell, we are changing our dense bodies for lighter ones. Our food requirements are changing. My own dogs are eating a lot more fruit and vegetables, I've noticed, and my cats have become even healthier with more vegetables and supplements.

And I think, for sensitive people, this is how it will be in the years to come. As our vibration increases, our dietary needs will change and evolve to a more compassionate way of eating. Eventually we won't need food to sustain our light bodies, and then we will have a world without predators.

Personally I have gone from vegetarian to vegan, to vegan raw food and smoothies. Our whole family enjoys the raw food recipes, including the dogs. It's a lighter way of eating, suiting our enhanced vibration.

It was interesting to me to hear noted paranormal author Dolores Cannon echo my thoughts that this diet of smoothies, juices and raw food, is one of the marks of moving into the New Earth of the 2012 prophecy. She said people needed to drop the heavy meats from their diets. I was thrilled when she said that! Dolores also said that eventually we would only need liquids and then no food as we ascended into lighter bodies.

If you can follow the Golden Age prophecy of the indigenous people – that we are making quantum leaps into what Dr. Alberto Villoldo calls *homo luminous*, or what I call human angels – you can see we are becoming more spiritually evolved, and so are our animal companions. And that in the future, anything is possible. I for one, envision a planet in sacred harmony where the idea of a food chain has been replaced with the idea of community and family. Where there is no longer fear from the hunt; where animals can live in herds as family.

One indigenous seer, a Native American woman elder called No Eyes, written about in *Phoenix Rising* by Mary Summer Rain, saw a future where the buffalo grazed together as family – young and old. I believe this is feasible if you change your thinking from what is probable, to what is possible. I do this on a daily basis.

You have to remember that the future is going to be very different, as we all become lighter, less dense beings.

There are a lot of arguments around about food, and having had an interest in nutrition for the last 30-odd years, I've heard most of them. Just when we think we've got it right, science comes along to tell us we're wrong again. Wheat, once a staple, now is a leading cause of allergies. Chocolate, once a treat, is now a super food. Well, cacao beans are. But not for animals. Until proven otherwise, chocolate is toxic for dogs, and any treats should be made with carob powder, which is highly nutritious and beneficial.

Nutrition can be very confusing, and everyone has different thoughts about what's good for you. Many of the ideas being bandied about now are circulated by the multi-nationals who just want to make money. We tell ourselves we know everything about nutrition and food, and yet both humans and our dogs and cats are succumbing to degenerative and other diseases at the rate of knots. Hmn.

So what is the answer?

For a start, nourishing food is the least processed you can find, food that doesn't glow in the dark, or come in tins and packets. Nourishing food comes from the organic garden mostly and a healthy variety is a key. Raw food provides the necessary enzymes for good health.

Second, if you understand that thoughts are things, then you can project whatever you want into the world and it becomes truth – a self-fulfilling prophecy. So instead of seeking out arguments and problems against a cruelty-free world where carnivores become plant-eating, perhaps we could all join together to visualise and manifest a world where our animal friends live healthfully and in harmony, without killing each other for nourishment. To quote the Bible, "The wolf also shall dwell with the lamb, and the leopard shall lie down with the kid; and the calf and the young lion and the fatling together." (Isaiah 11: 6)

We saw this with Little Tyke and Becky the lamb. And there are other stories where the animals are showing us the way and helping us use our powerful imaginations to dream in a better world.

There was a story from Best Friends Animal Society and the World Society for the Protection of Animals (WSPA,) with photos of a wolf who had been caught and was living in starving, dirty conditions as part of a two bit private zoo in Albania. A pathetic looking donkey had been thrown into the cage with the wolf to feed him. Instead, the wolf bonded with the donkey, grateful for companionship. Both are herd animals and this need for friendship, overran the so-called "instinct" to hunt and kill.

The situation of the wolf and the donkey befriending each other (and indeed the wolf hid behind the donkey and would pine when the donkey was let out to graze), attracted international interest from rescue groups around the world. Last I heard, the wolf was released into the forest, but the donkey remained.

So here we have a predator living with prey, as friends, and a vegetarian lioness. Surely this is a glimpse at what can happen when the conditions are right for social and spiritual change. To me, this is Great Spirit's way of showing us, through the animals, the kind of Eden, or Heaven, we can have here on Earth. If we want this Heaven, we need to start thinking about it now, and help it happen with our thoughts and actions.

To answer the vegan/vegetarian cat and dog diet question. In the here and now, perhaps not everyone can provide their animals this sort of diet in a healthy way – simply because perhaps not everyone is ready to. Some dogs really do need a bone, and some cats really need their meat to meet their dietary requirements.

But lots and lots of animals are definitely thriving on vegan and vegetarian diets, and many more are heading in that direction. The numbers grow daily. Further, because of the work of pioneers like the James Peden, Anne Wigmore, Sandy Anderson, and others of the raw food and vegan movement today, there are now food products and supplements to make the switch easier. This is a growing industry, and the way of the future.

I fully believe that from now on we will see a growth in this area until we finally reach a quantum leap into sacred harmony on the planet. What used to be weird and unnatural, will become the norm, and the world's food will become plant based for all species.

Further, I believe we can manifest miracles, and in the future, could be able to provide nourishing meals by the power of thought alone. And further still, we will rise to a level of vibration where we won't need food at all. After all, angels don't need food, so why should human angels?

So lets begin by working together on the vision of a cruelty free world where all animals live on a plant-based diet. Envision it in, and take steps towards it by introducing a balanced and healthy fresh, raw food diet for our companion animals today.

Taking Steps Toward A Healthy, Kinder Eating Plan For Domestic Animals

Any diet changes for yourself or your animal companions need to be done with care.

The first step is to stop feeding commercial canned and dried food. This will immediately improve the health of your beloveds.

Secondly, increase raw vegetable pulp and juice, and seek out organic meat, bones, chicken wings or fish fillets (no bones). Serve this raw and add yoghurt or cottage cheese. Dribble some rice bran oil, add yeast powder for vitamin B, and some vitamin C for dogs and you have a pretty good basic meal. There are supplements I would add like anti oxidants, green powder like wheat grass or barley grass, vitamin E, colloidal minerals and garlic tablets or Juliette de Bairacli Levy's Herbal Compound tablets. These keep the immune system well boosted and worms at bay.

Think about shifting the balance of the meal so that the meat is more a condiment than a major component. Then, once or twice a week, leave out the meat all together and serve meals of eggs, table leftovers, fruit, vegetables and cottage cheese. I'll often just make a huge batch of whatever we're having, and share it with the dogs, so its not "leftovers", it's their meal as much as it ours. This includes salads with hummus, and fruit salads with finely pulped seeds and nuts. My dogs relish it all and are vital and glowing. My 14-year-old dog has as much vitality as the three year olds, playing ball with as much vigour.

I also give my dogs and cats raw rolled oats with coconut milk, especially in winter when it's cold. You do need to be very careful of grains for some dogs, as they can be sensitive to them. In particular, I wouldn't feed grains to dogs prone to pancreatitis, arthritis, or allergies. Herbs like Uva ursi (Bearberry), and digestive enzymes can support the pancreas.

Thanks to the multi-nationals' practise of overfeeding cereals, we now have health problems and weaknesses in our animal friends.

Some people feed their animals rice with vegetables, legumes and sprouts. Make sure the enzymes are there for proper digestion and assimilation. They are certainly in the sprouts.

You can then increase the number of vegetarian and vegan meals per week, according to your dog's particular ability, and supplement with legumes like lentils. Watch their stools and note their health. My cats love lentils and my previous cat family adored pumpkin and yeast extract spread as part of their varied diet. Avocado is a food great for cats and dogs alike. Buckwheat is also good on occasions.

Dogs can't do well on chocolate, potato, onion, or more than a few raisins. Many have allergies to wheat, corn, soy, beef or dairy.

Good foods include coconut milk, avocado, dulse, apples, carrots, celery, beetroot, spinach, sweet potato,and parsley. There is a whole range of foods out there which support health, and you can use a trial and error system to work out what suits your animals. Some dogs thrive on raw cabbage and others on carrots and grapes. Our own dogs get whole carrots, apples, berries, and bananas to munch on as snacks.

I like to supplement with a good antioxidant, multi vitamin-mineral, (with B 12) or multi vitamin and colloidal minerals, garlic, omegas (from freshly ground linseed, chia or hemp seeds) and anti inflammatory (turmeric). Taurine and carnitine are very important for the vegan/vegetarian animal.

Without it you may see heart and eyesight problems.

Vitamin C is also important in times of stress, because this is when animals use more of it.

My mature dogs get Coenzyme Q10, Vitamin E, probiotics, enzymes.

Always, always, always, honour your animal. They will tell you if they cannot tolerate certain foods and if they repeatedly refuse something, listen to them. Alternatively, if you are switching from toxic foods which their bodies are addicted to, to fresh live foods, then you might try eating it first, to show them the way.

Our Blue Heeler Raffi was staying with us at a friend's place when he was making personal appearances at Finding Joy screenings. When our friend fed him some of her dog's dried kibble, he pulled a face and refused it. He did, however, enjoy the rolled oats she finally served him instead. It changed her way of thinking about animal diet.

So do your research and find the highest quality organic vegan foods for yourself and your animal family. Check out your vegan food products, but make sure you understand the needs and requirement of your animals, and that the diet you have them on covers everything they need. Not all companies will have the animals' best interests at heart, and not all will have done the required research. Ask yourself, if this is a high vibration food which is suitable for your animal?

The journey to feed your animals a high vibration diet will open doors for your own health as well. Many people feed their animal companions better than themselves. And the animals need you to experience vital health as well.

Many vets today don't understand nutrition, and the importance of feeding high vibration, living food which serves and nourishes cells. At Expos, I've been appalled at how many people have come to me with questions about their dog's skin problems and they haven't made the connection between "the best food on the market which was recommended by the vet" and the dog's skin. It has a lot to do with it. Animals, like people, need fresh food and a varied diet.

When I spoke to the holistic vets in Australia I most admire, the general consensus was that the multi-nationals have practically made the animals vegetarian with their tinned foods, which have very little meat in them. And this is killing them.

However, over thirty years experience of feeding dogs a mostly vegetarian diet with very little meat, I have to say that, despite their varied breeding and backgrounds, they have been shiny, glossy and practically disease free. The difference is that I feed mine food that nourishes and supports them, and tins do not. I also don't feed an imbalance of cereals. And there's certainly nothing toxic in fresh organic produce.

I'm not a biochemist but I would probably say it's the things in the tin which are killing the animals, like an imbalance of too much grain, the dreaded by-products and preservatives, and meat from diseased animals. All round it is dead food, not designed to support vital health. Let's face it. If you open the can and think, "This is gross", you're probably right.

I believe we can have true peace without the exploitation of animals when people have the heart, desire and awareness to make the shift into vegetarian and vegan living. And that time is coming now. I'm grateful to the people who have paved the way and made this possible for us all.

Finally, another word on thoughts. If we get stuck in the mindset that this cannot be so, then it won't be. Following the universal Law of Attraction, if you set the intention to raise your household's vibration around food, you will see miracles.

Animals, like people, are under the spell of the collective unconscious. However if we can shift consciousness, we can change the way food is assimilated and used by the body.

Little Tyke showed us the way. Here was a cat carnivore who refused meat. Her diet should have caused her to have symptoms of nutritional deficiencies. But it didn't. Why? Further, around the same time in India, (1936) lived another vegetarian lioness who refused meat in favour of rice and milk. Her human friend was a swami, Krishnananda. The story was recalled by Paramahansa Yogananda in his illuminating book *Autobiography of a Yogi*. And James Peden also mentions this in *Vegetarian Cats and Dogs*.

I fully believe these animals were enlightened souls with a command of the body that we dream about. They made up their minds to be so, and so they were.

A lesson from animals to be sure.

Recipes

Vegan Live Raw Food Recipes for Dogs

Ani Phyo is currently our favourite raw food recipe maker. In her book *Ani's Raw Food Kitchen*, I was delighted to find some vegan raw food recipes for her dog Kanga, a Rhodesian Ridgeback who has returned to health on this diet after Ani adopted her when she was very sick, nothing but skin and bone and very depressed.

Ani brought her back to stunning health with a vegan living foods diet in two months. She became vibrant and beautiful.

Inspired, we began experimenting with recipes for the dogs. The cats gave the nut pates a big thumbs down, but the dogs loved them. The cats didn't like the raw garlic so we are still experimenting for them.

Our base for feeding the cats is finely pulped raw veggies with lentils. They often have vegetarian meals of raw eggs, goat's milk and cottage cheese.

I'm a "vibrational" cook so I don't normally measure, and naturally we use a lot more ingredients for eight dogs. But have a play with the basic recipe and see how your dog benefits.

Basic Ballyoncree Nut Pate

1 cup of nuts – almonds, cashews, Brazil nuts, pecans or walnuts.

1 cup of sunflower or pumpkin seeds

½ cup linseed

2 cloves garlic

a tablespoon of turmeric (an anti-inflammatory)

2 – 3 cups of assorted vegetables – carrots, spinach, celery, fat hen – whatever is growing wild or in the garden.

To this we would add a tablespoon of tahini or hummus, or olive oil, or sometimes coconut milk.

And we would supplement with a green powder, a teaspoon of vitamin C (depending on the size of your dog), and some yeast powder.

Everything is thrown in a food processor and served raw.

The eight Ballyoncree dogs give this meal a huge thumbs up. It is nutritionally dense and fills them up, as well as tasting delicious.

Like Ani, we use up all our vegetable leftovers, stalks and ends to make the dog food, reducing our compost and providing fibre for the dogs. Edible weeds like fat hen and easy-to-grow veggies like spinach all go into the dog and cat food mix. The good thing about it is that it is fresh and organic.

We buy our nuts in bulk and make different vegan "cheezes" and pates with vegetables and herbs. Have fun experimenting with this food for yourself and your furry companion.

To make this sort of food, it is helpful to have a food processor and a dehydrator. Inspired again by Ani, we use sweet potatoes dried in the dehydrator to help keep the dog's teeth clean.

Here's another idea to try.

Lentils (cooked)
Pumpkin (grated or lightly steamed)
Pulped raw greens
Garlic
Spirulina powder
Turmeric
You can add yoghurt, cottage cheese and/or a raw egg for variety.

Enjoy being a creative and healthy food preparer for your beloveds! Plus your dog's special daily supplements!

Chapter 36:
Diet for Horses

As with other animals, horses do best on a natural diet. They are browsers, not grazers, and again commercial food is dubious for them as well. When my old pony needed a food to keep the weight on, I was shocked to find some brands of prepared feeds had meat meal in them. Yuck. There was another brand that was full of crushed up biscuits – obviously factory leftovers. Not great for us or our equine companions.

Keep it simple and raw.

According to de Bairacli Levy, horses do very well on barley. And there are a lot of wonderful herbal supplements you can give them like rosehip tea for their adrenals and hooves.

If you have land, consider growing herbal hedgerows as natural medicine for horses.

Hay is the most natural fodder, providing the all important roughage which horses need an abundance of. So any horse diet would have chaff and hay as a basic first step. And a good mineral block to balance deficiencies in local soils.

On top of that, you can research what is right for your particular horse. Most of my horses graze naturally, but for my "special needs" horses, I like to add seaweed meal, rosehip tea, rice bran oil, apple cider vinegar, garlic and coarse grain sea salt. And then it depends on the individual horse. Barley, French White Millet and Black Sunflower Seeds are also recommended. Keep it natural and do your research. I'd also add a tablespoon or so of psyllium seeds once or twice a week – especially if the horse is fed on sand. Sand in the gut can cause sand colic.

I don't like pellets or processed food, but teeth-challenged, elderly horses do very well on extruded feeds with chaff. We wet this down well to make a mash and feed two or three times a day, depending on the need. My experience has been that my mature horses who begin to have weight problems due to their teeth, have thrived on this. Sebastian, as I said, was 44 when he passed away, and he'd been on this diet for a decade.

Having said that, until the age of about 33 or 34, Sebastian did very well on boiled barley and boiled linseed or steam rolled barley, all wet down with herbs, supplements, water and chaff for a good, nutrient-filled mash. Some mature horses might need a probiotic and Australian horses definitely need an easily assimilated mineral mix because of our depleted soils. A good diet suited to your particular horse is vital for health and longevity – and all horses are different.

Bread and cardboard are both pretty unnatural: cardboard being a non-food and bread being toxic in its commercial, refined form. Apparently people have been known to feed horses cardboard in drought times, something I would never have believed until I read about it.

A lot of people feed bread that's left over from bakeries as a cheap source of horse food. I would never do this. It can swell in the gut causing problems, and cheap, white bread is a health hazard in itself, filled with chemicals and refined out of any goodness.

Chapter 37:
Age, Diet and Our Thoughts

Have you ever noticed how our society is obsessed with age, death and illness. Just because one is mature, doesn't mean one has to be struck down with any crippling diseases. And the best way we can prevent age in our animals and in ourselves is with better, more youthful thinking.

The normal age for a dog used to be 30 to 50 years old. But with our breeding, processed foods and thoughts, we've shortened their life span pathetically and made it unpleasant with degenerative diseases.

The oldest recorded living dog was Bluey, an Australian cattle dog who died in 1939 at 29 years and five months. Another Australian cattle dog died in 1984, reportedly at the age of 32 years and three days – but there wasn't an official entry.

In 2008, the contender for the title of oldest dog was Britain's Bella, a rescued Labrador who was 29 and only died in September 2008, from a heart attack.

The interesting thing about Bella is how she demonstrated secret animal business to perfection with her person Mr Richardson. Bella became ill and couldn't walk. So it was thought her last days had arrived and an appointment with the vet was made, and a hole was dug. But Mr Richardson says he couldn't sleep for thinking about Bella (actually Bella was communicating with him!) The next morning he'd made up his mind to let Bella die naturally in her sleep. He cancelled the vet and when he was filling in the hole, he turned around to find Bella standing behind him, watching him. I can feel her satisfaction with that turn of events!

Other reported dogs were a rescued Border Collie in Britain called Bramble who was 27 in 2002 and lived on a vegan diet of organic vegetables, rice and lentils. She was reportedly "remarkably free of health problems", and went swimming and walking. Another long-lived vegetarian dog is Tykie, a 23-year-old terrier mix who walks daily with her family members, and was only plagued by a little deafness.

And then there's Jerry, a cattle dog mix who lived in NSW with his Aboriginal people living on a diet of kangaroo, emu and table scraps at the ripe old age of 26, and heading into 27 in 2004. And also there was a 28-year-old Beagle called Butch in Virginia, USA around the same time.

I've personally had a pony of 44 who was spry and happy, and a goat who lived till she was 21 which the vet couldn't believe because "goats don't live that long".

As soon as we start thinking of our animals and ourselves as old, so they become. The Law of Attraction works with everything, not just our dreams and desires.

When Andrew and I attended the Harmonic Convergence in Glastonbury England in 1987, it dealt with the themes of physical immortality. The issues of youthing instead of aging are even more relevant today but what I picked up on then was the fact that when people were young and vital in their thinking and living, their animals lived longer. And this makes sense. When we are devoured by negative thinking or unresolved issues, we tend to create an energy field of ill health, which aging falls into. When we are vital, healthy and happy, so are our animals. Also, if someone is constantly telling you that you are old, it's hard to keep believing you are not.

I was staying with some people in the city once and they had a small dog they adored. She was spry and bossy and quick to tell me that she 'owned the place', and how she "took care of everything." That dog had a job to do and was very fulfilled and happy. Her person's husband however, told me over and over and over how old she was. He called her 'old girl" and was obsessed with her age. I can tell you she hated it and I could see how difficult it was for her to keep putting up a psychic barrier of protection against his thoughts and words. I wondered if he was simply projecting his own fears of aging onto her, or perhaps his fears of loss.

So let's keep affirming that both we and our animal family are young and vital and that as we mature, we can continue being youthful, active and spry.

Next time you meet an animal, instead of asking his person how old is he? Ask how young is he? Banish "old" from your mindset and everyone benefits.

Try This

Fred Lehrman was speaking at the Glastonbury Harmonic Convergence, and said, "I'd like you to try this. Please meditate on the worst disease you can possibly imagine every day for 20 minutes for two weeks." There was an uncomfortable groan in the packed town hall. Fred let it sink in.

"So," he continued, "if thought and manifestation works for us to become ill, why can't we use it to become well and vital? Why can't you devote 20 minutes of your day to thinking yourself well, happy and vitally alive?"

Good point. This is something I ask my students to consider, and if they can't do it for themselves – at least do it for their animal family who don't need to suffer just because we humans don't get the Law of Attraction and the power of our thoughts.

Help for Older Animals

Life is tough for an old homeless dog and while they may have many years ahead of them in the right hands, they often aren't given the chance. Our dog Dusty is a case in point. We took him in because we heard no other rescue outfit would – because he was old. He wasn't only old, he'd been abused and wore the scars and cost us personally thousands of dollars we didn't have at the time in vet bills. But we were committed. And today he is happy, healthy, rejuvenating and part of the family. And we adore him. He has become Andrew's special dog.

Another old dog was responsible for Andrew and I creating a forever home for the animals we came across. Pooh was called Pooh, not after a cuddly bear, but because he stank.

He lived across the road, and slept under the house in the dirt. He was happy enough and we didn't really notice him, until the neighbours moved from across the road into the house next to us. They left Pooh at the old house, because he was too dirty and smelly to be in the new one.

Pooh was often at the door of the new house, looking pathetic and that's when he came onto my radar. Up close I could see he had a terrible skin infection that had created coat loss over half of his back. He was also suffering badly from arthritis.

My heart went out to Pooh and I immediately understood where his health problems had come from. This was confirmed when the neighbours said his skin problem had started "around the time they moved."

I was furious, and immediately went into action. I knew Pooh could have a happy life. My neighbour on the other side was also concerned and we stole over to the empty house to give Pooh blankets and home made dog biscuits.

When Pooh's person told us he needed a new home, we found one immediately. Pooh was to be relocated onto a home on 15 acres to keep another older dog company. My neighbour and I were very pleased with ourselves. Pooh would be living in paradise. Why then, was he crying when I left him?

It tugged at my heart, but his new person assured me Pooh would be fine.

Why did I believe her, over him?

I made one terrible, terrible mistake and it took me a long time to get over it. It shaped my views on rehoming forever more.

From my extensive background in natural therapies, I understood that Pooh's health problems came from stress, neglect and poor diet. I only saw a healed Pooh. But his new people took him to the vet and the vet euthanased him. When Sonya rang to tell me he was dead, I was beside myself.

"The vet said Pooh was too hard, he had too many things wrong with him," Sonya said apologetically.

"Natural therapies could have fixed him," I said. I was heartbroken. I blamed myself. And Pooh's cries haunted me. He had known. He had come to me for help, and I had failed him.

The next dog I saw in a condition like Pooh's was Louie. I didn't make the same mistake. It took me less than a month to have him itch free, shiny, glossy and looking magnificent. Thanks to a healthy diet. And a vet who understood that.

Often the first question an unenlightened vet will ask is – how old is he and then make assumptions on that age, and speak them out loud in front of the animal.

Rebecca, a horse healer, and a student and good friend of mine, had this experience recently with her 14-year-old German Shepherd, Seamus. Normally healthy and vital, he became ill suddenly after a cold snap, and Rebecca and her husband whisked him off to the vet. After asking her Seamus's age and finding his high temperature, the vet proceeded to insist that the dog had cancer – because it was common with dogs of his breed at that age. Further he wanted to take out Seamus's spleen as soon as possible, because it was enlarged.

Rebecca kept telling Seamus not to listen. She was worried Seamus would take on board what the vet was saying. And she "knew" her dog didn't have cancer. All the same it was hard to make decisions against the voice of authority.

Rebecca rang me from the vet surgery, and when I tuned into Seamus, I found a vital dog who was more terrified of the vet than any illness. He told me he would *"die if I stay in hospital"*. I told Rebecca she needed to consider Seamus's thoughts, and Andrew piped in that she needed to trust her own intuition.

All this she had to balance against a vet who told her she was irresponsible if she took her dog home and he would surely die there.

" I kept telling Seamus not to listen to him", she said. "But when the vet showed me X-rays, Seamus insisted on looking at them too. He was standing by my side. The vet didn't notice, and kept telling me he was sure it was cancer.

"Instinct, or maybe Seamus himself, told me to take him home, and I did. Seamus was so relieved, and I'm sure that played a big part of his healing.

"Seamus proved the vet wrong by responding really quickly to a protocol of supplements. He is still alive, healthy and very grateful that he didn't have to stay the night in hospital!"

"And he didn't have cancer."

I had a similar story with my German Shepherd Twylah who I had taken to a vet for acupuncture. She was a 13-year-young lady at that time, still spry and happy but on that day she had a high temperature.

"This is a very sick dog," said the vet, a lovely young man who didn't know me or Twylah. " She'll have to stay in for a couple of days and have tests."

From looking perky when she went in to the vet, Twylah now looked devastated. I thought quickly. Twylah was our omega dog in the pack. She was sweet and gentle and never left our sides. It would make her worse if she stayed. I sent her a silent question mark. "*Home,*" she said.

I allowed the vet a blood test and escaped with Twylah to the car where I immediately rang a healer friend of mine, Susan Scott. The blood tests came back showing she was anaemic which Susan found very helpful. The vet said Twylah would surely have spleen cancer. Because I am a healer, I was strongly convinced I could help Twylah myself and took her home. I kept telling her that she would be all right and that Susan's stuff would make her better.

Twylah improved drastically, and when she did finally pass two years later, it wasn't from cancer.

Every animal is an individual, and just because they are a certain age, doesn't mean they have to be ill, dying or suffering a disease that "all animals get at that age."

The important thing is to listen to your animal.

Chapter 38:
More on Health and Healing

The Emotional Causation of Illness

Can you imagine what it must be like living in a society where no one understands a single thing you say? Animals, like people, need to be heard and understood, and sometimes all it takes to resolve a behavioural or emotional problem is someone taking the time to listen.

When they've finished speaking about what they need to discuss, I'll feel a tension released, mirrored in my own body. Their people will report they know when I've had a session with their beloved, because "he's a different dog!"

Empaths (people who can sense another's feelings) have an easier time with detecting the disturbances in the body of their furry brothers and sisters than people who are more visual or verbal. When you merge with another's energy field and turn your attention to your body, you can feel what is going on for them. It's important that you know your body well and that you can be clear and clean. It's important you don't project. And it's vital to understand the emotional aspect of healing.

I mentioned before that our Kelpie Suki created a mass on her throat, which disappeared after she got the outings she desperately wanted. *"You take us out in the car, but we don't really get out,"* she said. So I made a special effort to take her to outdoor dog-friendly cafes and for walks around the block whenever I went to town. I figured if this was her last request, it was worth the extra time. Suki thrived. She loved meeting new people and dogs, having new experiences and smelling new smells. And of course, it was her suggestion that I take all the dogs on a holiday and film it. At first I worried I was spending a lot of time organising the trip, and Andrew worried Suki wouldn't make it long enough to go on the trip. But as I said before, a week before the holiday the mass completely disappeared, and Suki lived on for another two amazing years.

A sheep in the USA had pneumonia. She was lying down in the barn, unable to stand. Her person was very worried about her and contacted me. When I tuned in, the sheep wanted to be a mother. This was her life's purpose. And her baby had been taken away.

I asked if the sheep's lamb was still on the property. But he wasn't. I felt the sheep's sadness. She was listening to my thoughts as I emailed her person.

Suddenly I had a brain wave – from me or her I don't know. But I suggested that there must be other lambs on the farm. There was.

Apparently, this sheep saw the lambs being herded into the door of the barn where she lay at death's door in the straw, and she struggled to her feet. Her eyes were filled with new purpose. She had a job and fulfilled her maternal urges.

Today she is the lamb nanny on that farm, and is happy, strong, and fulfilled.

Pneumonia showed up again in a rescue dog in the USA, who'd been left for dead by her family. As they drove off down the drive with the car loaded with their personal possessions, the husband shot the dog with a rifle out the car window.

Neighbours saw what happened and the dog was saved. But she wasn't responding to the best medical care available. When I tuned in to her, I learnt that she didn't understand what love and compassion was. She'd never experienced it. And she needed to, in order to live. I asked the rescue workers to go in to the vet hospital where she was, and to give the dog physical demonstrations of love – physical affection and tons of it.

She responded, and lived.

Soul Bonds And Emotional Healing

I've mentioned before that sometimes animals find themselves in homes which no longer work for them or serve their purposes. Many give up on the people they are trying to teach or give love to, and need to move on. Usually they allow themselves to get lost, and then found by someone else.

One example of this was a strict woman with two dogs who never let them in the house. They were for breeding purposes only. The dogs ran off and when I was called to psychically track them, the dogs had found themselves a new home and showed me themselves happily creating havoc on a double bed.

"We're happy here," they told me. *"We are loved."*

Now this is not to say that all lost animals are looking for new homes. Far from it. But some may be.

The Story of Sadie

Sometimes though, the lessons come through healing situations which ultimately shift the world and heal bodies. In any situation, take the high road, and let Spirit help the situations resolve for the highest good of all concerned.

Lori, one of my students, had fallen in love with Sadie, an older dog who she cared for on occasions. When I met Lori, she was torn to shreds because she didn't believe Sadie was happy or getting the right kind of care in her own person's home. As the carer and Lori had fallen out over Sadie, Lori felt even more distanced from this soul companion.

Sadie, I could see, was also working on Lori in the subtle way of the animals. Her person really didn't have time for her, and she loved Lori. There were lessons here, and even though I couldn't read the outcome of this particular case and it seemed hopeless, I counselled Lori to take the high road and trust in Spirit.

This meant that I suggested Lori work on the situation in the etheric, leaving the way for events to unfold for the highest good of all concerned, but at the same time to hold positive thoughts that she and Sadie would be reunited.

Lori tuned into Sadie constantly, telling her she loved her and affirming that the old contracts between Lori and Sadie's person were resolved for the highest good of all concerned. When she felt clear of emotions, she emailed the other woman saying it would be her privilege to care for Sadie in her old age.

The return email was pleasant, and included an invitation to visit Sadie at any time. Lori continued to tell Sadie she loved her, and tried to be calm and positive even though she knew in her heart and gut that Sadie needed her.

Two months later she received an email asking if she would like to adopt Sadie, as she had developed an anxiety order from being left alone and was too hard to look after with her allergies and old age. Her skin was a mess.

Lori was over the moon, and Sadie recovered quickly in the hands of someone who could give her true love, a nourishing diet, supplements, and acupuncture for her sore back and legs. When we last spoke, Lori excitedly reported that Sadie's eyes were clearing of their cataracts, her hearing was improving, and she was enjoying her morning walks. Sadie celebrated her 14th birthday younger than she had been for a long time.

Holding Onto The Past

Many people have rescued dogs who have suffered trauma which makes them behave a certain way. I have had many clients want to know exactly what this trauma was. Some animals tell me they don't want to relive this trauma – it's in the past. So I don't pry. As a shamanic healer, I take their point. It's not the story, the old baggage we want to engage with. Why reopen a wound just for someone's curiosity? When I get a "no", I definitely don't pry.

People have a habit of making their own story an on-going wound that they live by. It directs their actions and habits. "I was abandoned." "I was abused." "I was unwanted." It defines them and traps them in a holding pattern, so they can't move forward in life.

There's a saying I love to share, and I even wrote a song about it and used it in our film Finding Joy. "There are never any victims, there are only volunteers." When we really realise that we are volunteers in this life, we can make up new stories which empower and embolden us.

And so too can our animals.

In fact, I have counselled many animals to do just that. "Create your own reality" is a catchphrase for them, just as it is for us.

Praying For and Sending Energy to an Animal Who is Ill

With energy healing, always ask permission before you do anything. Humans, and particularly many energy workers, sometimes jump in and send energy to animals and people without asking permission or knowing what the result might be. Some cancers, for example, love energy and feed on it, growing instead of shrinking.

Prayers, however, allow for healing energy to work as it will. I personally work with lineages of medicine people who live outside of time and these days I simply ask them to do what is needed for the highest good of all concerned. "Thank you, thank you, thank you for doing whatever is needed to be done for Rex, for the highest good of all concerned." Then I trust that it will be done. I've had terrific responses from clients with whom I have worked with their animals in this way.

This is fifth dimensional healing – seeing the animal as already healed.

Other Modalities I Love to Use

There are so many modalities to learn at the moment I can only encourage you to find the ones which stir your heart. Because I have an interest in healing, but never wanted to be a healer I understand the rudiments in many different modalities. I'm glad I have these skills, and they have stood the animals of Ballyoncree and my clients' animals in very good stead.

My main tools are nutrition, naturopathy, herbalism, homoeopathy, aromatherapy, including Raindrop Technique, shiatsu (acupressure), natural horsemanship, TTEAM, massage, crystals, Emotional Freedom Technique, Reiki, Theta healing, and Shamanic Healing. I also dowse, and use many supplements.

Dowsing and muscle testing for the right modality is especially important at this time, as animals are very sensitive right now and may resist healing or even go backwards if the wrong modality or remedy is used.

Even natural remedies can become toxic if they are used the wrong way or in conjunction with other things which may cause a reaction. Don't give your animals a toxic cocktail. Ask them and their bodies first.

Some of my best healing has been done through simply helping an animal release their fears or concerns through listening to them.

Ascension Symptoms

In these changing times, we're hearing a lot about Ascension symptoms. These have to do with the shifting of our DNA and cellular structures, helping us move into the higher frequencies of higher dimensions, and become the fully realised human angel we are becoming.

Sometimes we might get strange flu-like symptoms, without the flu. We might get hot flushes, dizziness, panic attacks, bloating. It might be like menopausal symptoms, because we are going through a change. We are awakening to our divinity.

Animals also are sensitive to these energies, and might behave strangely with each energy shift. These energy shifts are often at strong full moons or the equinox or solstice – again times of great importance to the ancients who knew the power and understood the aliveness of the planet we inhabit. So an animal might resist healing or look as if he is going backwards, before he goes forwards to renewed health. Some animals may even look as if they are dying. And then suddenly they are not.

Our Great Dane cross Willow for example, had seizures around powerful energy shifts, like the winter solstice and the spring equinox. But she hasn't had any since and she is healthier and more vital than she has been for a couple of years. She is youthing!

Ascension shifts may also make animals more sensitive to chemicals and some natural products and supplements. Always check with your animal's body to what they need.

It appears we are going through a time where "less is more". Animals who may be evolving might have less dense bodies and therefore only need the higher energetic forms of healing to help them shift into health. But it takes an experienced practitioner, dowser or muscle tester to determine which animal this is.

I certainly would not recommend anyone ignore any symptom an animal is having. Many animals today are having real reactions to the toxins in our environment, and the solution is not to ignore them or casually say, "It's just an ascension shift." These things are poisonous to our dogs and cats, especially when the animals have been fed a commercial diet of junk food and therefore have compromised immune systems.

It really is time for a complete overhaul of the way people live. Animals and people are reaching a tipping point where they just can't cope with the household poisons we use every single day, the poisons in our food, the chemicals in our water, and so on. Unless we make a radical change now for the sake of ourselves, our Mother Earth, and our beloved animal companions, we are looking at disastrous results. Actually, I would say we already are – and we need to change immediately. So go the extra mile, and find the environmentally sensitive products.

The Hazards of Chemicals

This is a huge subject and one I can't do complete justice to here. But I do want to alert people to some basic thoughts.

If a dog wash screams "Poison", "Do Not Get On Skin", or any other nasty, don't use it on your dog.

Flea washes and mange washes are highly toxic and there are alternatives like neem oil and essential oils. I throw some drops of essential oils like rosemary or lemon into the neem oil. This keeps my dog's skin healthy and has made really nasty cases of mange disappear quickly.

I use herbs and homeopathy for fleas, ticks, heartworm, worms and vaccines. There's a natural remedy for most things and they have the added benefit of promoting health and not having side effects.

The vaccine issue is a contentious one. Personally I think conventional vaccines are given too young and too often. My experience is that homeopathy is just as effective, without the side effects. If you must vaccinate, consider dosing with vitamin C prior to the vaccination and giving homeopathic Thuja afterwards. This helps to counter the side effects which can be deadly.

I'll never forget when Reka had the early stages of distemper, the next-door neighbour came over with his dog. Reka was vital then and you wouldn't have known she was sick – except I was trained as a health practitioner, and knew. I warned our neighbour and asked him to take his collie back home with him because Reka had distemper. He went pale and took his dog straight to the vet for a vaccine. The dog who had been healthy and energetic that morning, died the same day after receiving the vaccine, which apparently sent him into seizures at the vet surgery.

Reka was treated naturally for the disease and lived with no lingering side effects at all. But I was deeply distressed and shocked by the incident of the neighbour's dog.

I've also noticed in many clients who complain about their dog becoming more aggressive, that the change in behaviour seems to stem back to the vaccinations, coincidentally. My perspective is that vaccinations are medical interventions, and need to be researched carefully by people before the choice is made to use that particular medical tool.

Mindful of the health of my family and animals, I never use conventional chemical cleaners. You can buy beautiful orange and lemon based cleaning products from the health food store, and more and more Earth-friendly products are hitting the supermarket shelves. You can use tea tree oil or baking soda.

In short, if you value the health of your animals, go natural.

Speaking of essential oils – don't use them on cats. Cats can't process most essential oils and they can cause liver problems. I use a lot of essential oils at home, but never on the cats' bodies or internally.

Entities

I often get clients who email and say their animal companion has changed since they came back from the vet. Perhaps they are suddenly aggressive or frightened or just sick. If the animal hasn't been protected, or was worried, despairing, or open in some way, there is every likely they have picked up an entity.

Vet surgeries are places where animals are euthanased and often these souls have not passed over correctly for whatever reason, usually trauma. They have become Earthbound. So the souls, especially puppies, can attach themselves to the body of another dog, for example. Once they are asked to go back to the Light, the host dog returns to their normal personality.

Normally you can see the entity with your spirit eyes and you can ask them gently to go to the Light. For more difficult cases you will need the help of a shamanic healer. I suggest consulting shamanic healer who has graduated from the Four Winds Society's Healing the Light Body school, because the extraction method used in this school of Andean healing is very sweet and certainly the best I have come across.

Once my daughter was ill with pain, diarrhoea and vomiting. I lay down in bed beside her and scanned her body as she rested. Sure enough, there was an entity of a small black dog – a rescue pup of ours who had died suddenly. I gently asked him to go to the Light, assuring him it was safe to go home. I left my daughter sleeping. Shortly after she joined us in the office and sat at her desk as if nothing had happened.

These entities usually do not want to cause harm or pain, and often don't. They can attach themselves because they are lost, they have a message, because the host is vulnerable, or because they are looking for love.

Part 6:
Death, Dying and Euthanasia

Chapter 39:
On Death and Dying

The hardest part of any relationship is the final parting. Don't let anyone tell you "*it's* just an old dog", "*it's* just a smelly old cat," "you can get a new one", or any other of the phrases people come up with when they don't understand the animal-human connection. The animals in our lives are woven into the tapestry, the very fabric of our being. And when they go, there is a tear, a wound in that tapestry of life that nothing else replaces.

Suddenly there are empty spaces all over the house where the animal used to be. There's no one in the chair by the fire, no one hanging over the fence looking for carrots. To lose an animal friend renders the human lonelier than she has ever been, and cuts like a sword deep in our solar plexus and our heart. The thread unravels.

Animals come into our lives for a reason and the truth is that sometimes they are with us for the long haul, and sometimes just briefly to be touched by the grace of our love. And for us to be touched by theirs. I've had animals share life with me for decades, and some only for moments. But each one has enriched my life.

I can't stress enough how important it is to love, to open our hearts and go the extra mile. Animals give so much of themselves to help us along the path. The Divine shines out of their eyes, begging us to see the light within.

More and more people recognise the soul bonds between themselves and their animals, and are finding solace in like-minded communities when their animal leaves them for the spirit world. It is natural to grieve your animal friends and to grieve them deeply.

I've lost too many animals over the years, and every death leaves a scar. But the death of my horse Sollie shook me to the core. It hurt to feed the other horses and not see his familiar form among them. It hurt not to see him grazing in the back yard, or to have him come into the house seeking attention and carrots. It hurt in general. Everything hurt. I was surprised at the pain I was in and how long it took to get over it.

Sollie and I had been together 22 years. He was only 26 when he died. I wasn't ready to lose him.

There are many stages to grief including anger, denial, guilt and finally acceptance. It was a year before I even considered riding another horse. And even though we've had up to 30 horses here at any one time, there's never been another Sollie.

There are, however, other horses who have opened and healed my heart, and I recognise them for the blessing they are, and freely shower them with love and joy.

Sollie, for his part, now works outside of time helping horses cross over. He says he will return one day "when the veil thins". He is around me all the time as a guide, and others see him clearly as well.

So if you have lost an animal and are in deep pain, please take comfort in knowing there are others like you. That the pain does pass, and time is a great healer of heart wounds. And so are other animals.

The last thing your animal friend would want is for their death to cause ice in your heart, to cause you to shut down and stop the love flowing. That would undo all the work they came here to do. Many animals who pass over ask me to pass on the message to their people that they must find another furry soul to love. They understand the importance of an open heart and how loving another takes the edge off the sharp pain of loss.

Further, sometimes another soul comes in to take the baton as it were, to help you on the next stage of your personal spiritual journey. You recognise these souls by a quickening of your heart. They may either force themselves into your life by appearing as a stray or an animal who needs an urgent home, or they will tug at your heart strings, asking you to take them into your family and your heart.

The important thing to remember here is that the one you lost was unique, and it takes time to get to know a completely different personality and build a bond of partnership. Many people have made the mistake of getting another animal and expecting the relationship to be the same or similar. The new animal is sadly held in the light of his or her predecessor and found wanting, through no fault of their own.

Finally, it is really important to grieve the loss of an animal kin. But just as important is the need to be mindful that the lower energies of grief, can hold a spirit earth bound.

Many animal spirits come to me imploring their people to celebrate their passing, not mourn them. To find joy in their freedom, the lessons and love they gave, and to celebrate their new beginning in the other realms.

So have gratitude for your animal friends – every day, including after death.

Grieving Animals

Animals also experience grief when one of the family dies. And they often know it is coming, far before we do.

Cedar

When our dog Louie was failing, his mate Cedar began sleeping under our bed every night for weeks. The night after Louie died, she again slept on a dog bed. I knew my dog Tala's time had come when Cedar, once again, slept under our bed, instead of in her own.

Of death Cedar says, *"Death is just another stage of life. It's nothing to be feared. Your friend leaves and it's always sad and the people are sad too. But new friends come and the sun shines again. Louie is still here for me, around. He is still my friend.*

"When he died it was his time because he was frail. He taught me to love life and to have courage and I'll never forget that. You can't ever really be 'over' someone you have loved. You just live with them in a new way. It's like they have gone on a journey without you, but you are still connected and still friends and you still talk – every day sometimes. Louie likes Dusty and thinks we should be friends. He thinks Raffi is a rascal. He talks to Raffi too. So do the girls."

I asked Cedar how she dealt with grieving. *"By being practical,"* she said.

Animals can mope, lose their own health and will to live, when they are grieving. Some of them can get frightened. I once went to the wake of a beloved dog of a friend and the sad-eyed face of the family's other dog came to greet me.

"I'm next," she said. My friend caught the exchange and demanded to know what it was. I was loathe to tell her to prepare herself for another loss, but the dog wanted me to, and I did. She passed within months of her friend, as often happens in both animals and humans.

Samantha the Shetland was Pixie the Shetland's best friend. Before that, she had been my horse Sollie's best friend. When Sollie died from Cushing's disease, Sam and Pixie both came over to me, asking me what had happened.

Samantha

"I'm sorry," I said. "He's gone."

Samantha was okay at that point. She had Pixie and the two of them were inseparable. They shared a stall in the stables and went everywhere together. One day we noticed that Pixie was a bit slow and then she was in dreadful pain. She had headaches. She was sweating. Sam was desperate for us to help her. We called the vet and used drugs as well as every other modality under the sun and Pixie still went down seizuring. The vets didn't know what was wrong.

Sam would push into the stall to see for herself what was happening with her friend. The day Pixie died, Sam was lying just outside the stable and you didn't have to be an animal communicator to understand the question in her eyes. When I broke her the news, Samantha lay down flat in defeat. "No Sam," I cried, tears pouring down my face. "We need you. You can't leave us too." It was probably a selfish thing to say but I saw how she gave up on life in that very moment, and I was in too much pain from Pixie's sudden and dreadful departure.

Samantha took a long time to heal and feel a part of the herd without Pixie. Like Sollie, she came down with Cushing's and its sidekick laminitis.

When my wonderful farrier friend came to trim the horse's feet, he took one look at her and suggested we end her life for her. She was that miserable.

But it wasn't her time. She was simply heartsick. We were doing everything we could to help her heal, knowing time really was the best medicine. As well as herbs to help her with the Cushing's and laminitis, we gave her flower essences to help her heal her grieving heart. We also gave her lots of individual attention and fussing over.

Two years later, Samantha is the Ballyoncree Animal Sanctuary mascot, and she's doing really well.

Of that time, Samantha says, *"The two most important beings in my life passed over. I loved them both deeply and they gave me company and friendship. No one has replaced them and I saw my life as a lonely journey alone. I wanted to cross over and be with them. I really didn't think Pixie would leave me. It was such a shock, and for her too. What helped was knowing I was so important to my people. "*

I asked her if she had any advice or insights to share with other people for what we can all do to help a grieving animal.

"It's hard. Sometimes you are lost in your own world of pain. But I think what helped me the most was that the humans never gave up on me. The humans kept giving me love and affection. I still see Sollie and Pixie, and I know you do too. It's different now, but they are a comfort. And my herd is Erin and Lea. They may be faster than me, but they care for me in their own way and we enjoy each other's company at night in the stables."

There are No Accidents

One of my clients had to move to a place where there was a busy road and she was very worried about letting her cats out. But the cats themselves assured me they would be very careful. *"It's not our destiny to die on this*

Dylan

road," they told me.

Similarly I was very shaken when Dylan, one of our rescued pups, was killed instantly in a horse "accident". I turned to his sisters, Daisy and Tusuque, and asked them if this was their destiny as well. I didn't want it to be. *"No,"* said Tusuque.

"I don't have a death wish," said Daisy.

Dylan, it turned out, had no need of staying longer. He'd found love, and that's what he'd come for.

Animal Views on Death

"Death is a doorway that only the dead and gifted can see. It depends on the evolution of the soul to where they go. I chose to stay outside of time and I will return in a human form when I'm ready. I didn't want to die, but I accepted it long before you. I knew you'd be lost without me and I didn't know how to hold you up. I wanted my death to make you strong. I didn't want you to crumple. I was grateful for Andrew.

"Our love bind is strong and you know when you want to see me, you do. It is the same for many animals. It is the same for humans. We all have the same journey. We all have the same eternal soul. There is no difference. I am here, I am there. I am everywhere. I am ascended. And you will be too.

"Death is fearful to those who should not die. To those who love life on Earth and want to stay for a chance to live with their emotions and their body. I wanted to live every last moment with you and not be taken before my last breath. Other beings who come in as animals feel the same way. Every animal has their secret animal business, and who ever knows another's soul? I can only tell you my heart, and how much I love you.

> "In death I am in the room beside you. In death I am your guide and companion. Death is a doorway to a new beginning. The ties of love are strong but they should not be binding. For the soul's journey is the soul's alone.
>
> "You want me to tell you of the animal's perspective on death. It all depends on how much they have been loved. Like a human soul, the journey is to ascend and to learn and to treat every other soul with kindness. Love uplifts us all, and heals the wounds of the past. It is good medicine, and powerful too. The hands of love. Humans have that capacity. They learn it from us.
>
> "There is a journey for you with other horses. Ask who wants you on their back. Go gently and go with strength. Keep your heart open. Death is life in another form. It is not the end, and you and I will be reunited in the physical, and until that day, we are never apart."
>
> – Message from Sollie, in spirit since May 2002.

Just as we face death with courage or fear, fighting it or accepting it, so do the animals. Different situations, different animals, different viewpoints. Most of my animals, however, have seen death as merely a doorway to another world when their time comes. And this is the key. Some animals have their own reasons for not wanting to leave at a certain time.

One elderly dog client told me he would stay for another year. *"It will be hard, but I'm needed."* He told me his male person had cancer. And he did. He wanted to provide comfort to his people and not give them grief when they had enough on their plate.

Euthanasia

'Help me."

The old white dog was standing miserably with his people at the vet. I was sitting across the room, impatiently waiting to collect Pucawan, who'd had a kidney problem.

"Help me."

I wasn't focussed but his distress was clear. How did he want me to help him?

"You're here at the vet. They'll help you," I said kindly but firmly.

The dog sighed and looked infinitely sadder. I was about to ask him some more when they were called and ushered into the depths of the vet surgery. While Andrew and I waited for them to collect our cat, I heard snippets of conversation.

"Just too old. They can't be bothered ..."

"A nuisance, they said ..."

The nurses were clearly distressed. And then they brought out the body bag.

I was operating on a very slow gear, being heavily pregnant. But Andrew wasn't.

"The old dog," he said.

We walked quickly through the surgery and found the vet already inserting the needle of death into the dog who struggled for his life while his two people looked on, impartially.

We were too late.

Andrew quickly steered me outside where I could cry, great heaving sobs of tears. He held me close.

"I should have helped him", I wailed.

"What could you have done?" he asked.

"I don't know. Asked him why he wanted to be helped. "

"Then what? Turn to the people and tell them you'd take him?" Andrew gave me a gentle squeeze.

"Well they obviously didn't want him."

I was shattered. I'd completely failed that dog. It was a hollow, empty feeling. I just wanted to turn back the clock.

"He didn't want to die," I sobbed into Andrew's chest. "They just couldn't be bothered to look after him anymore".

"I know". Andrew's voice was tight.

I was aware of a presence near me. The dog's spirit was hovering. Andrew started walking me to our truck. "Why?" asked the spirit." Why did they do this to me?"

"I don't know", I answered honestly. " All I can tell you is that not all humans are like this and if you come back as a dog, try and choose someone who will commit to you properly. Now all you can do is forgive your people and go to the light in peace. Please know that Andrew and I honour you and send you our love."

The dog's spirit left us. I cuddled Pucawan to my chest, and cried some more. Again I pledged to the animals that I would try to do more to help people understand.

– Excerpt from Billie's journal, 1995

The subject of the moral right to take the life of an animal is a big one. Our society is sadly numb and ignorant to the psychic and spiritual problems around killing animals, but I will take that up in another chapter.

Euthanising animals we think are suffering is also a tricky topic, because sometimes what we think is a kindness is actually impeding their soul's journey, and sometimes it is a kindness to help them out of pain. We need to ask permission and to honour the animal's personal journey. Sometimes they ask for help and it brings relief and release. Other times it interferes with what they need to do, and brings fear.

The clearest example any animal has ever given of this was my horse Sollie, who made it obvious to both me and the students who were there that he did not want help dying. It's a natural process.

So many times I've had people contact me in distress because they are under pressure to kill their animals from other people who only see what they want to see – an animal with little life left. But sometimes these animals aren't ready to leave for their own reasons, and their people will know this intuitively. Often these animals are spending lots of time out of their bodies.

The most important thing we can do for any animal is to honour their soul's journey and give them the unconditional love they have always given us. Above all, trust yourself. You know your animal better than anyone. Most animals prefer a natural death, but you will know if they ask for help, and when. Trust that.

Chapter 40:
When Your Animal Friend Is Dying

The first thing to do is to ascertain if your animal friend is actually dying or just thinks she is dying, or if the vet thinks she is dying or has simply run out of answers. Many animals have their lives cut short because the medical profession has run out of options.

But if it's not an animal's time, miracles can happen! And often an animal wants these miracles to occur just to prove to their people that there are other ways, and that miracles indeed should be part of every day life. I've had animal clients say, *"I'll live if I'm given alternative therapies."* And their human has been encouraged to explore a different medicine road which has actually helped their own journey of health and healing.

When Suki told me she was going to be my "miracle", I knew she would recover even though the vet had told me it was her last days, and there seemed no obvious solutions. She had a mass on her throat, and a heart condition which prevented surgery. I could only pray she wouldn't choke or not be able to breath, or suffer this way. In the end the mass completely disappeared – indeed a miracle.

This is in no way to disparage the veterinary profession. Most vets provide wonderful, caring service and come from a place of the heart. But too often over the years I have met vets who thought an animal's life should be ended before their time. This is what I'm questioning.

How to Tell if an Animal is Dying

I was boiling linseed for the horses when a magpie flew into kitchen, sat there for a moment, and flew out again. "Do you have a message for me? " I asked him.

"A man is coming," he said as he disappeared.

I thanked him and figured I had better clean up if I was getting visitors!

Hours later, I was making a cup of tea when an old man lizard limped in. He'd been scratched up by cats, was injured and in shock.

"I just want to die," he said.

"Do you now," I said. I went to work on him, giving him some rescue remedy and following the strange instructions I received from Grandmother Logan of my spirit tribe. This required me to create a safe dark spot for him to heal, and to ask the eucalyptus tree for some leaves on which I was to put some water. I followed her instructions and put the "dying" lizard into a shoebox soft with leaves, and the eucalyptus water. I left the box in a safe spot where the lizard could choose to live and wander off, or die in peace.

The lizard lived. He was shocked and "felt" like dying but as soon as he felt better, he realised living was a better option. To me it was a big lesson in never giving up hope and that miracles can occur.

You can tell an animal is dying:

- By the colour of their aura. Usually you can see a black or dark aura around a being who is dying. Edgar Cayce tells a story of how he refused to get into a lift when he noticed all the other people in the lift had dark auras. The lift had a malfunction and those people fell to their death. Even today I'll scan people's auras before getting on a plane. Usually I see lots of pink and green. Like Cayce, I have seen the black aura of a dying animal.

- If they have spirit friends by their side. When friends who have passed over appear near a seriously ill animal, it is one of the clues I use to gauge the severity of the situation and whether or not it is time. But even this can be overruled by an animal's will. For example, our horse Sarki once led the herd with her mate Monty, who passed away several years before her. In life, they were inseparable and when she was dying, I wasn't surprised to see Monty's spirit by her. But Sarki was stubborn. The herd was everything to her and she didn't want to leave them. So we honoured her and provided hospice care until she was ready.

I nursed my Dad in his final weeks, and knew the day he was dying because his hospital room filled up with so many spirits I could barely breath. That last day was very difficult for me on many levels. My mother's spirit was there with open arms, pushing away his departed spirit sisters, who had all come to him in his final hours! I told Dad there was so much love in the room he had nothing to worry about, and indeed he died peacefully.

Provide Hospice Care

Even though Sarki was lying down most of the time (even to eat) and her systems were beginning to shut down, she didn't want to go. Not yet. So we nursed her. We took the van into the paddock and made sure someone was with her the whole time. Andrew and I slept with her through the night and Tamsin would take her music and books and hang out with her during the day. I realised it was exactly what I did for my Dad when he was in hospital dying. He took six weeks to realise he was dying, stop fighting, reach acceptance and leave. Sarki needed more time as well.

The day before Sarki died, she told me she was grateful we had honoured her process. She was glad not to be rushed. For some reason her soul wanted to linger. She hadn't been ready, despite her body slowly giving up.

Hospice care can be challenging in today's world, but it is a necessary part of service. Your animal friend has given you love and served you in ways you don't even know. Toward the end of their life, it's time to give back and in that service step up in compassion, love and commitment.

What You Can Do

The most important part of hospice care is to make sure the animal is clean, comfortable, warm and has food and water. Painkillers may be an important part of hospice. But you have to be careful with some drugs. Some of them make the animal feel worse. Suki, for instance, hated the drugs the vet gave us for her heart condition. I used them a couple of times because I was afraid she would drown in the fluid from her failing heart. But she went down hill on them and told me they were too strong for her. I ended up giving her homoeopathic Spongia, and dowsing other natural remedies for her condition on a daily basis.

Sometimes an animal who is making their transition just wants to be left alone. Others need company. Most need a bit of both.

When my daughter's pony Tammy was making her transition, we nursed her for three weeks. She had an open stable to go in and out of, friends to be with or not, plenty of food and water – and Tamsin would read to her out loud, sitting in the open stable with her.

The day Tamsin came into the kitchen to tell me Tammy hadn't eaten her carrots that morning, was the day I knew she would no longer be with us. She died peacefully in the paddock within an hour.

Finally, think about what it is like when you are feeling frail and unwell. You want peace and cleanliness. You don't want someone hovering around you with loud, clanking energy. You don't want people talking about you as if you aren't there, about how you should be killed, and how horrible you look. That's the way it is with animals too. Be like a really good nurse. Gentle, quiet, patient, loving, attentive and calm.

Dying is such a taboo subject in our society, and it shouldn't be. The animals are much more matter of fact. They understand the journey and many find the process "fascinating". I have had more than one animal tell me they didn't want to "miss a minute of it!"

Dying is simply the end of a journey in a particular body, and the beginning of a new journey.

Most importantly, call in your angels and guides, and ask that your animal friend be able to live until they die, that they die peacefully and naturally, for the highest good of all concerned.

You might just find they help.

While we were waiting for the vet for our horse Maverick, who was in trouble, I called in the angels and guardians and anyone else who would come to assist. With my own eyes I couldn't tell if they were there or not and I was very distressed because I knew Maverick wasn't going to make it. I took last photos of Maverick and later realised that the stable was full of orbs. The luminous ones had come to my call!

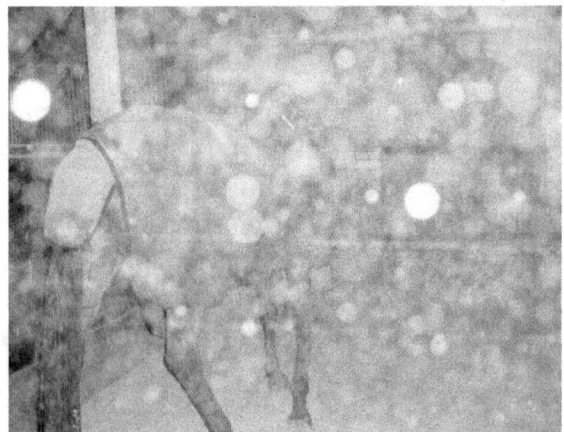

Maverick with orbs

Ask for Last Requests

Many of my clients ask me to ask their animals for last requests, and often an animal will leave peacefully if he has been taken for one more car ride to visit the sea, toddle along the beach, or the garden or a park. Some want Reiki. Some want to lie in the sun.

Sarki wanted to see the herd again, and indeed, even stood up when they came galloping over. The herd knew she was "dead" and were shocked when they saw her standing. They wheeled away as one, racing off toward another part of the paddock. To hear Sarki summon a weak neigh almost broke my heart, but it was necessary to break her bond with life. She had asked for it, and the herd did what they knew they had to do. And on that level, Sarki felt complete. She had said goodbye.

Give Permission to Leave

Animals, like people will cling to life sometimes because they are worried about their beloved ones or other reasons. So sometimes you just have to say, "It's okay to go. It's all right, beloved. Thank you so, so, so much for our time together. I'll be all right, I promise."

This is also a time to ask for last messages.

The Dying Process

Animals prefer to die peacefully and naturally. Like birth, death is a natural and important process, but sometimes assistance is needed. Forced euthanasia can create problems for the soul's journey. So assisted death needs to be their choice, not yours, and it's really important they don't die in fear. Animals make the choice to die with assistance for many reasons. Their souls may be complete with life, like the goat Valentine, or they might have given up the struggle with pain. Permission must be sought because we can't assume. There are countless stories of animals coming back from the brink, having been on some secret animal business of their own, like processing an energetic shift. If euthanising your animal friend, trust your intuition. They will tell you when they are ready. They make it clear. Don't let anyone bully you and when in doubt, don't.

The shamanic death rites and other skills are precious tools to assist an animal through euthanasia and natural death. Euthanised animals often remain earthbound and need assistance.

My website has links to practitioners who can help with this last and most important journey. www.billiedean.com

When people contact me about whether it is the right time or not, it generally isn't. And they know it, but just need confirmation. I always tell people – you will know. The animal makes it very clear. Trust your intuition.

Often an animal gets more energy before they leave their bodies. There is a restlessness and an inability to settle and be comfortable. If this happens, know it is part of the dying process, and allow it to happen. I've also seen many animals look around saying goodbye to the place where they were loved, and I've seen others looking at things we can't see.

I had no idea when Suki would die. She would pant and toddle around and was basically in good spirits despite her health. Then one morning I woke up and "knew" she was leaving. Suki had "told" me. I cancelled all my appointments and hung out with her for the next four days. On Day Four, she had the restlessness, a strength in her frail body which hadn't been there. She exchanged deep and meaningful conversations with several of the other dogs and made sure she was complete with her favourite spots in the yard.

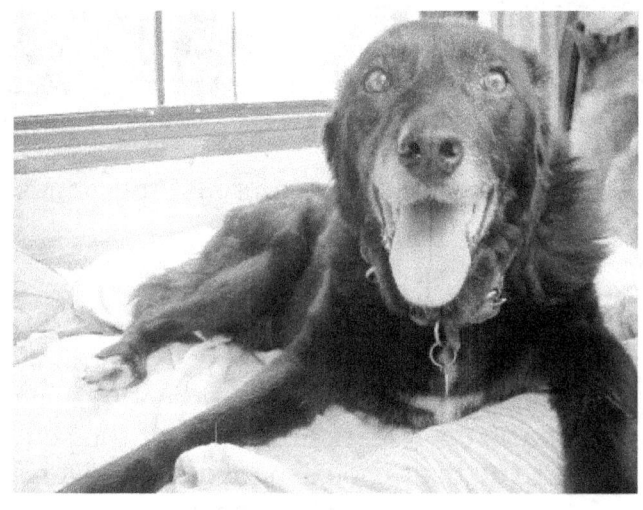

I sat with her in the sun, just being with her. In the evening she watched as Andrew took the other dogs up to feed the horses and I realised she wanted to "work" too. So I popped her in the car and let her out to wander around. She was happy and grinning all the time. We popped her in the front seat of the car for one last drive and she died peacefully in my arms as I took her out of the car. It was a grand ending for a grand old lady who lived until she died.

Ceremony

After death is a time of ceremony and ritual. We do shamanic death rites to make sure the spirit is safely out of the body. Then we do ceremony in the way Grandmother Kitty taught us. We cleanse the body by smudging (with sage smoke), and then release the spirit through the crown chakra by inhaling three times seven breaths of sacred tobacco and on each of the seventh inhales, blow all that smoke onto the crown chakra with the intent of the spirit riding the smoke to the heavens. Most of the time the spirit has well and truly left, especially if we have done the death rites, but we like to do this ceremony anyway.

I have often seen spirits flying off with glee once they have been released.

During the burial ceremony our family says words of gratitude for our time together with that animal, how much we loved them, how much they will be missed.

Note that you need to make sure the animal's soul has left the body before the burial ceremony. I have come across earthbound spirits who have been buried and had to help them cross over.

Once the body is buried, and there's nothing left to do, it is time for a wake. Because we live in an isolated location, I will either email or call my friends and tell them of our loss, and we will flop down in front of a light-hearted movie and eat something chocolate. The next day our family ritual is to head to the beach with the dogs for a day out, and the next day we clean the house, stables, yards and everything, so we have a fresh start. Other people do other ceremonies with friends and families and then create altars with photographs or bury their animals with their favourite things, like a ball or rug.

One of my friends had her dog cremated and divided her into small purses which she put on her favourite places in the house.

I always take some hair to keep, and where it is appropriate, I plant trees or a small garden. This was hard during the drought, but Andrew and I know the position of every animal lost to the sanctuary, each of whom we have loved.

It doesn't get any easier emotionally, and we've tended many, many deaths. But now I have added tools to help the transition process, I feel a bit more equipped to be a good shaman for this last and most important journey.

Memorials

Do a ceremony or memorial for your animal companion. This could be as simple as lighting a candle, or saying a few words of gratitude for a life shared.

Keep hair and/or name tag. Keep this somewhere special. Consider a scrapbook journal of memories or a special box or altar.

Hold a wake with all your animal's favourite human and animal friends, and film this. You can gather together photos and footage of your beloved to create a special film or an altar, and share this at the gathering.

Plant trees or create headstones and beautiful gardens for your beloved if you have buried them.

If you have cremated them, put the ashes on a special altar in a beautiful vase or box. Alternatively, you can scatter the ashes somewhere that was special for your animal.

Channel your grief into self-expression for your animal like writing, dancing or painting.

Only share your loss with people you know will understand what you are feeling. This is a time you will feel raw and you need nurturing, support and advice.

Orbs

Orbs are an increasingly common phenomenon as the veil between the worlds thins. These are circles of light which can be seen on digital photographs. At first they seemed to only hang around spiritual happenings, but more and more they are everywhere. They are luminous beings. Some are fairies. Some are angels.

Tammy's Orb

Some are from other worlds. And what we've noticed at Ballyoncree, is that some are our dearly departed.

When Tammy left us, Tamsin took some random photos in the paddock which included a very large orb. "That's Tammy", she said.

Years before I was taking pictures of the dogs after my beloved dog Tala died, and there were a

Tala's orb

host of orbs, including a large one which I knew was the spirit of Tala. And that was before I had heard of the phenomenon. And when our rescue horse Maverick was dying, the stables were filled to the brim with orbs. And that's a real comfort to know – we are never alone.

Animals in the Spirit World

Many clients ask me to check in with their beloved animals who have passed. Some want to know where they have gone. Others want to know they are okay.

There is a world, a dimension, where the dead live. If an animal has left this plane in love, I see them as golden and etheric. They have indeed crossed over to the other side. Many animal souls, however, need healing.

Some become Earthbound. This is often an animal who has died suddenly or before their time. They might have been killed by a car, or euthanased prematurely. Sometimes people hold them here with their intense grief. Confusion and terror can also chain an animal's soul to this plane.

However an animal who had been loved will often tell me how this love has helped him ascend and healed some wounds of his soul psyche. They tell me this is the most important work of all and the best thing a human can do for their animal friends.

These days, much of my work comprises requests from animals in spirit to do healing on them so their luminous energy field doesn't carry the energetic imprints of disease or trauma. That way they can come in with a fresh slate. It's a wonderful gift.

I also assist the Earthbound to go to the Light. Sometimes this is as simple as gently encouraging them to do so, reminding them it is safe. Sometimes calling on their friends, guides and angels helps them make the shift. Sometimes they need me to take final messages to their people, before they move on.

Bringing Spirits Home

Some people unwittingly bring spirits home with them. This is different from entities attaching themselves. Earthbound spirits are often at vet surgeries and kill pounds where they have been euthanased, and also on the roadside where they have been killed suddenly by cars. Well-meaning people connect with these beings. The dead animal's spirit, being lost, may follow the person home. These animal spirits need to be lovingly sent to the Light.

So if your animals start acting weird at home, you might have attracted some spirit visitors!

Part 7:
Creating a Better World for Animals

Chapter 41:
2012 and the Fifth Dimension – The New Earth

Only after the last tree has been cut down,
Only after the last river has been poisoned,
Only after the last fish has been caught,
Only then will you find that money cannot be eaten.
　　　　　　　　　　　　　　　– Cree Indian Prophecy

The Mayans were an amazing people. They were timekeepers. They kept calendars. Lots of them. And one of their most important calendars runs out on Dec 21, 2012. Why? There's a lot of speculation.

On Dec 21, 2012, there is also a major galactic event, one that hasn't happened in 26,000 years. This is when the sun aligns in the middle of the Milky Way. Like many others, I believe this will have a profound effect on us.

The ancients knew this and have passed on this knowledge down through the ages.

The Hopi people have a prophecy which talks of a fifth world, a new time where the world is in harmony, peace and unity. It comes after a chaotic time –like we are currently experiencing.

The Inka have a prophecy about the world being turned right side up again. They say there will be a tear in the fabric of time, and a new human will appear on the planet. They call it the return of the children of light.

So many traditions around the world say similar things. Looking around, we can see we are in the process of immense change. I believe we being prepared for the fifth world or what is often called the fifth dimension – the time of the new human.

Many 2012 writers liken the new human to a human angel. Not only do they walk in love, compassion and joy, but quantum leaps in our evolutionary process are expected, allowing our former "junk" DNA to be activated, giving us access to our full psychic nature.

This is the predicted Golden Age of indigenous prophecy. It's an evolutionary shift in consciousness from warlike human beings to beings of peace. It's a shift from being "asleep" to spiritually awakened. It's a time when humans remember their Divinity, the feminine principle comes back into balance, and all animals, nature and humans live in peace and sacred harmony.

However it is not automatic. We need to do our personal healing work so we can become the best people we can be, and step up into this higher frequency. This is a challenge and an invitation. I believe the fate of humanity rests on our ability to say "yes."

As mentioned previously, many people are experiencing what are called ascension symptoms, and animals are definitely affected by energetic shifts. The symptoms are varied and largely menopausal in nature, and the shifts seem to mostly occur around the full moon, equinoxes, solstices and eclipses. So at these times, susceptible animals may exhibit health or behavioural problems. Some will look like they are fading, and then bounce back. They may become aggressive. It's a new time and new experiences, and health practitioners are having to be very discerning.

The new time is about being "light", as in "light-filled". While it may seem like a dark time of suffering and negativity, with old paradigms collapsing and Earth Changes or natural disasters occurring around the world, it is actually a time of growth and opportunity for those who have the courage to make personal changes.

This means we have to drop the heavy stuff we carry around, the dark negativity, the anger, the pain and especially the fear. Drop that and you can step into a world which is lighter, easier and filled with joy, because you will be lighter.

This is what the animals want for us. This is what they want for themselves.

The thing is, how attached are you to your stories and your pain? Many people feel they have done a lot of healing and clearing on themselves, but they are still caught in a world that is chaotic, fearful and painful.

This means there is more work to do.

Paranormal author Dolores Cannon has a simple remedy: forgive others, forgive yourself and create no more karma. Plus, drink lots of water and eat a lighter diet of raw food and liquids, like smoothies.

Creating no more karma is a big one, as is the forgiveness. How do you walk in the world? Are you in right relations every day? Are you walking in integrity? Do you give a value in exchange for what you receive? Do you treat others with impeccability?

How do you treat your animal companions? How do you treat the Earth? Do you honour the Mother Earth and all her children? And if you think you do, could you do it even more or better if you knew there was another way? Think about what you are putting out in the world.

There could be a lot of fear around the 2012 end date and the challenging times in between. But I don't believe December 21, 2012 will herald in an automatic shift. We are already under the influence of change from many directions. It's happening now. (See my film This Sacred Earth: The 2012 Phenomenon for a deeper explanation). So by 2013, I believe there will be many people of light and peace, because they have had the courage to meet the challenges and have had the heart and desire to change.

I urge all of you to find that courage, if you haven't already, for the sake of your animal companions and the animals around the world. Given that the animals in your home mirror your health and harmony, wouldn't it be better for them to have us evolved and awakened? If emotions are at the root cause of illness, then surely the gift of happiness that they try to impart to us every day could be something we accept and embody, for their sake as well as ours – and the future of our planet.

The Earth Changes we currently experience were foreseen by indigenous peoples, and they have been warning us for a long, long time. This time has been called a "culling" or "harvesting of souls". Sadly for humanity, animal and insect souls are leaving the planet in droves. Just think of the millions of souls who perished in the 2009 Victoria bushfires alone.

When natural disasters come, I know in my heart that humans will take care of each other. It's not fun, but they have help to rebuild their lives. But what of the animals who have lost their lives, their loved ones, their homes, their habitats? It is their fates which pull at my heartstrings. Nature has a habit of renewal, but it takes time. And in the meantime, the world is a much sadder, lonelier place without those animals.

Of course, on one level, their souls signed up for this mission here at the end of time as we know it. But my connection to animals is such that I want to make a difference. I want to honour their souls' journeys and make that difference. I want to be the best I can be – for them.

I believe you do too.

So please join me for the transformational section of this book, where we begin to shed the layers of density and disconnection that hold us back from being all that we can be, and all that we truly are.

There is a probable future – and a possible future. The choice is ours.

Chapter 42
Dreaming in the New World of Peace

The spirit painting took on the familiar shape of the man I know as Grey Wolf. He was a member of my spirit tribe from the life when Andrew and I were together as warrior and medicine woman. Grey Wolf looked at me with compassion in his eyes and handed me a peace pipe.

"You must now carry this," he said. "And Dream the Dream awake."

– Excerpt from Billie's journal, 2006

Indigenous people are big on the concept of Dreaming. Western society is big on the concept of nightmare. We are fed images of fear daily, constantly. And when we are constantly focused on fear, we create more of it.

To step out of the collective unconscious nightmare, you must understand that the world is simply an illusion – a projection of our thoughts. When we individually and collectively visualise a world of peace, we will have peace.

But so many well-intentioned people focus on peace in their minds, but not their hearts, because they haven't yet learned to dream peace by being peace. They still carry their violence within.

We live today in a time of tremendous opportunity. And we chose to be here at this time to help the entire world become a peaceful one. It might start with our own garden, but it ripples out like a pebble in a lake and touches others.

The world is changing. Yes, we are having Earth Changes and wake up calls. But already there is a huge search for spirituality and a life with meaning. There is a vast desire for personal change. And things *are* changing.

I already feel lighter. If I put my awareness on my body, it definitely feels more spacious and less dense. I have undergone a change. The light is brighter. My luminous field is cleaner. I notice a difference in the way the animals know me and greet me. There is greater harmony here and I feel there is so much more to come. I see it in the promise in their eyes, and in the current of their thinking.

Nature talks to us and guides us like a benevolent spirit – in the magic of an eagle, or a rainbow or a raven at just a certain moment. It comes in the rustle in the trees, the arrival of the wind or the rain.

The more peaceful I become, the more I walk in harmony with the world. This is the Beauty Way I want to share with you – a path of possibility. And all we have to do is follow the trail of our heart and our senses, and drop the denseness of our pain and suffering to become beings of light.

The animals have asked me to tell you that it is time for us to step up. Many of them are leaving. But the veils are thinning as we approach that tear in the fabric of time – the arrival of the New Earth of consciousness and peace. I already see many spirit animals zooming around the place with my spirit eyes. I feel like I walk in Avalon, but the crossing of the river of mist is a short one. Sometimes I feel as if I have a foot in two worlds. The veils between the worlds are coming down.

I have seen the return of animals to this new world, and have been asked also to tell you that there will be others, and the return of what appears to be our original species – forms that appear to be hybrids – like my own Christos – the spirit friend with the head of a lion on the body of a man.

So imagine a world full of possibilities, magic and miracles. Imagine a world if you will, of people who are free. The feeling I have experienced of the future is lightness and grace, happiness and joy, humour, and yes, freedom. All feelings of density were gone. There was no room for the tarnish of negativity or fear.

In this future, the earth is a peaceful blue planet, her inhabitants honour her daily in gratitude, animals are abundant, there is plenty for all, and Earth's children live together in sacred harmony and right relations.

Imagine that, and join with others around the globe, to dream it in. Step out of the collective nightmare and dream consciously.

Allow nature and the animals to help you because that world is here now, whenever you choose it to be. And as we go deeper in the Mystery of the 2012 Phenomenon, we can just choose a life that gets better and better, as we peel away the dross.

The animals will thank you for it.

Chapter 43:
Help an Animal – Change Your Diet

We've talked about diets for animals, and touched on diets for humans. But diet is a tool for transformation, and the choices you make affect you, the animals who share your life, and the planet.

"You are what you eat" is not a cliché, it is a truth. To truly become the human angels or children of light that prophecy speaks of require some shifts in dietary thinking for many people.

As an animal advocate, I have lived a vegetarian life for over 30 years and been very happy and comfortable with that. And then suddenly, I couldn't eat eggs any more – or dairy. They felt heavy and had the wrong vibration. The energy of the animals they came from didn't mix with mine. It made me feel sick if I even thought about eating them.

I made the switch to veganism and was very happy and comfortable with that. Except there was still something not quite right with the way I was eating. I could sense it. When I tuned into my spirit guides, the one I call "Grandmother", a round, Native American Elder with long plaits and a serous disposition, said, ""No sugar, lots of water."

So I did that. Most of the time, anyway. And I knew she was right. Sugar is not only acid-forming, but science shows it contributes to the aging process. And that's not what I wanted. Water, as we all now know, is vital for cleansing and replenishing. People need good, clean water for our health and well-being.

I had heard of the raw food movement for some time, and was attracted to it. But suddenly, I discovered raw food recipes I could make without hassle, and just as suddenly, so did my husband. Our bodies felt lighter and I knew that an alkaline raw food diet would keep cancers, arthritis and other diseases associated with aging well away. We were excited. This was the diet our bodies had been searching for.

Breads, pastas and other carbs had been feeling too heavy for a long time. I was very happy with smoothies and raw foods – as much as we could.

Thanks to the pioneers of the raw food movement, there were (and are) lots of recipes out there that delighted not only our palates, but also the palates of our eight dogs. Nut "cheezes" and pates are definitely a big hit.

With the dogs embracing this kind of food, I could see the beginning of my vision for a non-predatory world beginning to take shape. Imagine a world with no predators – animals and humans living in sacred harmony. The end of killing, the end of suffering, the end of anguish and pain, and definitely the end of dis-ease. Yay.

The pain and suffering of animals contributes to what has been called an "Earth Shadow". This is a field of negative energy which keeps us firmly in depression and anxiety. It's built up over the centuries to become a big, thick mess and it doesn't exactly mesh with the idea of joyous light beings dancing away on the New Earth. This is why I hold the vision of a non-predatory world. To me it feels like a must.

I mentioned before that Dolores Cannon said that to become lighter and raise our vibration, we needed to eat more lightly. She also said that water, smoothies, juices, and raw foods was the next stage diet. She did mention chicken and fish if people had to make their transition more slowly – but cows, sheep, horses and pigs were definitely off the menu. Once our higher frequency bodies had settled into this diet and shifted some more, we'd be onto liquids – smoothies and juices – until finally our light body wouldn't need food at all.

And then the New Earth will be completely predator-free, and my vision of animals and humans living in sacred harmony would be a reality.

I know for some people the thought of a world without coffee, meat and sugar might be a bit hard to take initially, and there might be a gut reaction against the thought. But believe me when I say that the raw food movement is a delicious one and getting easier daily. Starting slowly and building up your raw food intake is one option. But if you have health problems you want to heal you might want to go a bit more gung ho. Raw food provides the necessary enzymes and high nutrition needed to allow the body to heal itself. The occasional juice fast also benefits the process of healing, anti-aging and encouraging the light.

Raw food eating also deepens your connection to the natural world and increases your compassion for all living things.

Further, when the body is well nourished without the chemical overload of processed food, people become more chemically balanced, happier, energetic and peaceful. Like New Earth people! So I like to promote the use of organic fruits, veggies and nuts, and super-foods like cacao, spirulina, maca, coconuts, goji berries, hemp, chia seeds, and so on. Chia and hemp seeds are rich in the all important omegas, which have always played a vital part in health, brain function, and healing.

The more work people do to shed themselves of their heavy emotional baggage which keeps them firmly third dimensional, the lighter they become. The need for heavy foods lessens. This makes perfect sense to me. Imagine eating the New Earth raw food diet. You might find yourself shedding a lot of the old gunk naturally and hastening the evolutionary process.

Another way to hasten the shift is called the Forgiveness Diet. Forgive everyone you know you have issues with, including yourself. You'll find yourself lighter in more ways than one.

We're changing as a species now, becoming far more enlightened and awake. It's an exciting time to be alive. Roll on the New Earth so that animals and people can walk forward together in sacred harmony and peace.

Chapter 44:
Animals and Spiritual Practice

Like most people today, finding time to do spiritual practice is a challenge for me. But because it is important to my stress levels and my evolutionary growth, I find myself multi-tasking as I do the animal chores.

Even as my peace is shredded with excited kelpies and demanding baby goats as soon as I put my foot out of bed in the mornings, I cherish stepping into the early morning sun. I'll feed the baby goat kids, throw balls for the dogs and thank Spirit for all that I am grateful for. Another trick I have is to lie in bed to visualise my day and give thanks for it, and then get up!

My time with the animals out in nature is a practice in mindfulness. When I'm walking the dogs in the back hills, checking horses, I'll watch for signs in nature, and feel grateful for everything I have. As I'm filling water troughs, I'll go through my breathing and yoga practice. This way spirituality threads through my day, instead of being something else I'm trying to make time for.

This is something you can do too. And sometimes that's exactly what the animals are asking us to do. You might enjoy a walking meditation as you stroll along the beach with your dog, or experience an exercise in joy as you play games with him. Whether you are having a calming conversation with the cat on your lap or the thrill of a ride on your horse, consider it an opportunity for spiritual practice.

With animals by our side, we can shift our chemistry and come into better alignment with our higher spiritual selves. The animals in our homes touch the wild within us, and help us re-connect to the natural world. If we move away from what television and advertising tells us is important in life, and focus on what the animals tell us is important, we'll make huge headway in spiritual growth.

Chapter 45: The Power of Right Thinking

Over and over in sessions with animal clients, they stress that it is time for people to lift their game. This means finding the courage and will to do the personal work to become a better human. They need you to understand they are holding a mirror up to you, and demanding healing and growth.

Further the collective unconscious of the world tends to the negative. Wars, hatred, crime, suffering, disconnection and disharmony are easy to find all over the planet. But we can come to understand the power we have within and available to us, and we can change the world with our thoughts.

Personal transformation can only be touched on here, but in my school it is something which is deeply experienced. My Rainbow Fianna animal shaman students are encouraged to not only work on their personal healing, but also to receive shamanic initiations, which work on cleansing the sludge from the luminous energy field, and help them fast track their spiritual growth and healing. My goal with my school is to create human angels for animals, and doing transformation work like this is the key.

But really, we need a world where every animal loving person is a human angel.

Here's an excerpt from a recent conversation with client Lesley's horse Rosie, who wanted to help Lesley become a "better, more confident person."

..."this is one of the teachings of horse. We demand leaders who lead with their heart and light hands. We stand for no violence, only peace. We fall in love with strong people who are radiant lights.

"I love to dance and sing inside. My job right now is to lift this one to her feet. Tell her to join (energy) fields with me. We can take it slowly, but I see her sitting lightly on my back with glee in her heart, instead of the *leaden, lumpy fear. Ask her to think why I am the way I am, and to come inside my mind and body. By blending our energies, we become one. We are one. We are together."*

Rosie wants to lead Lesley into happiness (her words) and she wants to be a teacher. She wanted to be quoted here so that people could *"understand the magnificence of horse teachings."*

So let's talk about how we can create a world of peace, bringing to awareness how we can live life more consciously and more beautifully. When people Walk in Beauty (explained below) they live a life of miracles and grace. Synchronicities abound and life is magical. When we are happy and living a life of Grace, the animals in our lives do too.

This kind of life is waiting for all of us who see through the illusion of the dream or nightmare we have created with our thoughts, deeds and actions. The world we create affects the animals in our care. So let's get off our butts, and create a wonderful world for the animals we love.

Once you are aware that "life is but a dream", as we sang when we were children, then you can change your dream into what you want.

I've found many people will act positively to change themselves when their animal friend is at stake, more so than if it is just for themselves. This kind of compassion is admirable, even if it is a sad reflection of how we treat ourselves.

When people stop blaming and complaining and open their hearts to love and peace, the animals (and people) will be literally in heaven on Earth.

Resisting Change

If you find yourself never keeping your spiritual practice promises, preferring to watch TV, check your email, or getting caught up on the phone – it could be that your ego is running the show, and resisting the change it fears.

The ego resists change. But like a sprite slipping through a forest, you can use things like poetry and ceremony to move yourself forward without the ego noticing or feeling challenged.

Walk in Beauty

The Navajo expression "Walk in Beauty" has always been one I aspired to. It speaks of not only spiritual enlightenment, but a beautiful connection and way of being in the world.

There is another meaning to this beautiful phrase "walk in beauty". It means walking in what the indigenous people call the sacred hoop of the fifth dimension, the dimension of spiritual enlightenment where a human walks through this world in a state of bliss, humour, happiness, and power, wielding that power with integrity, wisdom and gentleness.

This is a state of grace our animal friends would like us all to be in.

Some indigenous traditions call this state of grace the fifth dimension or the fifth hoop. There is indigenous prophecy that says Mother Earth is demanding us to be in this fifth dimension, and that is why she is unsettled. It's time to wake up to our spiritual selves – indeed our God and Goddess self.

One way I ask my students to walk in beauty is by seeing the beauty in nature and animals, and by using poetry to capture that. As an artist, I have always written poetry, and have had a fascination with nature's light and beauty, which I capture on film. To me, being a part of the breath-taking splendour of life that is all around us constantly informs my soul and lifts me to the higher dimensions. Depressions and earthly concerns are transformed when I take the dogs and go outside for a walk. My favourite is walking in the mountains where the eagles fly.

I found it intriguing to have my experience echoed in *The Celtic Way of Seeing* by Frank MacEowen. In this book, he talks about the advocacy of the Celtic poet. "Through making a profound connection with the spirit of place, Celtic poets have always expressed their love for the land, becoming a voice for the land."

He also talks about the Celtic art of "love talk" or *geancannach*. This praise poem is a form of meditation hailing from "the deeply inspired states of consciousness of the wandering bards".

From his friend, the Celtic mystic and author Tom Cowan, Frank shares the praise poem formula : *Beautiful…. Beautiful too.* You capture beauty around you in phrases that start with those words.

I find doing this immediately puts me in a state of enormous love and gratitude for nature and the animals. You don't make up these poems sitting at the kitchen table. You go outside and experience it. It isn't about writing poetry. It's about seeing the world through the eyes of a poet, and letting beauty fill your cells. You can even say the poem aloud and write it down later. I find it has quite a profound effect on the people who do it.

Here's an example I wrote:

> *Beautiful is the rain on the window pane which shelters the ancient orange cat from the cold, grey skies*
>
> *Beautiful too are the horses running in the wild, wet grass, snorting into the mist. I feel like a centaur filled with strength and grace, my body long behind me.*

My Grade Two students get to enjoy this exercise.

From Lisa McFadyen:

> *Beautiful is...........*
>
> *.....the thick winter fog rolling in through the valleys of the mountains circling and embracing my home with the most delicate of touches*
>
> *Beautiful too..........*
>
> *.....the sound of the bordering creek, rushing around and over rocks and logs, after a night of rainfall with the purest of purest icy cold spring water.*

Of writing the poetry, Lisa said:

> It felt "beautiful". I felt connected to nature and at one with everything. I felt humble, grateful and awe inspired. I felt loved and in love.
>
> It helped in my relationship with the world, animals and nature, because I wasn't connected to my ego. I was able to be a part of the big picture from a point of selflessness. It helped me to "be quiet" and listen with all my senses.

From Rebecca Booth:

> *Beautiful is the silhouette of a majestic equine face against the*

crystal clear night as it is slowly gives way to the coming dawn on a winter's day.

Beautiful too is the luminous mauve and amber of the sunrise reflected in his deep soulful eyes as Father Sun returns to warm all his children.

Rebecca said:

I think it makes you feel more aware, alive, connected. It allows you to see the beauty that surrounds you. It allows you to walk in beauty and harmony.

From Rose Mackinnon:

Beautiful is the majestic Macrocarpa rising from its roots in the womb of the Mother, its silhouette reaching to paint the sky up above

Beautiful too is the tiny white shell that lays on the sand so delicate, yet perfectly formed, self contained yet connected to all

Beautiful is the black swan as it glides on the calm sea, its long slender neck bowed gracefully

Beautiful too is the seagull which glides, dipping and soaring on the eddies of wind.

Rose said:

I enjoyed the poetry homework. It was quite interesting observing how doing it increased my feelings of well-being. This was particularly noticeable when I was able to observe the beauty around me for a reasonable period of time.

I like to think I'm quite conscious of the beauty around me a lot of the time, but this work also reminded me of how often I become unconscious of beauty and the possible effect this has on my psyche and the realist that I help create. It is a very mindful practise and 99% of the time it helped me stay out of my head and just be present in my surroundings. It also increased my sense of appreciation and gratitude, which is always good. I will definitely keep doing this as a practise simply because it feels good!

Try This

To be reconnected to the natural world, go outside in nature to your back yard, to a park, to the beach, to a paddock, to the bush... and make up your own "love talk", with a praise poem Beautiful... Beautiful too.

Chapter 46:
Ritual and Ceremony

Much can and has be written about ceremony. But if you think of life as a prayer to All My Relations and a salutation to beauty, then ritual and ceremony become a natural part of life. This might be as simple as the ritual of getting out of the house early in the morning with your dog or horse and experiencing the peace of the new dawn. You can welcome in the rising sun, sensing its beauty and giving gratitude for all you have in that moment. What a way to start the day!

Perhaps you have created a beautiful altar in your home with photos of your animal friends and family, special stones, feathers and crystals. You might pull a daily tarot card in the morning and leave it there for the day, as you think about its meaning for you.

In the evening, you might walk in the dusk with your dog, checking out the neighbourhood and looking for fairies. You might light candles and incense as you prepare the evening meal, and play spirit-lifting music.

You might have a ritual of reading to your family of animals in the evening, or tucking them all into bed as you offer your love to them.

An obvious ceremony is a fire ceremony, but even lighting a candle in a sacred, conscious way, becomes ceremony. It has nothing to do with religion or the occult; it has everything to do with raising your vibration to Walk in Beauty in the world by living mindfully and deliberately, instead of being caught up in a tangle of thoughts and emotions. Step outside the tangle, and into life.

Chapter 47:
Making a Commitment to Happiness

Happiness is always around, you just have to choose to find it.

– Joho, the dolphin in spirit, excerpted from Billie's journal, 1987

Animals in the home are very sensitive to the energies of their people. I had one depressed client who demonstrated this very, very clearly when both her dogs got cancer. *"It's a heavy load just for the two of us,"* one said, showing me the weight of the dark energy in the household. It made me realise how important it is that we keep our vibration up for the health and happiness of our animal family. So I encourage people to embrace the idea of making a "commitment to happiness".

How many people do you know who are truly happy? How many people are filled with fire and passion for life? Who do you know who is truly committed to their own well-being and happiness? I bet you can count them on one hand.

How many people do you know who are sad, depressed, complaining and blaming others? A lot, eh? So, what does it take to make a commitment to happiness? And why don't people do it?

Many people are just plain stuck. We are filled with toxins from our world, our thoughts, and our food and water. There is too much pressure to "have" and to "spend, spend, spend". And what we are encouraged to spend on is meaningless and doesn't bring us happiness. Let's face it, do we really need designer clothes and McMansions to be happy?

It's time to shake off the conditioning of our society, and instead include some basics, like simple pleasures and nourishing food. Depression might be a thing of the past if more people took vitamin B complex, especially niacin. This is an important nutrient to replace if you drink alcohol or eat sugar. The "B's" are called the happy vitamins, and we might just be seeing an epidemic of a vitamin B deficiency with people replacing real food, with processed food, and not supplementing their diet with extra vitamins and minerals.

As I said previously, in this day and age, we don't get all our nutrients from an ordinary diet. We're under too much stress, the food is too old and the soils they come from are too depleted.

I think we need to visualise a day where community organic gardens and orchards are the norm, where the backyard veggie garden and herb patch return, and people start taking responsibility for their own health and happiness instead of thinking that an over-the-counter medication with side effects is going to do it for them.

Humanity needs to give reign to artistic souls to help create more beauty in the world. Developers have gone overboard creating soulless deserts of cheap box housing, which does nothing to feed the spirits of those dwelling in them. Studies have shown that this kind of living creates anxiety and depression. Instead, allow nature to nurture – plant trees, veggies and flowers.

It's certainly okay in our supposedly advanced civilisation to want nice things and to be comfortable, but at the end of the day, it's about balance. Poverty never did a soul any good. We were made to live in an abundant world. But you must have a life that is meaningful to you and filled with joy. It's about finding happiness and contentment in the simple things. It's about spiritual community – a strong sense of like-minded people who share your values and beliefs. It's about love, companionship, communion, and connection with nature.

As a species, we are not meant to live isolated lives in cities, staring at computer and television screens, and drowning the voice of nature in sirens, traffic, radio and blaring TV. We are supposed to live in nature – in celebration of and communion with her. We need to have the long vision of scenic landscapes, the time to be still and to listen to the whispers in the silence.

As most people do live in cities, we can still make that reconnection to nature through our animal companions, through beaches, backyards, flowers, parks, and gardens. You can make your home your altar, and make outside time a ritual, You can dance, sing, and enjoy good entertainment which lifts your vibration with humour and laughter.

We are also meant to value life not just by the amount of money we earn, but by the service we offer. That's what pays us. Good service fills the pockets and also the heart.

Try This
What are ten things you absolutely love to do? How can you make a wonderful lifestyle and career from combining these? I first heard about this exercise from the Loving Relationships Training in the mid 1980s. One of the examples used was a couple who loved parties, balloons, children and each other. They made a successful business out of creating children's birthday parties together.

Try This
Make a Treasure Map or Dream Board by putting pictures and affirmations of the way you want your life to be either in a box or on a board. I create mine on cardboard and make it a work of art, with pictures and photos of everything I want in my life. It is a prayer to Great Spirit, made in the present, thanking Great Spirit for the beauty of my life and the abundance I have.

Create-a-Mate
And love? The first quest for humanity is to learn to love the self, before we can truly attract another. A lot of people struggle with their love relationships. For a long time, many men, in general, have lagged behind women in their search for spirituality, and the women have broken free from these marriages in search of mates who vibrated at their new level.

When searching for a life partner, it's important again to consider lifestyle. There's little point in falling for someone's physical appearance if one of you loves city life and the other can't stand it. Love is a funny thing, and often we are attracted to karmic partners to finish up old business. In this new spiritual shift of consciousness that we are currently experiencing, that time is over. It's time to attract the partner who resonates at the same vibration you do.

Another tool I learnt from the Loving Relationships training was the Create-a-mate. It was important in the 1980s and even more relevant today to be clear about the sort of person you want in your life. And if you love animals, that had better be high on the list.

When I made my Create-a-mate list, I wanted someone vegetarian, free of addiction and vices, who loved animals, and was in the same industry as me – at that time, comedy. I wanted him to want to work with me, be into health and fitness (but not be glued to the footy on weekends), spiritual and willing to surf. I wanted someone single, loyal, free of emotional attachments, and willing to commit to a relationship. I got Andrew, who was all this and more.

Try This

Even if you are in a relationship, the Create-a-mate exercise works to help bring out the attributes you most love or desire in your partner.

Write down all the attributes of a perfect life partner. Make sure they are phrased in the positive (so, not "Doesn't live too far away", but "Lives in my area."). Be specific and if you don't want a long distance relationship, then you better include "willing to live where I live", or something similar. Make sure they are single as you don't want the karmic fall out of dating someone tied to another. Make sure you add "for the highest good of all concerned, thank you Great Spirit." Sign it, date it and put it away.

Be patient. Andrew was my third relationship after doing this process. I kept refining my list until I got it right – and the Universe delivered.

The Importance of Play

Sarah and Winston on the slide

Let's remember the importance of play in our pursuit of happiness. Good old-fashioned fun. This is something the animals teach us, especially dogs who are simply masters of play and enthusiasm for life. If we can't take this on board from them, then humanity has reached a sad place indeed. There's nothing more soul stirring and heart lifting to me than watching the horses in my care race around their large paddocks kicking up their heels in a fantastic display of health and happiness. It's contagious! It feeds me to see the dogs racing around after a ball or chasing birds flying in the air. I love playing with my cats with bits of string, or playing chase with Sarah the sheep and the goats. Even just walking with them in the hills behind my home is play for me. I love watching the goats and sheep do their "happy dance". It fills my heart with joy.

Joy is contagious. How many people are attracted to the people who radiate fun? Imagine how much more fun it is for the animals when we are in joy.

Try This

Do something different for fun. What does your animal companion like to do? Do that with them. Try and be an animal, embody the attributes of an animal you love or admire, and have fun.

Laughter is indeed the best medicine. Laughter creates endorphins, exercises our lungs, lowers blood pressure and increases the immune system. Sadly, much of our comedy today is simple, nasty sorcery – poking fun or ridiculing others. When Andrew and I performed comedy, we developed a reputation as family fun, because we'd made a pact not to do offensive humour. Instead we created humour from situation and irony, and let other people see our panic and determination as we fearlessly improvised from the suggestions they threw at us.

More recently, I had a wonderful laugh out loud moment on a horse ride with a friend. We stopped to watch a young fox playing with a butterfly. The moment was so endearing and so funny, I had to laugh. It's a memory I cherish and thank the fox for, as I'd been working too hard and the ride was a joy I'd been denying myself.

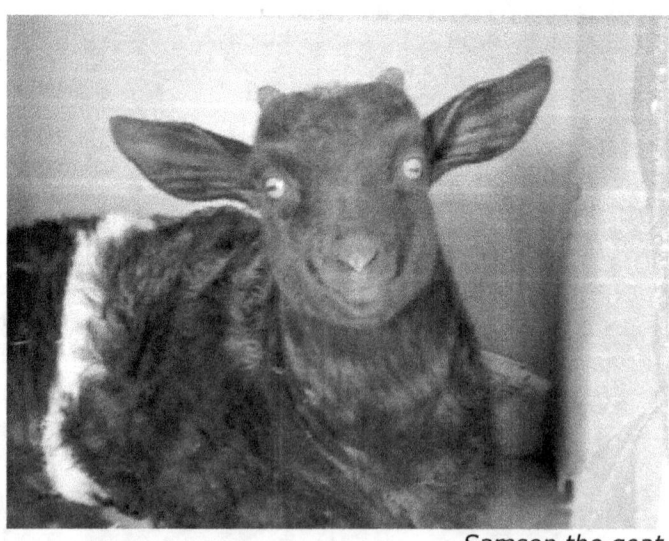

Samson the goat

Make a commitment to happiness. Maybe you can't do it all at once, but maybe you can take a step towards it today. Maybe its taking a book out into the sunshine and reading out loud to your dog, cat or horse. Maybe it is sitting on your horse's bare back and doing nothing. Maybe it is walking in the forest or along the beach, your dogs beside you. Perhaps it is that contented feeling you get from watching your cats curled up in front of the fire.

Try This

Write down all the things which touch your heart, make you laugh, are fun and nourishing to the soul.

For example:

I love watching my horses race down the paddock, tails up, pig rooting with joy. I love the sound of them contentedly munching on hay on a cold winter's night. I love watching my dog's chasing each other, or making me laugh with their antics and the same goes for my goats, sheep and alpacas. I love watching the geese swimming on the pond and the cats cuddled up beside me in bed, or by the fire.

I also love reading out loud as a family, dancing, surfing, listening to good folk music, especially Celtic bands, or drumming. Taking photos makes me happy, catching the light illuminating the beauty of the landscape or the animals.

These are just some of the things which make me happy. Now what about you?

What You Can Do

- Make the commitment to be happy at least 10 minutes a day.

- Do something for 10 minutes with your animal companion, and then 10 minutes for yourself (with or without your animal companion), like singing, dancing, drumming.

- Do endorphin releasing work like exercise or laughing.

- Watch good uplifting movies.

- Read good uplifting books.

- Be in your garden or a park.

- Do something for someone else, like throw a ball for your dog, or take your horse for a bonding walk, not riding.

- Get a career or job which makes your heart sing.

- Always follow the call of your soul, that song from spirit which sets your heart beating wildly. If you need to make a decision about something, does your gut clench with disappointment or does it make your heart race with excitement.

- Have the courage to follow your dreams, because that's the siren song of your soul.

Finally, humanity has that rare gift of hope that things will get better. I once interviewed the late Norman Cousins, who healed himself with comedy. He told me the most important tool in healing is hope.

I have hope that people will take responsibility for and make a commitment to their personal happiness. And that life will improve significantly for the animals in their care.

Our Shadow Side

Shadow work is a big subject, but for here I just want to make people aware that there is much within us that is subconscious and unconscious.

Our shadow is everything about us, that is hidden or unseen to us. It is not hidden from the animals or from other people, although they may not know how to put a name or a finger on it. To be free of the binds of the shadow, you must acknowledge those bits of yourself.

The best way to figure out what your shadow bits are is to be aware of what plugs you in about other people or animals. Feeling irritated with someone? Angry? Annoyed with the dog, or cat? Hmn. Maybe it is time to search within and figure out why. That's your mirror.

Once you have shone light on it, the shadow bit is no longer shadow. You have become conscious of it.

Shadow bits can be things we don't like about others mirrored back to us, and likewise, the things we do like about people and animals. No one person is all black or all white. We may have hidden good attributes as well.

Be ready to recognise when you find yourself irritated with someone. What sets you off? Catch yourself and figure out what attribute is triggering a reaction in you. What is it about them that annoys you? Thank those people and animals silently for being a teacher and a mirror. And look at yourself honestly to see where those attributes are within you. It could be that it is the self-sorcery you do to yourself – like not nurturing or paying attention to your own needs.

Projections

People tend to project their shadow onto other people, and sadly, also onto animals. I see this a lot with people who are afraid of a certain animal, like big dogs. What we fear, we attract. The big dogs will keep coming into your field, until you change your thoughts. It has nothing to do with dogs, and everything to do with your thoughts.

Take 100% Responsibility

If you are making a commitment to growth, then take 100% responsibility for the thoughts which are making your world.

Complaining and blaming only hold you where you are. And in fact, they increase your likelihood of getting more of the same. If you want change in your life, say thank you, thank you, thank you and affirm you are already in the new space you want to be in, and be grateful that the situation is better – until it is. Listen to the voice of the heart, and take the actions you are guided to take.

A few years ago, people in our district were up in arms. The avenue of trees on the road into town were really dangerous. They were running into cars and causing deaths! They should all be cut down! And not only that, compensation needed to be paid to all those people who's cars were ruined because a kangaroo got in their way. Cut down the trees, and cull the kangaroos! Of course, the fault doesn't lie with the driver. No way!

Hmn. Would we say the same thing if a child ran out on the road? Do we sue the child too?

Humans are really good at blaming others for everything that's wrong in their world. Instead, when something is out of sync or alignment with Grace, take steps to put it back into right relations.

Change your thoughts. Instead of thinking something outside of you is creating your world, take responsibility. If you haven't got enough money, love or career satisfaction, then what are the thoughts or contracts that you have playing in your mind? What unhealed part of you is waving a red flag at you and saying "come and get me!"

If something happens to you or your loved one, how do you react? Are you angry? Do you want revenge? Or maybe you consider what unconscious or conscious thoughts attracted this event.

There's the difference between a strong life urge and a death urge. Many people and animals, on one level, have a yearning for release. This could be because they are unhealed. Two decades ago when I was travelling through America performing stand-up, I stayed with some friends who had a dog with distemper. I recognised the symptoms immediately and because I had healed my own dog of the condition, outlined a healing program for them, which did not include a vet visit. Every morning the dog would come and place his yellow, gunky eyes under my hands for healing. The dog healed. But I learnt later that he was run over by a truck and killed. He had a death urge.

When my friend Maryanne was hit by a car and died, I was shocked. She had seemed so full of life and was a powerful animal advocate. But I learnt she was leaving her husband that day, and therefore vulnerable to lower vibration thoughts. Perhaps on one level, she was completed with this life, for there are no accidents.

Sit in the driver's seat of the car of your life. Take charge. Start thinking about what you want, and focus your attention on that. Energy follows thought. And thoughts become things. So by blaming and complaining, you put your focus, energy and intention on creating more of what you don't want! Again, think about what you do want and start creating that with your vibration, imagination and action.

And here's a hint: the more you heal yourself of the wounds which create the unconscious patterns in your life, the higher you will vibrate, and the easier it will be to manifest what you want.

There are numerous techniques for change which you can use. These include shamanic healing, neuro-linguistic programming, hypnosis, Theta healing, magic tapping in all its forms – the list goes on. Study the Law of Attraction, and work from there.

Being Mindful

A roadrunner danced in the corner of desert where the ladies bathroom stood. I signalled to the other women around to be quiet, and we watched silently with big smiles. The bird appeared oblivious, but I knew that he knew there was a crowd of women watching in delight. I sent an enquiry asking what message he had for us. I was told to be patient and aware.

Suddenly, a young couple pushed their way through the gathering and strode out into the desert, intent only on their walk and their togetherness. The roadrunner disappeared into frightened hiding. The women all sighed in disappointment. Ah, I realised, this was a huge lesson in being mindful, for the young couple missed magic that day, and spoilt it for others.

– Excerpt from Billie's journal, 2007

Mindfulness is the art of being aware, awake, considerate, observant and deliberate in our actions. Everywhere I go these days I see people plugged into their iPods and mobile phones, frowning as they rush to get somewhere ten minutes ago. How does Spirit make contact with these people through the messengers of nature and the animals? There's too much noise in the way. People need to take some time to switch off every day and be observant of nature.

After a day's work indoors, I took my class outside to a park and asked them to find a tree who called them, stand against the trunk, get into rhythm with the tree and contact the tree spirit. A magpie sat high in one of the trees and squawked to get our attention. When I called the class together to share their experiences, one young woman complained that she couldn't concentrate because of the magpie. Everyone laughed, and the look on her face was priceless when the penny dropped. Everyone else had a message from both their trees and the magpie – and the magpie's was to "see Beauty in everything".

Right Relations

The two most important steps you can take to keep in right relations are:

- Keep your promises, and don't make promises you can't keep, otherwise Spirit gets mixed messages about your intent.

- Always give back. When someone gives to you, give back. There must be an energetic exchange to create balance and right relations. When you take from nature or an animal, you must give back. Some traditions call for sacred tobacco or corn to be sprinkled on the ground as an offering. Others offer prayer and ceremony. When I'm out in nature, I place my hand over my heart, fill it with the intention of love, and place that hand on the earth with the declaration, "From my heart to your heart." I'll also do an Andean-style *despacho*, or prayer offering.

In the old way of teaching and mentoring, the seeker always took the wise one a gift, like blankets or food, in return for their teaching and wisdom. There was an exchange. When we drove two native Americans to the airport unexpectedly, they gifted us sacred sage in return. The size of the gift isn't the issue. The intent is.

Mother Earth supports us in every way that is important. In return, we must honour her and steward her well. That's what's wrong with the planet today. People take and take and do not give enough back. Now is the time to return to sacred harmony and balance. White people have been always known as those who walk empty handed. Let's change that sentiment right now, and stay in right relations.

Keep Your Promises

How many promises do you keep? How many promises do you break? For a long time, I made promises to the Universe that I would clear out the clutter in my house. But I never had enough time, or made time. It remained something I felt out of alignment with the Universe with. Until I finally did it.

Do you promise walks, ball games, or more time with your animal friends? Do you keep those promises? Do you promise things to your career or to your human family? Keeping promises is important in human relationships. If you break your promises, you break trust. And without trust you have no foundation which you can build a relationship on.

By keeping my promises to my animal companions, I've found a trust builds that is like no other. And that's rewarding!

Nourish Your Soul and Theirs

There's nothing more important in this life than being kind to your soul. Many of us get so caught up in life and our busyness. But what could be more important than running your dog, curling up with your cat for a nap, or hanging out with your horse? If we put things into perspective and did things we know they need, and really, we need as well, both parties would be better off. Is checking your email first thing in the morning a fair substitute for a walk for the dog?

If you find yourself yearning to do something, take the time to do it. Because grieving for not having done it will create disease in your body. So even if you don't go for a ride with your horse, take the few moments to just brush him or give him some carrots. And schedule some time to do the bigger thing when you can. We may not always feel we have the time for the bigger things, but we can take the smaller steps and that's better than nothing at all.

Gratitude

The greatest gift to ourselves and our animal companions is gratitude. This is the path that puts us into alignment with the universe and perks us out of the denser emotional states. In the morning, even before you are out of bed, give thanks. "Thank you for this new day. It's awesome!" By the Law of Attraction, you are more likely to have a good day than a bad day if you start the day with gratitude.

Then, before you go to bed, thank the day. Being grateful is a wonderful way to shift you into a better state of mind and keep you there as you go to sleep. It also opens the doors for more good things to happen – because your focus is on what is good.

I daily thank my animal and human family for being in my life, because I want them and the Universe to know how much they are loved and acknowledged for who they are.

Chapter 48:
Animals as Shamanic Teachers

I call animals shamanic teachers because they give us experience and make us work out what it means. They're subtle and tough, and they teach with great dignity and love.

Learning from our animal friends and from nature requires we develop stillness, mindfulness and the art of communication. If your head is busy somewhere else, it is unlikely you will see the bird in the tree who has a message for you. It's about being aware all the time.

As I have said over and over, animals are great teachers through their behaviour and the way they mirror back to us our health issues, emotional states, and our shadow sides. This, to me, is the essence of their shamanic nature.

Other ways animals are teachers:

- The way they are very in-the-moment is a huge lesson. While they remember the past, they're more likely than humans to forgive and move on – bygones.

- They embody qualities that we can all mindfully embrace, like the nobility and endurance of a horse, the playfulness of a puppy or kitten, the mature presence of an elder dog.

- They lead us into life experiences that we otherwise might not have had, like forcing us to delve into natural therapies when allopathic medicine has no cure, or dealing with death and dying. These are lessons that are easily transferred into other parts of our lives.

- They can show us the value of good habits, like exercise, as well as bad, such as obsessing (I've **got** to dig another hole in the yard). If they are bored and obsessing, this is a clear sign to you that both of you need more in your life. Perhaps not work, but definitely play of the animal kind, like more walks and more intelligent animal education and games.

- When they behave in ways we don't like, they hold a mirror up to us that reflects how we handle things. Do we scream and yell at them? Do we deal with them with quiet patience and persistence? (And which would we prefer used on us or on our children?)

- They provide us with company and love unconditionally. A huge lesson.

- They can help us see value in the simple things in life, like lying in the sun, running, or eating.

- They're loyal and love us for our authentic essence, not what we pretend to be.

Animal Guidance for the Current Times

Some of the requests, messages and guidance people have received from the animals over the years has been very specific to their particular person's higher purpose or a stage in their growth. But the following are very common, and I think, relevant to helping everyone prepare for a New Earth.

House Clearing

One of the messages I get a lot from my animal clients is the need to keep the house clean, both physically and energetically, and at a high vibration. Sometimes they disappear and won't return until the "house is ritually cleansed." This is usually because the house holds the energy of anger, distress, anxiety, irritation and all those lesser energies. If arguments have taken place, some animals are very clear they don't want to live in that dense energy. Or you might have visited somewhere and unwittingly come back carrying an energy or entity that they can see and you can't. You might have even brought home something you bought which is carrying an energy the animals sense and don't like. I once studied with an Aboriginal Elder who encouraged us to smudge (burn sage) absolutely everything that was brought into the home to clear it of unwanted energies.

Cleansing a house is essentially the same as sacred house clearing. You can get as Feng Shui or shamanic about it as your intuition tells you, but here are the basic steps.

- Set your intention to clear the house of negative and unwanted energy, and to raise its vibration to the highest which can be held for the highest good of all concerned.

- Open the windows and doors so that energies may leave.

- Give the house a thorough physical clean. You can actually "see" stuck energy in corners and places you haven't been to for a while. See all that junk in that corner that's been there for years and that no one even sees anymore? That's an energetic black hole. Clean it up.

- After giving the house a thorough physical clean, bang a drum, ring bells, or cymbals, or clap your hands into the corners to move about the energy.

- Burn sage, wormwood or sweetgrass sticks to get rid of remaining negative energy. This is called smudging. Please be aware of animals in your presence when you do this. Some of them may be sensitive to the smell.

- Play some light, bright music to raise the vibration of the room. This has an added effect of lightening your own mood and boosting your metabolism. Please note, heavy rock and music with dark or negative lyrics is not beneficial.

- Finally, burn high quality rose incense in the room. I'm not comfortable with cut flowers, but if you ask permission and it is granted, then a vase of carnations or roses placed in the room also has the effect of raising the vibration, roses being the highest vibration.

Express Yourself and Raise Your Own Vibration

I have had many requests from animal clients for their people to stop drinking alcohol. When you drink or do drugs, you aren't actually really present to stop entities from coming into your body. Or maybe you become belligerent or aggressive, and that's why the animals don't like it. But whatever the reason, personally I would take it on board because animals have keener senses than we do.

A radio announcer's dog once told me to tell him to "drink less beer", and other people have been told "drink more water". Some people have been told to change their diet and include more raw food. Raw food is alkaline and it could be the animal's way of telling people to shift their body chemistry for either weight loss or to prevent cancer.

Some people are told to go for more walks by the sea or in the bush, and some are told to dance or do some form of self-expression like writing or painting. One client was amazed that her elderly cat told her to draw cats – as this is what she once loved to do! When she returned to the practice, she found deep satisfaction – made all the more meaningful because she had been guided there by her cat!

Turn off the TV

Two messages I get for many, many people is "turn off the news" and "turn off the TV". I personally stopped watching the news a long time ago, as I don't want to have those images burned into my brain so that I end up creating more of it! If you understand that everything inside us is reflected in the outside world, then the baser shows and frightening images only serve to create more of the same.

As I increase my own vibration, I've noticed neither the animals nor I can tolerate what I call third dimensional TV. I find it loud on many levels and it irritates my pack of dogs to the point where they won't settle. Switch to romance, comedy or something intriguing and uplifting, and suddenly the room is a lot calmer. I see this settling behaviour as a seal of approval from the animals which shows me I'm not doing anything harmful. Best of all, I have to say, is when the TV is completely off!

Chapter 49:
Animal Medicine and Messengers

The second wheelbarrow of horse manure was almost full when a small brown sparrow flitted to the ground in front of me. I knew she was trying to get my attention.

I stopped my shovelling. "Do you have a message for me?"

"They're not coming," the sparrow sent. And she flew away.

I muttered my thanks, threw my shovel onto the wheelbarrow and walked into the house. As I walked in, the phone rang and I knew it was the real estate agent before he spoke.

"They're not coming," he said.

I grinned and sent further thanks and blessings to the sparrow who had saved me hours and hours of work cleaning horse manure to make the paddock look neat for prospective buyers who weren't coming.

Thank You, Spirit.

– Excerpt from Billie's journal, 1996

Do you have a message for me?

Once we are in right relations and mindful in nature, we begin to see that the Universe conspires to put us on the right path or give us the information we need. We are all one and we are all connected. There are no co-incidences.

There are many shamanic books and card decks which talk about the sacred meaning of the animals, but a particular deck's particular interpretation of a particular animal may or may not have significance to you in the moment when you are out in nature. Understanding an animal's medicine can be very helpful in tarot readings and when understanding totem and power animals. But worldwide, the same animal means different things to different cultures. And sadly, their medicine can be misconstrued when interpreted.

To understand animal medicine at this level takes study of the individual animal and their gifts in a cultural context.

When an animal catches your attention by crossing your path, there is something specific you are meant to receive personally. It could be a warning. It could be an affirmation. And it could be a personal message. That message might be a response to a question you might have been silently asking. What were you thinking or talking about when you saw the animal?

Each animal is an individual and speaks individually.

When owls turned up several times in close succession in my life, I didn't turn to animal cards to figure out what the message was. I went to the owl herself.

"Do You Have a Message for Me?"

I have owl medicine in my field, but owls mean different things to me at different times when they appear. It's important to open yourself to your intuition and the silent whispers on the wind.

When an animal appears for someone, they sometimes try to read too much into it. And other times, they don't read enough into it. Secret animal business tells us that animals are messengers of spirit, and act as our guides through life. So don't run to a book looking for a message which may or may not relate to you. Instead, ask the animal what message he brings. You may be surprised at the answer, and glad you did.

Chapter 50:

The Need for Social Change in Animal Welfare

"The greatness of a nation and its moral progress can be judged by the way its animals are treated. I hold that the more helpless a creature, the more entitled it is to protection by man from the cruelty of man."

– Mahatma Gandhi (1869 - 1948)

"If you have men who will exclude any of God's creatures from the shelter of compassion and pity, you will have men who will deal likewise with their fellow men."

– St. Francis of Assisi

"Not to hurt our humble brethren [the animals] is our first duty to them, but to stop there is not enough. We have a higher mission: to be of service to them whenever they require it."

– St. Francis of Assisi, from God's Covenant with Animals, Lantern Books, 2000, xii

The For Life Campaign

If you have picked up this book, you probably love animals and are sensitive to them. You want to understand them better and want to be the best you can be for your animal and the animals in general.

So I probably don't have to tell you that all around the world, animals are suffering. I'm not going to go into specifics too, too much, because I am clear that if we all focus on how much suffering there is, then those grizzly images go out in the world and we create more of them.

Far better to focus on the good stories, and what we can do to help create more of those. However, what I want to do in the following pages is help you understand why we need to focus on social change for animals and how we can do that with the power of our intention, the healthiness of our thinking, our focus on the positive, and our actions.

So I will outline some stories and some spiritual thinking that I hope will help you understand why I created the For Life Campaign as part of the call to end the euthanasia of healthy animals, why I join the call for a vegan world, and why I have a vision for a world free of predators.

Spiritual Thinking

If we understand that what we think creates our world, then we have to understand the great big melting pot of thoughts creating the world we currently live in. There's a lot of fear, negativity and limiting thoughts. There's a lot of cultural conditioning.

The shamanic viewpoint sees the world as interrelated with everything else. Humans are connected to Nature and to the weather. What the 2012 phenomenon is doing is fuelling our manifestation capability, so that we are creating our realities more quickly. We are in the time of instant karma. With the acceleration of time, and the collapsing of old paradigms, people are under more pressure than ever to change. But many people don't know that. They just find themselves in their own private turmoil or dark night of the soul.

This affects our animal friends on many levels. For a start, if the weather responds to us and our emotions and lifestyle, then what does it say about our severe imbalance as a species, when we have the Earth Changes we are currently experiencing. As well as human suffering we are causing immense animal suffering by this imbalance.

And it's not nice living with people under stress, with their increased tempers and friction. The potential for animal abuse in those kinds of homes is high.

We also see more animal companions made homeless through these difficult times.

This is why it's important to make finding peace within a priority. Love and joy help propel us to the higher frequencies needed for the shift in the planet today, but the lower frequencies of animal and human suffering hold us firmly in the old world of pain and negativity.

Animal suffering causes a massive stain on our collective unconsciousness. And more and more people are waking up to this. If we want to walk into the Golden Age of prophecy and peace, we have to stop murdering animals in their millions, destroying their habitats, exploiting them for profit and gain, and throwing them out when they are too much trouble. And I use the term "murder" deliberately, as in to kill intentionally and with premeditation. Because that's what we do.

And this is from cultures who proclaim to love animals.

Here's the crux of it: we will never have true peace on this planet until we change our thinking about animals. There will not be true peace until the slaughterhouses around the world are silent of the cries of dying animals, until the death chambers in the pounds are empty, until all the animals know that they are safe in the hands of men.

Simply put, we need to stop hurting the animals we claim to love in the name of science, vanity, fashion and food. It keeps us from the realm of angels and condemns humanity to a continued culling process by Mother Earth with the Earth Changes, hurting the innocent animals in the process.

It's time to change things. We can choose to change. We can choose to work on healing ourselves and shining our light more brightly. We can make a decision to use our intelligence and be the best human we can be.

Sacrificial Lambs

A few years ago some Australian sheep were stranded in the ocean on their way to becoming meat in another country. Their plight touched a nerve in sensitive people all over the world and also brought attention to the horrors of the live export trade.

The souls of these animals had signed up for that torment in this life to help humanity wake up to the plight of animals. Did people feel compassion for these helpless beings? Yes. It caused an outcry.

Similarly, whales beaching themselves is another way they sacrifice themselves in order for us to open our hearts. The Japanese killing of humpback whales in 2007 brought a similar outcry with humans risking their lives to save the whales.

When I tuned into these magnificent beings of the sea, they were sad that they would suffer losses, but pleased that the humans who acted with compassion and love were responding with the intended outcome of their sacrifice.

We really are in a time of great separation of consciousness – those who are waking to compassion and love and those who are not. The desired outcome is that once enough of humanity responds appropriately and walks in the fifth dimension of beauty, there will be a tipping point – and we will indeed have a Golden Age of peace.

In this way the animals are sacrificial lambs. In this way, they help humans shift from mindless cruelty to true humanity.

Earth Shadow and Man's Collective Karma

There's another Doctor floating around the unseen worlds, who isn't a figment of the BBC's imagination. Dr Lascelles is a man beyond the veil who was ably channelled by the late Mr C. A. Simpson. I came across his work in a tiny booklet called *A Pilgrimage with the Animals*, by Stanley King.

The book hid in my bookcase for over two decades, a relic from my first trip to England. It suddenly came to my attention when I began to write this book, and was asking myself the question, "How can I make people care enough to change?"

I found myself one day unable to write. All I wanted to do was sleep, but a deadline was near and I caught sight of the booklet on my pile of research books. The good doctor was guiding me! If I hadn't been overcome with fatigue, I wouldn't have stopped to read. I figured he was in cahoots with my spirit tribe!

Although I talk a lot about the collective stain on man's unconscious because of the way we treat animals, Dr Lascelles, speaks more plainly and more graphically, and is particularly vehement against vivisection, the testing on animals for any reason, and the killing and torture of animals for fashion and vanity. He says we are creating a "morass of retribution", and that if we knew the enormity of it we would "recoil with repugnance."

He refers to what he calls the Earth Shadow. According to occult thinking, fear doesn't go away. It hangs around in a thick, etheric blanket, affecting people's minds and bringing about anxiety, guilt, regret and depression. This Earth Shadow is not only from humanity's fears and sufferings, it is also the result of nature's suffering, especially the agony of animals who are killed in "fear and horror".

According to Lascelles, this thick blanket of fear has built up over the centuries and is now almost solidified. It affects everyone. And the earth-bound psyches of killed animals also serve to increase the "secret dementia which haunts human beings without their knowing it."

Animals are supposed to die peacefully at the end of natural lives. As we all are. By the murder of the animals we claim to love, in pounds and slaughter houses all over the world, we condemn humanity to unhappiness, depression and phobias.

We are all connected. By the killing and inhumane treatment of animals, we violate their sacred rights, and this in turn sabotages our "sacred peace".

Creating Social Change By Changing Ourselves

Native wisdom says that by changing ourselves, we change the world, and when we don't do our personal work, we hold the world back. So it is up to all of us to do our work of personal change.

If we don't want to see the future suffering of animals, then rid yourself of the violence and anger within, by doing your forgiveness and striving towards replacing your fears with love and peace.

Break through the cultural amnesia and remember how to live in right relations with the world. Until we can live in sacred harmony with our furry brothers and sisters, how can we live in harmony with each other, and indeed, among the galaxy in peace?

We are living in exciting times of change, but it is up to us to make a change for the better. Every single one of us. It is up to us to make sure the prophesied Golden Era of peace comes into being through humanity shifting their attitudes – towards each other and our animal brethren.

Things You Can Do

Here are some things you can do to create a better world for animals.

Mental, emotional and spiritual things:

- Forgive everyone for everything.

- Think of all the beings you fear or consider "pests", and find things you love about them. Honour them. Acknowledge them. See them as Divine beings. Ask yourself what it is within you that might be mirrored in your reaction to these beings. Shine some light on that. Ask them for some wisdom.

- Meditate on a world which honours animals. "See" it as already happened – and if enough of us do this, it will become so.

- Practise mindfulness.

- Use stress meditation tapes to help you be more peaceful in your reactions.

- Love yourself.

- Journey to the Other World.

- Understand that whatever is in your outer world is from your inner world, and so instead of blaming and complaining, accept responsibility and work to change. This could be as easy as saying, "Oh, I now release this issue." Or you might need to seek help.

Physical and practical things:

- Become vegetarian or vegan.

- Lobby for For Life sanctuaries (no kill shelters), saying "no" to euthanasia of homeless animals and assessment testing. Write to your local council, your local members and the RSPCA. If enough people do it, we can make a difference.

- Refuse to buy factory farmed products.

- Write to all of the above about the horrors of factory farming. Write to the press about your feelings.

- Support your body chemistry with nourishing foods like fruit, vegetables and whole foods – instead of chemicals and fast food. This way you will become more peaceful and less irritable and reactive.

- Get enough sleep.

- Schedule play time.

- Become an animal foster carer or work with wildlife rescue groups.

- Spread the word that we need to each focus on a positive beautiful world for animals, not focus on how bad things appear to be.

What can you add to the above lists?

Animal Advocacy: The Current Problem with Pounds and Shelters

It was love at first sight for Leeor, one of my students. The dog was in an animal shelter and Leeor was under her spell. She called the dog Blossom because she knew Blossom would indeed blossom under her care. She just had to wait the seven required days for Blossom's carer to appear, or not. Leeor was incredibly excited about her journey with this dog.

But something went very wrong. Blossom failed the behavioural assessment. Leeor felt a growing dread. She offered to pay for a second test with an outside assessor. No deal. Blossom was off to the death chamber. She was murdered even though she was desperately wanted.

Leeor went into shock. She couldn't believe the nightmare of it. As a student communicator she understood the connection she had with Blossom and she knew it was important for both of them for their spiritual growth. How could her soul partner be snatched away? How could Blossom be dead? How come she was so powerless to do a thing to stop it?

Leeor began an animal advocacy group to try and change the mindset that chose death over love and commitment just because the dog had supposedly failed a stringent behavioural test under stressful conditions.

Many people have the idea that pounds and shelters are places where people love animals and will do their best for them. And, yes, some people there *are* loving, and they *are* trying their best. But most are unaware of the sentient and psychic nature of the animals in their care, or have closed themselves to this so they can do their jobs.

The draconian idea of killing dogs if they fail to pass stringent behavioural tests is disrespectful and a great disservice to both animals and humans. It shows ignorance of the animal's sentience and psychic nature, and the spiritual bonds they have with humans.

Sadly many people are locked into thinking that this is the "only" way to deal with the problem of too many homeless animals. I disagree. In Germany, for example, three vets have to sign off on a dog before she is euthanased. A very different system, indeed. And to my eye, much less barbaric.

If we stop killing animals in pounds and showed the world that all life is precious, and that animals were valuable members of society, it would filter down to the rest of humanity and people might stop thinking of animals as toys or disposable commodities.

What we also have to understand is that some people need to take on a less than perfect animal for them to heal themselves. Some people need to go on that journey for their own spiritual enlightenment or healing. So if someone has an urge to take on an animal in need, let them.

Once I was contacted to try and help save a young dog who'd been surrendered. This shelter had been told that people were interested in the dog, but when we rang at 9 AM to tell them we were going to collect him that day, the dog was already murdered. We were all shocked. The council worker in charge was new and zealous, and made the decision to murder the dog based on her own thoughts that he didn't get on with other dogs. My friends who were trying to save the dog protested. They said they hadn't seen any evidence of that behaviour, and even if they had, he could have been given a chance to be educated, and he might have been homed as a single dog.

There was another story of the elderly man made homeless. He took his old dog to a shelter in the hope that she might find a good home, as he couldn't provide her with one. He was crying as he handed her over. She was killed the same day because she was old and therefore considered unrehomeable.

These are just three stories out of pile that come across my desk every week. I believe assessment testing is archaic and must be ended. If you are unfortunate enough to end up in the pound with frightening smells of death and are able to read people's minds, how on earth can you be expected to "behave" appropriately? I believe many of the dogs who pass the tests, already know they have a chance to live.

When I have spoken to people about the pound situation, the response has been that the public are "stupid and irresponsible" and that education is the key. The problem is that we already have an "education" that says it's okay to throw things away when they don't work properly. Because it is understood that it's okay to euthanize healthy animals, we devalue their lives. It makes it okay to throw them away.

That's why you get breeders who think the solution to puppies and kittens not sold is to kill them. That's why you get racehorses and greyhounds being killed when they can no longer race, and people dumping their animals in the pound or just abandoning them because really, their life is of no value and they are too much hassle. Allowing animals to be killed just because they are homeless is a major stumbling block to getting people to care and commit.

There's discussion in some religions as to whether or not animals have souls. We're taught that the biblical idea of man having dominion over animals, means domination rather than stewardship. We're taught that animals are less than us.

We are full of education.

If it were law to care for an animal and euthanasia wasn't an easy way out, more people would consider their animal commitment before going into it. If we changed our language around animals and helped more people understand their secret animal business, life would be better for animals all around. They would be revered instead of a cute toy for the children or something to profit from.

As someone who has been on the ground floor of animal rescue work for over two decades, I have to say that it tarnishes the way you view your fellow species. The only thing that has kept me going was the belief and hope that people would change, and I see that now. People are changing and more people are standing up for what they believe is right – that all animals are worthy of love, compassion and life.

We do have to educate people. But it has to be a different education to what most people think.

Unless a pound or shelter has a *for life* or no kill policy, it is an unsafe place for animals and they know it. It affects their behaviour and temperament. It causes unnecessary suffering, and it causes a dark stain on our collective unconscious because we know it is wrong, and yet we look the other way.

Why do we sit around and accept the decision that animals have to die because they are homeless? We blame the numbers, the back yard breeders, the expense of neutering and spaying, the ignorance of people who don't make a commitment to the animals. We say there are too many.

To all of that, I say balderdash.

It doesn't have to be that way.

And a change is long over due.

To me, it looks like nothing less than a failure of will and determination. If Best Friends Animal Sanctuary can do it, if the San Francisco SPCA can do it, if the entire country of Germany can do it, then why don't we do it as well?

A pound is not the place to put your dog or cat if you have any love for animals. Surrendered animals are usually murdered anywhere from immediately to around two days. Lost animals who are microchipped get 14 days. Without a microchip, they get seven. Who makes this decision? And why aren't the people of microchipped animals contacted? And if they are, why can't they take some responsibility? Allowing your dog or cat to go to the pound is as bad as committing murder yourself. Sorry, but it is.

No animal should die just because they are homeless. Why, when the Bible everyone keeps quoting says, "Thou shalt not Kill" do we blithely ignore and kill daily? Wouldn't it be better, for example, if the pounds and shelters of our society made a stand and refused to kill animals in their care. Then what?

I only hope we can find out one day.

The Sad Plight Of Old Animals, Including Horses

Our society could value the elderly more, both human and animal. If a horse can no longer be ridden, he is considered useless and sent to the knackers. Older dogs and cats are easy targets for the death chambers. It's not much of a reward for a lifetime of service. I would like to make a plea here for the older animal who is homeless.

It would be lovely to see people making a long-term financial commitment to their older horses, and for more retirement homes for aged horses to be supported. Here at Ballyoncree, we have a large number of older and special needs horses, and none of them are "in work". To me riding is fun, but the real gift of horse is being around their energy, and the opportunity to serve, observe and learn. Older or retired horses don't deserve a miserable end. They are family, they are kin. And we need to take care of them.

The Story of Dusty

The woman from the Crisis Centre had heard of our work. She was looking for a home for a dog from an "at risk" home. The woman "at risk" wouldn't leave her situation without a new home for her dog. She wouldn't leave the dog with her violent partner.

They rang when I was teaching and Andrew helped them out by rattling off the rescue organizations he knew that fostered and took care of animals.

When he told me about the conversation that night I had that flash of insight which told me the dog would come to us. He needed us and he needed us urgently. "Ring them back, Andrew, and tell them we'll take the dog."

I was full of admiration for the dog's person. She had courage to stay with her violent partner for the sake of the dog. By taking the dog, we would also free her. The dog had to get out of there.

Andrew rang back the next day. And when he was told that none of the rescue organisations would take Dusty because he was too old, Andrew saw red. "Do you want me to get him now?" he said.

It was a month later when the call came. The dog had to be collected that day. Andrew was there in half an hour. Dusty clung to him, and has been bonded to Andrew ever since.

Dusty is a gentle, sweet dog. Sadly he had been badly beaten and had many injuries. His nerves are shot, he walks with a permanent limp, and he nearly died from a hole in his diaphragm. He ended up costing us thousands of dollars despite some very kind sanctuary sponsors, but we were always pleased he came to us, and is living the rest of his life in health and happiness. It just makes you feel you are living your life well when you can do something for another.

There's a lot of people who say, "Oh, I wish I could do what you do, but...." Andrew and I are just two ordinary people with a high level of commitment. We do it. And so can you.

I think there's nothing more satisfying to me than to see happy, healthy animals in my care with sleek shiny coats and loads of vitality. Dusty's limp will never change, but his coat has gone from unhealthy orange to deep dusty red. He is shiny and healthy and his happiness is evident from the big grin on his face. And that's priceless.

The Alternatives: The Good News

Fortunately, things are changing fast through the commitment of wonderful people all over the world. I believe kill shelters will soon be a thing of the past, and that past will be considered barbaric indeed, when public pressure finally undermines this old paradigm. While some people still think no kill shelters can't possibly work, these kinds of shelters are popping up everywhere, created by people who care and commit.

In the past we've found excellent homes against seemingly impossible odds through the network of caring people who read my newsletter Animal Whispers. Imagine trying to find a home for a 10-year-old, blind, diabetic fox terrier who's person had burnout and didn't think she could find anyone to take care of him while she went overseas for a break. What she needed was the right kind of advice and help, not the normal kind, which was pressuring her to euthanize him. We had the week between Christmas and New Year to re-home him. One of my students took him on gladly as a friend for her dog, recently bereaved, and the relieved woman has become a supporter, and still visits her dog as an aunt.

Another of my students found a good home with a Labrador for an elderly Lab whose people were moving overseas. We've had homes found for horses with a day to go, and two dingoes (read: needs special people) who had three days left.

And the list goes on and on. I'm just one person with an email list. Lots of people are working on behalf of the animals (but we need more!) If we spread the net wide enough, we can help *all* the animals in need. And if we change the system to a more animal-honouring one, this would truly be possible. Humanity has to step up. And more and more are heeding the call to action.

Some of the Many, Many People-Driven Organizations to Inspire You

This is simply a small selection of some of the fabulous organisations and individuals who are making a difference. It is inspiring to see how individuals can work together to do good. As I said, it's just a matter of heart, desire and will.

Let's consider the so-called cat problem. In many, if not most pounds, the percentage of cats who are placed is miniscule compared to the number murdered. One city newspaper had a picture of a shelter worker with a box full of kittens, all marked for death, because they had too many kittens and cats who were homeless, they said.

The Cat House on the Kings
www.cathouseonthekings.com

Lynee Lattanzio single-handedly designed, funded and built The Cat

House on the Kings, a sanctuary on six acres. The Cat House on the Kings is California's largest no-cage, no-kill, lifetime cat sanctuary and adoption centre. Since its founding 16 years ago, this unique shelter has saved over 16,000 cats and 4,000 dogs, and currently cares for more than 700 cats and kittens.

Note that these animals, including dogs, live free on the six acres in harmony. And that includes feral cats, too.

Now a non-profit corporation and supported by volunteers and donations from the public, Lynee started alone but with a responsible vision. She was convinced she was put here on Earth to do something worthwhile and cats became her calling. She is an incredible inspiration.

Search YouTube for the inspiring video about the Cat House on the Kings.

Best Friends Animal Society
www.bestfriends.org

In America, Best Friends Animal Society is leading the way in animal advocacy. A small group of committed people bought 3,000 acres of land in Utah for use as an animal sanctuary, and made a commitment to never turn an animal away. At first it was funded from their own money, and now they receive donations and their service is phenomenal and nationwide. At any one time they have more than 1,500 animals in their care. They are committed to a program called No More Homeless Pets.

Here's what Michael Mountain, President and one of the Founders of Best Friends, had to say about his program when I asked him:

> *Up until the early 1990s it was almost universally accepted, here in the United States, that there was simply no alternative to killing millions and millions of homeless pets in shelters every year – about 15 million every year.*
>
> *Here at Best Friends Animal Sanctuary, we hadn't thought about the issue very much. We'd been busy building the sanctuary and caring for the animals who came here – but weren't really focusing on the wider issues. Then, one hot August day in 1992, a young German couple on their honeymoon came driving into the sanctuary. They'd been hiking at the Grand Canyon and had come across a mother cat and her newborn kittens, abandoned on a*

trail, huddled up against a rock trying to seek protection from the blazing sun. The German couple picked up the whole family and raced to the highway, where they stopped at a gas station and were directed to Best Friends, about 60 miles away.

We were able to save the mother and two of the three kittens, whom we named Hansel and Gretel. The young couple waited around for the rest of the day to be sure all was O.K., and while they were waiting I gave them a tour of the sanctuary. They were impressed with what we were doing, but puzzled about how and why the dogs and cats and other animals came here. I, in turn, was puzzled by their puzzlement.

"They come from shelters all over."

"But why do they need to come here?"

I explained about the special care they could get here, but nothing quite seemed to make sense to the couple until it gradually dawned on them what happened to homeless pets in this country.

"You mean ... you mean ... that in this country they KILL homeless animals?"

When I said that there were about 15 million dogs and cats being killed every year, their mouths dropped open.

"In our country," one of them replied, "it is illegal to kill a homeless animal."

I later learned that it took three vets signing off on the fact that a dog or cat needed to be euthanased for their own good (terminally and painfully ill, and with no quality of life).

In other words, killing all these animals wasn't a "necessary evil." It was just an evil.

For us, here at Best Friends, this was the beginning of the No More Homeless Pets campaign, which would work with shelters and rescue groups and communities all over the country to bring an end to the killing of shelter animals.

The main keys to this goal were hardly rocket science. The basics are:

Encouraging people to get their pets spayed or neutered, and providing low-cost and easily accessible sterilization for low-income families.

Encouraging people to adopt their pets from shelters, rather than buying from stores. This means making adoption easy, accessible and fashionable.

And making a firm commitment within local communities to bring an end to the killing.

Within 10 years, the numbers being killed in shelters had dropped from 15 million to below 5 million. We still have some way to go, but the progress has been remarkable. Few people now seriously maintain that the goal of bringing that figure to near-zero cannot be reached.

The San Francisco Society For Protection against Cruelty for Animals

This is also no kill, relying on the good hearts of people who foster and help the animals in need. Their no-kill policy was inspired by Nathan Winograd, an excellent example of one person inspiring a huge change. Check him out on Google.

Angel's Gate

www.angelsgate.org

One of the USA homes for animal hospice and rehabilitation.

Senior Dogs Rescue in Australia

www.freewebs.com/seniordogs

The Senior Dog Project in USA and Canada

www.srdogs.com

Edgar's Mission

www.edgarsmission.org.au

Animal advocacy for farm animals

Good Samaritan – Donkey Sanctuary
www.donkeyrescue.org.au
Turning donkey suffering into donkey serenades.

Horse Rescue Australia Inc
www.horserescue.com.au

Devoted to the care and rehabilitation of horses who have been abused.

Get Involved

These are but a thimble's worth of the people the world over working hard and in some cases risking their own lives to help the animal kingdom. Some people go without food, sleep, rest or money for the animals. The burnout turnover is high and it takes dedication, commitment and support.

But their stories are phenomenal. And what they are achieving is phenomenal. These are people of courage and motivation, seeing a need and filling it. They have to be applauded. There are lots of positive stories around of people who are just seeing where the problem lies, and stepping up.

When the heart is willing, the answers come. We just need people who will go the extra mile and make their passion for animals a commitment for life.

Try This
Make a list of other rescue organisations and no-kill or For Life shelters around the world.

For Life Sanctuary

I was pregnant with Tamsin when I had the vision for Rainbow Fianna and the For Life Sanctuary. In the vision, I saw an enormous property where, for example, old horses could live out their retirement in large paddocks with other horses, instead of being turned into dog food. There, animals of all kinds could find a home for life if they couldn't be re-homed.

This vision included a shamanic education centre at the heart where students learned first hand from the animals they cared for, based on our personal credo of caring for animals with love, compassion and commitment. The people working with the animals would all be educated in telepathy, diet, holistic healing and the shamanic viewpoint.

The vision also saw For Life sanctuaries the world over, linked by the net, so no animal in need was ever without a sacred haven.

This vision is coming into being. Our own Ballyoncree Animal Sanctuary is a small private, forever home for the animals who have asked to be with us. Not all do. We've run up to 30 horses here and eight dogs. It's given us practise and experience for the bigger vision. Indeed my school Rainbow Fianna already attracts the animal carers of tomorrow – human angels who Walk in Beauty, who have the courage to work on their own healing, who see animals and nature for who they really are, and who treat them accordingly.

Farm Animals

It was on a Sunday morning when I first met Sarah, a tiny bundle in a box. Her mother had died and her farmer person didn't want her. Someone suggested us. So down the drive came two strangers who called themselves "soft in the head" for bringing us a stray lamb. I took the lamb gently in my arms.

"Soft in the heart", I said to them smiling.

Sarah came into the house to be raised with our eight dogs, four cats, two budgies and two goats – the latter had also been orphaned and needing a mum. Sarah, Winston and Samson loved standing by the fire place to keep warm and Sarah would also cuddle up with the dogs on their beds.

Like all sheep, Sarah is intelligent, bright and funny. She and the goats come for walks with the dogs and us in the morning, skipping around, jumping in delight and head butting for good measure. They bring us a lot of delight.

We fed all three on goat's milk and later they developed an appetite for hay. To ease the goats out of our living room and into their new home in the back yard, we'd leave them there with Totem, our first hand-and-house raised goat, and the alpacas, Zeeka and Benji for longer and longer at night. We'd then invite them back into the house for the warmth of the fire and cuddles. Eventually we moved our sofas into the old goose shed, much to their delight, and they settled easily into a full-time life outside. Goats need shelter, and they love to jump and climb.

Sarah was a different matter. She took some time to move out, being a bit younger. She made it known that she resented having to sleep in the mudroom with the bikes instead of with the fire and the dogs. So we compromised. Sarah slept on a dog bed for the rest of her stay as an inside animal.

When she finally made the transition to the back yard, she'd greet us enthusiastically in the morning, demanding to run and play with the dogs. She could climb and jump as well as any goat, and had a wonderful sense of humour.

Today we have a delightful herd of farm animal family, who are friendly and funny and very, very loving. The bond we have with them was worth the winters with newspaper on the floor instead of rugs, losing our sofas, and hundreds of dollars worth of goat's milk powder. It's a bond that transcends.

When she was younger, Sarah would come in the car with us and the dogs when we went grocery shopping. I was very grateful we were a vegan and vegetarian family because there was no way I could have packed lamb's fry or lamb chops or anything lamb or sheep in the car with Sarah. That would just be yucky. Sarah is family. Sheep are her relatives. That meant all sheep are our family too.

I keep thinking about the herds of sheep who live around me on neighbouring properties. Some of the sheep are very, very smart. I often find stowaway sheep with their lambs on our place, avoiding separation.

And during the drought we had whole flocks who found a hole in the fence to our place which was more lightly grazed. Part of me didn't want to tell the farmer they were here so they could be safe and able to graze in peace.

And yet some farmers do things like shear them in winter so they'll find shelter. I was once staying with some friends who shocked me by coming into breakfast every day with a tally of the dead sheep they'd found that winter morning. "Two hundred deadies today," they said. It was harsh open country they lived in and the poor sheep had frozen to death.

Cattle are no different. I once had a herd of cows come running up to the fence to speak to me when we first moved to Ballyoncree. They told me they were pleased to meet me and wanted to know more about me and my family. They told me they had been there for years and their person liked them very much.

Apparently my neighbour had been watching and the next time she saw me she asked me what I'd been doing to her cows. I guess it must have been strange to see them all crowded at the fence, chatting to me. I told her we were just saying hello!

Each animal in a herd or flock, or squashed into trucks for the abattoirs, or sitting in the hot sun at the sale yards, or living any kind of a life, has a mind and a voice. They have emotions. They are not interchangeable commodities to be exploited, and treated like things. It's time farmers also stepped up and saw themselves as guardians of their sentient animals. Wouldn't it be great if animals were asked if they wanted to be milked or their eggs collected? And if sheep were shorn with dignity and respect instead of in a race between shearers.

I believe as a species we are able to make the shift into humane and respectful farming, especially if we drop the killing-for-meat aspect of farming. We just have to find that part of us that wants to go the extra mile. The part that recognises the Divine in all life, and honours that.

Chapter 51:
The End of Animal Suffering: Brave New World of Animal Stewardship

Louis showed me himself as a wise man. A teacher or a sage. He had been a father once to his person, Susan. When I asked him what he had to teach her in this life, he said, "That love is all, truly. Love is everything.

"Humans often really don't know what it is to love unconditionally. In this they are our children, and need to be guided. This is why we often come in a cute and cuddly form – to show them the way."

I asked Louis for a message for Susan – some guidance she could use.

"Tell her that wearing dresses doesn't make a woman. A woman is female, the divine feminine. This is lost from the earth right now. And needs to return. What is divine feminine? It is love, heart consciousness, intuition, intuitive guidance, listening, respect, honouring. On earth there is a lack of balance and the scales need to be tipped in the balance of divine feminine. In a world of compassion there is no suffering."

Louis told Susan that he wanted her to follow the path of the divine feminine and become a warrior for compassion. He said animals have had enough and it is time to make a stand. He said hate and anger were not the key, love was.

– Excerpt from Billie's client journals, 2008

My students sit around a circle looking at me to speak. The room, however, is filled with spirit animals and people. I pause for a moment checking in. A spirit dog called Louis reminds me of a communication I did with him not that long ago. "The animals have had enough and it is time to make a stand," he told me. He explained that animals were finished with suffering. "Hate and anger are not the key, love is."

I thank the dog and relay the message to my students. This is the cornerstone, the foundation upon which my teachings lie. It's time to take animal care to a whole new level, and we can do that by honouring animals as sentient, spiritual and psychic. But most of all, we can do that by improving ourselves and our understanding of the deeper mysteries of life.

In our society, most people don't realise the impact they have on others – the earth, the environment, and the animals in their care. Spinning in their own orbit, people have forgotten they are connected to all of life in an etheric and enormous spider web. People aren't taught about the luminous energy fields around us and all of life. Or to take 100 percent responsibility for their actions.

The students in my class are keen to know how to help animals who are suffering. It's a question that comes up more and more now. It's also a sign of the times, as people become more compassionate and aware of the plight of our brothers and sisters.

But it's a tricky question. On one hand, we do need to act and change things. And the best way is to educate people about the treasures that animals are, and how they like to be treated and handled.

But as I have been saying, to really effect change, one must understand the Law of Attraction. If energy follows thought, then thinking there is a lot of suffering, and putting energy into that, will bring more.

So instead of putting energy into how bad things are, just put energy into what is good. Be an animal advocate who has strong intentions for social change, visualises the world of sacred harmony and creates that by being peace and harmony yourself.

As Mother Theresa said, "I was once asked why I don't participate in anti-war demonstrations. I said that I will never do that, but as soon as you have a pro-peace rally, I'll be there."

This was the thinking behind creating a For Life campaign instead of saying "no kill", which still places an emphasis the "kill" part in a "no kill" situation.

We can effect change by creating real sanctuaries for animals where they are safe for life, change the euthanasia policy to make it against the law to kill a healthy, homeless animal like it is in Germany, and educating people to value the lives of animals and to understand their needs.

While understanding that animals, like us, have free will as souls to choose their destiny, also understand that like us, they have many different possible futures and it is important we steward well.

Chapter 52:
Animal Communication as a Business

Animal communication was never a business for me – it was always a sideline. It was something I did because the animals needed it and because I could do it. My real field is in communication, education and the arts. I became successful with this non-business because I cared, because I'm passionate about the welfare of animals. I also saw every animal who came to me as a teacher who would help me learn all I could about animals. People who say they know all about animals, are sadly kidding themselves. Who can ever know another soul without really communing with them first?

The animals need people who can interpret the language of silence with dignity and integrity. People who come from humility and who have worked on themselves so they aren't projecting from that unhealed place.

To walk in the world as an interpreter of the silent language is a very responsible and privileged thing to do. It is not something you want to come from that space of ego with. Sadly a lot of people walk around unaware they are ego driven only, and not understanding the truth of words like ethics, integrity and impeccability.

After trying to teach these words and have them take in the soil of my students, I realised that each person had their own filters on, and in many of them, the seeds wouldn't take. They were convinced they heard the silent language, acted in integrity and that's all there was.

Sorry, it is much, much more.

As a screenwriter it was drummed into me that it was never what a character said, it was what actions they took and how they behaved in the world that revealed the truth of who they were to the audience.

Many people talk the talk but they don't walk the talk.

Secret Animal Business

How do you walk in the world? If you can communicate with animals, how do you serve them?

Do you live in right relations? Do you keep your promises? Do you keep in balance with your energy exchanges? Or do you take more than you give? An animal shaman doesn't steal, and acknowledges the work of others. She walks her talk, lives her truth, does her personal work and lives impeccably.

Going to a single class in animal communication, and maybe reading some books doesn't mean you are a professional animal communicator. Sadly there are people who do a disservice to the world of animals by being untrained and unprofessional.

Rex was a classic example of the kind of work I had to undo from an animal communicator who obviously wasn't trained correctly. The client sent me a picture of her dog Rex, with the words "I'm not telling you anything because we don't like animal communicators."

Even with all my experience, that made me feel uncomfortable. There was a test here and I had to pass it to be able to help the animal. So I clicked up the picture of a gorgeous German Shepherd onto my screen, and opened myself to receive everything he sent me.

"I don't want to die." These were the first words Rex said. He felt toxic and lethargic. I instinctively knew he was on chemotherapy, and that he needed to get off it and go onto a natural, immune boosting pathway to health. Rex showed me a man crying when he walked the dog and sent me a wealth of information for which I was grateful.

And he was right. His person confirmed he had cancer and was on chemo and let me know an animal communicator had told her and her husband that Rex would die in four months, so they'd had a miserable four months expecting him to.

This is contrary to everything I teach, and I believe it is against the ethics of this particular service. This was a dog who hated being on chemotherapy and didn't want to die. And the chemotherapy was killing him as much as the cancer.

There is the probability of death, and the possibility of life. If changes are made and the being wills it, life can be a possibility because miracles can happen. Where there is life, there is hope and if the animal wants life, do everything you can to support that wish.

Professional animal communicators don't go around predicting death. They support life and healing.

And sometimes an animal *is* coming to the end of his time, but you really have to make sure you're not projecting your particular fears of death and personal limitations on the understanding of true healing.

As a shaman, I have travelled beyond death and also called animals back from the grip of death. It has given me not just an intellectual understanding, but a grounded experience in miracles. Miracles can happen.

One of my students reported to me that a dog had been killed because he had told an animal communicator that "people were evil." Was this the communicator's projection or what the dog actually said? And if the dog did say that in context with whatever his soul had suffered, surely counselling and lots of love would have been a higher option.

Another animal communicator reportedly said that a woman's cat was peeing because he was "spiteful". Another claimed every animal spoke of their human "masters", and still another claimed she met animals who were evil.

I'm sorry, but this just makes me sad. In over 20 years of speaking with thousands of animals around the world, I've never come across a spiteful one or an evil one. This is projection. And it comes from ignorance.

There is a lot of responsibility in being an animal communicator. It is not something you just do because you are intuitive. You need to be trained, and at a level where the animals are not at risk because you don't know enough.

Having said that, the world needs more professional animal communicators and I hope *Secret Animal Business* and Rainbow Fianna: Wisdom School for Earthkeepers can help be part of that journey.

Don't be just a good animal communicator, become an animal angel. Excel at what you do for the sake of the animals and the planet.

How to Be a Human Angel for Animals

- Get trained in secret animal business.

- Work on your self-healing. It's important to be a clear channel and know that you are not projecting your shadow, emotions and feelings onto the situation. How do you clear the space to be good at this work? My Rainbow Fianna students all work on their self-healing with shamanic techniques gleaned from around the world.

- Be a clear channel. I have been a vegetarian for over 30 years. I don't drink, smoke, take any drugs – recreational or prescription. I exercise daily and work on myself, my stuff and my emotions so that I can continually be the best I can be. As I ask my students not to kill, many of them become vegetarian also.

- Have a sound understanding of fifth dimensional healing, natural medicines, tracking the body for illness, and understand that miracles can happen.

- Have a network of healers to draw upon to give the animal the best chance there is. Don't let your ego get in the way. This is about co-operation for the sake of animals, not competition.

- Always walk your talk, and understand the messages in this book. When faced with a decision, take the high road of ethics, integrity and impeccability, for the highest good of all concerned.

- Make your business a spiritual practice and a spiritual service.

- Abide by a code of ethics and remember we are in the time of instant karma now. So do no harm. And help animals and people shine.

Chapter 53:
What I've Learned from Animals and their Secret Business

Being able to hear and sense the voice of animals and nature has defined my life, my animal advocacy and my vision for peace on the planet. My love of animals is what has made me walk that path of animal and human interconnection and spirituality. The animals have set me challenges which led me to search for answers so that I may best serve them. I sought out teachers of the highest ways of animal care in diet, healing and education. These, in turn, brought me deeper understanding of my own and the human condition. In short, my path with animals has made me a much better person. And that's their secret business in a nutshell.

Willow, with her challenge of epilepsy, has made me look at the way I deal with stress. She also sent me on a path hunting ancient fairie healing techniques, and she's taught me patience. Sollie, in his dangerous phase, taught me assertiveness, how to manage my emotions and be a leader. Feeding 44-year-old Sebastian before I went to bed at night made me appreciate the universe and the starry night. Finn, the wild brumby stallion, taught me subtle nuances of the dance of energy between horse and human.

Through years of observing and being around animals, I've learnt a lot about people, and I've learnt a lot about myself. From the dogs of Seven Days with Seven Dogs, I learnt to be quiet and unassuming about my work because it's just work. I've learnt a lot about the death and dying process and how to give the best hospice care I can. That's also taught me strength and resilience.

Twylah, Tala and Louie all taught me to trust in them and in Spirit.

At every step of the way, the animals have held my hand and guided my progress through life, most of the time without me even realising it. They've presented with obstacles that forced me to overcome my personal shortcomings, the biggest of these being low self-esteem and the typical artist's poverty consciousness – something all too common in my generation and in our society. When you have 30 horses to feed, there's no room for no self-confidence. You just stretch yourself and find the courage to do things you normally wouldn't dare to do – for the animals you love. And for the animals you love, you turn around the thoughts that hold you in anything less than the highest vibration.

The animals have pushed all my buttons and made me stretch and stretch my wings searching for answers. They have made me an animal shaman.

Nurturing myself and thinking abundantly have been my hardest life lessons so far, and indeed, they are part of the reason I'm here this time around. But by honouring the animals in my life, I have watched myself shift and grow and overcome these challenges.

I hope through the reading of this book, you understand better the Divine relationship we have with our animal kin. As a shaman, I feel called to shed light on the unseen and the misunderstood, so that animals may themselves live in Beauty, and enjoy the Beauty we create as we step into becoming the

Human Angels they ask us to be.

Because

ALL LIFE IS PRECIOUS!

Acknowledgements

It feels like this book took a ridiculously long time to come into being. Sollie and my guides have been at me for years, shown me the finished books, and pushed me to the computer. But I kept putting the task aside. So we all have to thank Maggie Hamilton for asking me to begin my journey, Lisa Hanrahan for encouraging me further and expanding the idea to include my teachings, and Patricia Hamilton for asking, "What else is possible?" and setting a deadline. I work well to impossible challenges. Without the three of you, I might still be putting other things in the way. So thank you.

A big thanks to my daughter Tamsin for letting me take over her room while I wrote. Thank you, Tam, for understanding my absence and supporting the process. You are awesome and I hope I left a good writing vibe in your room!

The book wouldn't have been birthed without some very special people working around the clock and to you I am incredibly grateful. It showed me the power of spiritual community because we all rolled up our sleeves and got to it with high thoughts in mind. What a joy! So enormous thanks to Wendy Slee for the awesome cover, and to the wonderful Liz Campbell for the lovely, lovely design and her willingness to press on into the night. The book is delicious because of you.

Most importantly, I couldn't have written this book without my husband Andrew Einspruch. I owe him for everything – his huge support, his willingness to do a double load of animal care, parenting and food preparation, his keen eye for publishing professionalism, his long days and nights of book editing, the index, and his eternal encouragement. You are my rock and my heart.

Finally, the book wouldn't have been written without my clients, students, teachers and friends - and of course, the animals themselves.

Much gratitude to all.

Bibliography

Boone, J. Allen. *Kinship with All Life,* Harper & Row, New York, 1954. ISBN 0-06-060912-5.

Boone, J. Allen, Leonard, Paul and Blance (editors). *The Language of Silence,* Harper & Row, New York, 1970. ISBN 0-06-060913-3.

Calhoun, Marcy. *Are You Really Too Sensitive: How to Understand and Develop Your Sensitivity as the Strength It Is,* Blue Dolphin Publishing, Nevada City, California, 1987. ISBN 0-931892-10-4.

Deane, Ashayana. *Voyagers II: Secrets of Amenti*, Granite Publishing, 2001, ISBN 978-1893183254

Emoto, Masaru. *The Hidden Messages in Water,* Atria Books, New York, 2001. ISBN 987-0-7432-8980-1.

Exley, Helen (ed.). *In Beauty May I Walk...,* Exley, New York and Watford, UK, 1997. ISBN 1-8505-838-X.

Harner, Michael. *The Way of the Shaman*, Harper & Row, New York, 1980 and 1990. ISBN 0-06-250373-1.

King, Stanley (ed.). *A Pilgrimage with the Animals*, The Seekers Trust, Addington Park, Kent, 1982.

MacEowen, Frank. *The Celtic Way of Seeing: Meditations on the Irish Spirit Wheel*, New World Library, Novato, California, 2007. ISBN 987-1-57731-541-4.

Martin, Ann N. *Food Pets Die For: Shocking Facts About Pet Food*, NewSage Press, Troutdale, Oregon, 2003. ISBN 0-939165-46-5.

Megre, Vladimir. *Anastasia*, Ringing Cedars Press, Columbia, Missouri, 2005. ISBN 0-9763333-0-9.

Peden, Barbara Lynn. *Dogs & Cats Go Vegetarian*, Harbingers of a New Age, Hayden Lake, Idaho, 1988. ISBN 0-941391-01-6.

Peden, James A. *Vegetarian Cats & Dogs*, Harbingers of a New Age, Troy, Montana, 1999. ISBN 0-941319-03-2.

Phyo, Ani. *Ani's Raw Food Kitchen: Easy, Delectable Living Foods Recipes*,

Da Capo Press, Cambridge, Massachusetts, 2007. ISBN 978-1-60094-000-2.

Roads, Michael. *Talking with Nature and Journey into Nature*, New World Library, Novato, California, 2003. ISBN1-93207305-1.

Sheldrake, Rupert. *Dogs That Know When Their Owners Are Coming Home and Other Unexplained Powers of Animals*, Arrow Books, London, 1999. ISBN 0-09-925587-1.

Summer Rain, Mary. *Phoenix Rising: No-Eyes' Vision of the Changes to Come*, Hampton Roads Publishing, 1993. ISBN 978-1878901620.

Villoldo, Alberto. *The Four Insights: Wisdom, Power, and Grace of the Earthkeepers*, Hay House, Inc, Carlsbad, California, 2006. ISBN 978-1-4019-1045-7.

Yogananda, Paramahansa. *Autobiography of a Yogi*, Self-Realization Fellowship, Los Angeles, California, 1975. ISBN 0-87612-079-6.

Additional Books of Interest

Adams, Pamela Talbot. *Angels Who Came with Fur and Four Paws,* Soul Companions, Clunes, Vic, 2007. ISBN 9780646480077.

Baïracli-Levy, Juliette de, *The Complete Herbal Handbook for the Dog and Cat*, Faber, London, 1992. ISBN 0571161154

Baïracli-Levy, Juliette de, *Herbal Handbook for Farm and Stable*, Faber, London, 1973. ISBN 0571048056

Billinghurst, Ian. *Give Your Dog a Bone: The Practical Commonsense Way to Feed Dogs For a Long Healthy Life,* Ian Billinghurst (publisher), Lithgow, NSW, 1993. ISBN 0 646 16028 1.

Billinghurst, Ian. *Grow Your Pups with Bones: The BARF Programme for Breeding Healthy Dogs and Eliminating Skeletal Disease,* Ian Billinghurst (publisher), Bathurst, NSW, 1998. ISBN 0 9585925 0 0.

Ferguson, Victoria. *The Practical Horse Herbal*, Carlton Books, London, 2002. ISBN 978-1842225653

Goldstein, Martin, *The Nature of Animal Healing : The Path to your Pet's Health, Happiness and Longevity,* Knopf : Distributed by Random House,

New York, 1999. ISBN 0679455000

Martin, Ann N. *Protect Your Pet: More Shocking Facts*, NewSage Press, Troutdale, Oregon, 2003. ISBN 0-939165-42-4.

Middle, Clare, *Real Food for Dogs and Cats*, Clare Middle (publisher), Bibra Lake, W.A., 2007, 9780646478456.

Mindell, Earl and Renaghan, Elizabeth. *Dr. Earl Mindell's Nutrition and Health for Dogs.* Basic Health Publications, Inc. Laguna Beach, California, 2007. ISBN 978-1-59120-203-5.

Pitcairn, Richard H. *Dr. Pitcairn's Complete Guide to Natural Health for Dogs and Cats,* Rodale Press, New York, 1995. ISBN 0875962432

Index

2012 phenomenon 23, 92, 120, 172, 227, 273, 275, 279, 310

A

adrenal burnout 28
advocacy 315
aggression 181, 186
aging 237
animal communication as a business 332
animals
  advocacy 315
  as angels 91
  as shamanic teachers 173, 303
  caring for 173
  lost 192
  older 239
  spirits 270
  views on death 258
  wild 169
animal welfare 309
ants 14
Are You Really Too Sensitive? 12
ascension symptoms 226, 248, 274
attacks 110, 184
Autobiography of a Yogi 232

B

babies 190
Baïracli-Levy, Juliette de 25, 221, 226, 229, 235
behaviour, demanding specific 148
being sold 197
Best Friends Animal Society 228, 318, 322
Binah 23, 45, 47, 120, 191
body language 151, 157, 205
body swapping 115, 118
Boone, J. Allen 23, 24, 108, 131, 134, 167
breeding 203, 237

C

canned food 154, 192, 217, 219, 220, 221, 229
Cannon, Dolores 227, 275, 281
caring for animals 173, 216, 326

Cat House on the Kings 321
Cedar 93, 217, 218, 255
Celtic Way of Seeing 286
ceremony 267, 290
change, resisting 285
chemicals 182, 217, 236, 248, 249, 282, 315
Chief Seattle 104
Chinta 13
Chockmah 23, 24, 209
Christos 102, 278
Chronic Fatigue Syndrome 33, 176
comedy 22, 26, 27, 28, 34, 140, 294, 295, 297, 306
commercial animal food 154, 217, 220, 221, 229, 235, 248
connectedness 130
Create-a-mate 293
creature 107
crystals 15, 78, 162, 247, 290
Cushing's Syndrome 73, 256

D

Daisy 111, 115, 123, 258
Deane, Ashayana 102
death 29, 50, 58, 89, 101, 152, 173, 253, 258, 262. 267, 303, 319, 334
demanding behaviour 148
desexing 203
diet
  cats 220
  dogs 218
  horses 235
  natural 219, 229
  raw 280
  vegetarian 228, 229
distance communication 163
distemper 25, 249, 299
dog attacks 184
donkey 228, 325
doubling 118
dreaming 277
Drury, Neville 26
Dusty 218, 239, 255, 319
dying 75, 145, 253, 262, 266, 270, 303, 336
Dylan 257, 258

E

education 107, 108, 182, 200, 317
Einspruch, Andrew 27
emotional causation of illness 243
emotional healing 244
Emoto, Masaru 130
energy healing 246
entities 92, 250, 271, 305
euthanasia 145, 159, 250, 259, 266, 310, 314, 316, 317
exercise 187

F

farm animals 107, 326
Finding Joy 102, 109, 231, 246
Food Pets Die For 220
For Life campaign 310, 318, 330
For Life Sanctuary 314, 325
Four Insights, The 129
frustration 175

G

Gingko 215
Grandmother Kitty 33, 99, 210, 267
gratitude 146, 302
grief 254, 255, 270
group mind 115
guidelines for apprentice human angels 83

H

happiness 291
Harner, Michael 102, 128
healers 120
healing modalities 186, 216, 247
herbs 249
Hidden Messages in Water, The 130
holistic healing 215
homeopathy 249
homo luminous 227
Hood, Robin 70, 143, 178
Hopi 273
hospice care 264
house clearing 304

I

illness, emotional causation 243
improvisation 138, 140, 142

Inka 273
it 107

J

Jaffah 135, 179
journal work 141, 144, 160

K

kahuna 128
Kai 28, 29, 30, 177, 196
Kinship with All Life 23, 24, 108, 131, 134, 167

L

language 106, 205
Lascelles 312
laughter 295
Law of Attraction 126, 165, 173, 206, 216, 232, 238, 239, 300, 302, 330
Lehrman, Fred 239
Lekota-Lesa, Pawnee Chief 1, 103
Little Tam 130
Little Tyke 224, 228, 232
lost animals 44, 192
Louie 93, 209, 218, 240, 255, 336

M

MacEowen, Frank 286
Martin, Ann N. 220
Mayans 273
meditation 93, 98, 137, 139, 140, 186, 283, 286
mindfulness 93, 131, 137, 188, 205, 217, 283, 290, 300, 303, 314
modalities of healing 186, 216, 247
Mountain, Michael 322
multi-dimensional nature of animals 119

N

names 200, 206, 207, 208
natural diets 218, 200, 235
natural horsemanship 32, 70, 151, 202
neem oil 249
neutering 203
new arrivals 198
No Eyes 227

O

older animals 239, 319
orbs 265, 269
owner 106
ownership 104

P

Parelli, Pat 70, 184, 201, 202
Peden, James 223, 224, 229, 232
permission 58, 83, 145, 153, 157, 169, 246, 261, 266
pests 165, 314
pet 106
Phoenix Rising 227
photographs 163, 268
Pip 9, 12
Pixie 256
play 294
pointing 204
point of view, animal's 110
pounds 315
prayer 97, 99, 216, 290, 293
problem animals 105
projection 180, 298, 334
promises 301
prophecy 23, 172, 227, 273, 280, 286
Pucawan 23, 45, 68, 259, 261

R

Raffi 109, 155, 156, 205, 231, 255
Rainbow Fianna 81, 84, 325, 334
Rain, Mary Summer 227
raw food 35, 166, 188, 218, 220, 225, 227, 229, 233, 275, 280, 305
recording communications 160
reincarnation 79, 113, 116
Reka 25-30, 47, 67, 115, 189, 196, 197, 249
relationship pressure 201
rescue 315
rescue organisations 321
responsibility 298
right relations 301
ritual 290
Roads, Michael J. 167

S

sacrifice 311

Samantha 72, 256
Saraid 76, 135, 160, 199
Sebastian 26, 76, 135, 151, 159, 236, 336
self-fulfilling prophecy 206, 228
separation anxiety 195
service 146
Seven Days with Seven Dogs 97, 113, 336
shadow side 297, 303
shamanic teachers, animals as 173, 303
Sheldrake, Rupert 124
shelters 315
silent language, learning 138
Skidboot 178
snake 210
Sollie 23-24, 26, 33-36, 66-79, 116, 133, 159, 160, 202, 253, 254, 256, 257, 259, 261, 336, 338
soul bonds 244, 253
soul family 179, 215, 216
soul journey 176, 203
space clearing 304
spaying 203
spells 118
spirits 270, 271
spiritual practise 283
star animals 119
stock 107, 326
stones 15
Suki 35, 40, 59, 93, 97, 113-115, 116, 161, 191, 205, 243, 262, 264, 267
supplements 215, 224-226, 229

T

Tala 30-32, 77, 93, 115, 177, 205, 255, 270, 336
Talking with Nature 167
Tammy 130, 264, 269, 270
telepathy 123-125, 133, 140, 150, 153, 164, 169, 206
thought 284
Time of the Drum 137, 140, 153
tinned food 154, 192, 217, 219, 220, 221, 229
training 107, 200
Tribe 28, 33
tribes, animals as first 102
TTEAM 70, 143, 178
Tusuque 113-114, 123, 201, 258
TV 202, 306
Twylah 31, 32, 35, 93, 101, 205, 241-242, 336

U

urinating 180

V

vaccines 182, 217, 249-250
validation 138, 159, 161, 164
veganism 220, 222, 223-234, 237, 280, 314, 327
Vegetarian Cats and Dogs 224, 232
vegetarianism 22, 159, 220, 222, 223-234, 237, 280, 314, 327, 335
vibration 148, 165, 168, 205, 208, 211, 216, 226, 229, 231, 280, 281, 290
Villoldo, Alberto 129, 227
vocabulary 106, 205

W

Walk in Beauty 147, 285, 286, 288, 290, 326
walk-ins 115, 117
Way of the Shaman 102, 128
whispers in the silence 133, 140, 292
wild animals 93, 169
Willow 108, 248, 336
wolf 185, 186, 228
words 205
World Society for the Protection of Animals 228
writing down sessions 160

Y

Yogananda, Paramahansa 232

World Society for the Protection of Animals 228
writing down sessions 160

Y

Yogananda, Paramahansa 232

About the Author

Born with an innate understanding of the silent language of nature and animals, Billie Dean always knew she would write and help animals. Her career first took her into the world of journalism where she discovered a love of photography and film, and a deep regard for alternative healing and indigenous spiritual teachings.

Billie's apprenticeship into the world of the animal shaman began at a young age with her dog Pip. Later she realised there was an animal guiding her at every turn.

Billie has been communicating with other people's animals in Australia and around the world for two decades. She has regularly been interviewed on radio, and has been featured in a wide array of magazines and newspapers, from Bark!, Dog's Life, and Woman's Day to Insight and Conscious Living.

Along the way she's been a comedienne, an actress, a filmmaker, writer, teacher and shamanic healer. She is a graduate of the Four Winds Society's Healing the Light Body School, and has studied with the Order of the Bards, Ovates and Druids, Lynn Andrew's Centre for Sacred Arts and Training, and other indigenous teachers around the globe.

Billie's first film Finding Joy was the launch feature for the Spiritual Cinema Circle and won Billie an AFTI Best Actress Award for her role of Joy. The "dog-umentary" Seven Days with Seven Dogs was next, followed by This Sacred Earth: The 2012 Phenomenon. Billie is the author of 10 children's books, countless magazine articles, and has written for children's television, including the multi-award winning series Hi-5.

Billie lives on a farm in NSW, Australia with her writer/filmmaker husband Andrew Einspruch, their daughter Tamsin, and a collection of rescued animals, including horses, dogs, cats, geese, ducks, budgies, goats, alpacas, and a sheep called Sarah. When she's not working, she loves to surf, study shamanism, read fantasy and hang out with her family of animals and humans.

You can read more about Billie on her website, www.billiedean.com, and you can contact her on billie@billiedean.com.

More From Billie Dean

Billie Dean's Web Sites

Please come by our web sites. You might like to sign up for our email newsletters to keep up with everything we are doing.

www.billiedean.com

www.wildpureheart.com

Coming Soon from Billie Dean

Secret Animal Wisdom

Following on from *Secret Animal Business*, animal shaman Billie Dean shares more stories from the animals and fairies, going deeper into the wisdom that will help you navigate the chaos of the current times by aligning you to your authentic essential self. Join her as she communes with the animals of Ballyoncree and her clients from around the world.

Path of the Wild Pure Heart

Billie Dean's shamanic adventures in the non-ordinary, multi dimensional reality. In this book Billie shares the wisdom and experiences of her shamanic path of visions, journeys and communion with nature and animals.

The Deep Peace Project

In this ground-breaking and truly visionary work, Billie outlines new paradigms for peace for all species from the animals, the fae and the tree people.

Time of the Drum

If you want to communicate with your animals, join Billie as she skillfully takes you on meditation journeys to the uplifting music of Tribe World Ensemble. Travel to the Time of the Drum, a world of ancient forests and caves, Native American elders, fairies and water spirits, magic rock pools and empowering unicorns. Meet your wild self and your animal friends as you bring your innate gift of telepathic communication to present day consciousness.

Use this meditation CD to relax and connect you to your deep memories of telepathy. Get your pen and paper ready to write down your messages from the animals and natural world around you.

Tracks:

1. Introduction

2. Hyayno Ah

3. Grandfather's Meditation

In this meditation, Grandfather, one of Billie's guides, helps you reconnect to your ancient gift of telepathy – the universal language of nature and animals. Set deep in the forest, Grandfather takes you back into the past, when you once had this gift and helps you bring it into the present.

4. Water Spirits and Magic Unicorn Meditation

Designed to wash away negativity and doubt and put you into the frame of mind to receive silent communication, Billie calls upon the water spirits and the magic of unicorn to heal and empower you. |

5. Forest Meditation with Shamanic Drumming journey.

In this last meditation, we travel to the forest where we meet a special animal who journeys with you on the beat of the drum.

Available from

www.billiedean.com

Secret Animal Business

Seven Days with Seven Dogs
A Dog-umentary

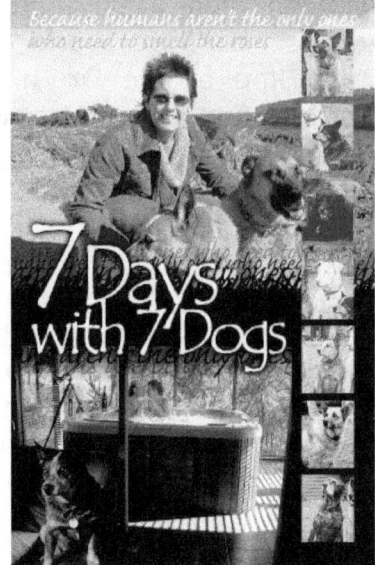

In Seven Days with Seven Dogs we bundled our seven rescued dogs into our old Bongo Bus van, and took off on a road trip to fulfil mature-aged kelpie Suki's supposedly last request - to go on a holiday and film it.

This is truly a heart-warming and uplifting story, chock full of joyful dogs exploring life and having fun, and we manage to weave in lots of helpful hints on dog care along the way. Meet and learn from late animal homoeopath Jackie Fitzgerald, and alternative vet Bruce Syme.

Filmed in some of Australia's most beautiful places, and shot by AFI Award winning cinematographer Anthony Jennings, the documentary follows Suki, Louie, Tala, Twylah, Cedar, Willow and Raffi as they do everything from stay in five-star, "Five Paw" resort accommodation to taking a horse-drawn gypsy caravan ride.

Because humans aren't the only ones who need to smell the roses.

Available from:
www.billiedean.com
www.wildpureheart.com

Finding Joy

This feature film won Billie an AFTI award for Best Actress and was the launch feature for the Spiritual Cinema Circle. Billie also wrote and directed the film -- an upbeat love story about finding your song and having the courage to sing it.

Stephen Simon, founder of the Spiritual Cinema Circle said, "It makes you feel good about being a human." Laugh and cry as you follow Joy along the bumpy road of self discovery, courage and love.

Set to the backdrop of the folk music scene in an arty country town, the story shows how the love for a stray dog can change your life. When Joy says yes to Raffi, she steps onto her path of destiny with friends like tarot-card reading Tessa (Janet Watson-Kruse), true love Peter Wolfman (Andrew Einspruch) and bucket loads of doubt.

This film celebrates universal themes of friendship, low self-esteem, love relationships , and the joy of dogs. It features us wearing our comedy hats, and is filled with fabulous foot-tapping and soul-stirring folk music to keep you uplifted, inspired, entertained and enlightened.

Available from:

www.billiedean.com

www.wildpureheart.com

Finding Joy Sound Track

We are thrilled to have been able to put together a soundtrack CD. It features the "Finding Joy" title track from Rick Grossman of the Hoodoo Gurus, the rollicking music of Katysha and Malumba, the haunting sounds of Tribe World Ensemble (who have also done much of the music for our documentary This Sacred Earth: The 2012 Phenomenon), some of the pieces that Peter and Joy perform in the movie, and much, much more.

The album delivers over 1 1/4 hours of fabulous music.

Available from:

www.billiedean.com

www.wildpureheart.com

This Sacred Earth: The 2012 Phenomenon

What is 2012, and is it the end of the world as we know it?

This is the documentary which looks at the 2012 prophecies from the perspective of a shift in human consciousness and a reconnection to nature. It asks how can we fall back in love with Mother Earth to save both ourselves and the planet.

Imbued with our trademark lightness of spirit, love of beauty and reverence for the natural world, this film takes you beyond fear and into hope and feel-good!

From our belief that a disconnection from nature is at the root cause of our planetary crisis, the film asks 17 wisdom keepers from around the globe what each one of us can do to ensure the 2012 indigenous prophecy of a millenium of peace becomes a reality.

Enjoy and learn, be empowered, uplifted and inspired, tap your feet to the music of Tribe World Ensemble and throw away your uncertainty about tomorrow.

Among the speakers are author Dr William Bloom (UK), Philip Carr-Gomm, author and Head of the Order of Bards, Ovates and Druids (UK), Dr Allberto Villoldo, author, shaman, medical anthropologist (USA), author Dolores Cannon (USA), Dr Geo Athena Trevathen, Celtic shaman and scholar (UK) Karen Ward and John Cantwell, Irish Celtic shamans, (Ireland) , Lucy Cavendish, author and white witch, (Australia) and Billie Dean, author, shaman and filmmaker (Australia).

Available from:

www.wildpureheart.com
www.billiedean.com
www.thissacredearth.tv

Rainbow Fianna: Wisdom School for Earthkeepers
and
The Australian Centre of the Munay Ki

Rainbow Fianna: Wisdom School for Earthkeepers is designed to train Earthkeepers, human angels for animals, and to help people through the 2012 Phenomenon with transformational shamanic teachings and initiations.

Our classes are a combination of on-line studies and retreats at Braidwood, NSW Australia where students are taught through lecture, discussion, animal experiences, nature walks, ceremony and celebration.

The purpose of the Rainbow Fianna school is to create individuals of integrity and compassion who work and live with animals in the highest possible way.

This is a school for animal guardians, communicators, healers and light warriors. It is a school for anyone who wants to understand the language of Mother Earth and all her children, and how to access their guidance, wisdom and knowledge. It is a school for wisdom keepers and Earth keepers, true stewards of our planet for our children's children and all those to come for the next seven generations and beyond. It is a mastery school, helping people evolve into *homo luminous* – and become human angels for animals and the Earth.

Take the evolutionary leap!

For More Information, See
www.billiedean.com

www.ingramcontent.com/pod-product-compliance
Lightning Source LLC
Chambersburg PA
CBHW080724230426
43665CB00020B/2602